J.K. LASSER'S™

FINANCE & TAX FOR YOUR FAMILY BUSINESS

Look for these and other titles from J.K. Lasser—Practical Guides for All Your Financial Needs

J.K. Lasser's Pick Winning Stocks by Edward F. Mrkvicka, Jr.

J.K. Lasser's Invest Online by LauraMaery Gold and Dan Post

J.K. Lasser's Year-Round Tax Strategies by David S. DeJong and Ann Gray Jakabcin

J.K. Lasser's Taxes Made Easy for Your Home-Based Business by Gary W. Carter

J.K. Lasser's Pick Winning Mutual Funds by Jerry Tweddell with Jack Pierce

J.K. LASSER'S™

FINANCE & TAX FOR YOUR FAMILY BUSINESS

Barbara Weltman

John Wiley & Sons, Inc.

New York • Chichester • Weinheim • Brisbane • Singapore • Toronto

Published by John Wiley & Sons, Inc.

Published simultaneously in Canada.

No part of this publication may be reproduced, stored in a retrieval system, or
transmitted in any form or by any means, electronic, mechanical, photocopying,
recording, scanning, or otherwise, except as permitted under Sections 107 or 108 of
the 1976 United States Copyright Act, without either the prior written permission
of the Publisher, or authorization through payment of the appropriate per-copy fee
to the Copyright Clearance Center, 222 Rosewood Drive, Danvers, MA 01923, (978)
750-8400, fax (978) 750-4744. Requests to the Publisher for permission should be
addressed to the Permissions Department, John Wiley & Sons, Inc.,
605 Third Avenue, New York, NY 10158-0012, (212) 850-6011, fax (212) 850-6008,
E-Mail: PERMREQ@WILEY.COM.

This publication is designed to provide accurate and authoritative information in
regard to the subject matter covered. It is sold with the understanding that the
publisher is not engaged in rendering professional services. If professional advice
or other expert assistance is required, the services of a competent professional
person should be sought.

Library of Congress Cataloging-in-Publication Data:
Weltman, Barbara, 1950–
    J. K. Lasser's finance & tax for your family business/ Barbara Weltman.
      p. cm.
    Includes index.
    ISBN 0-471-39623-0 (pbk. : alk. paper)
    1. Family-owned business enterprises—United States. 2. Family-owned
business enterprises—Taxation—United States. 3. Family-owned business
enterprises—Law and legislation—United States. I. Title.
HD62.25 .W45 2001
658.15—dc21   00-061958

Printed in the United States of America.

10 9 8 7 6 5 4 3 2 1

To my husband and children—
my main family business

Contents

Preface

If you're starting out or already own a family business, you're in good company. Three out of every four businesses in the United States today are family businesses. But just because there are numerous family businesses does not mean there are an equal number of answers to the tax and financial questions you face about your business. Your concerns are unique. No other family is just like yours. No other business is just like yours. You need financial and tax solutions tailored to your situation.

Family businesses face all the same financial and tax challenges as other businesses. They have to monitor cash flow, stay on top of collections, improve marketing efforts, hire and fire workers, comply with tax laws, and handle a variety of federal and state regulatory issues. But family businesses also need to deal with a number of problems or opportunities that have a unique spin. For example, every business needs to raise capital to get started or expand. But a family business may have a ready source of cash in relatives eager to join in. Every business needs to consider what happens when an owner retires or dies. But a family business needs to balance the interests of family members—those participating in the business as well as those who aren't—in making succession plans.

Some businesses may be concerned with fair compensation to

relatives, while other companies focus on how to transfer ownership in the most cost-effective way. As an owner of a family business, you must assess your personal circumstances and identify your own problems. This will allow you to devise special solutions to suit your situation.

Not every family business faces the same problems or problems of the same severity. Every situation is different and is influenced by unique dynamics of the personalities involved in the business, with all their competitiveness, jealousy, and other strengths and weaknesses. In addition, the interests of extended family members, such as spouses of relatives working for the business, can come into play. These dynamics certainly need to be addressed and, in some cases, may even require family counseling now offered by business consultants to work out issues satisfactorily.

It's up to you to take all your special factors into account and then tailor your business plans and strategies based on the information provided in this book. As an attorney, I've worked with many family businesses and have seen the problems that can develop without proper planning. I've also seen how level heads and a commonsense approach can solve most difficulties that arise.

This book is designed to assist you in understanding the potential monetary pitfalls and opportunities of a family business. While family businesses can run the gamut from modest to huge, public to private, this book is intended primarily to help small, privately held family businesses grapple with tax and financial issues. The book covers three general areas of concern:

1. Starting a business with family members—what you're up against, how you should set things up both legally and as a matter of practicality, how to put together your management team, and how to raise the money you need to get started.

2. Running a family business—fixing compensation both for family members and nonrelated employees, optimizing the use of fringe benefits and retirement plans, working from home, and protecting business ownership in case of divorce.

3. Selling or transferring a business interest—making a succession plan, going on when one relative leaves the company, planning for death and taxes, and selling the business to outsiders.

In the appendixes you find some additional resources to assist you in solving your problems. In addition to resources for handling personal issues, there is a listing of university-based family business institutes providing seminars, counseling, and information.

Throughout the book you'll see highlighted information that you should pay special attention to—an explanation of a technical term, a word of caution to help you and the business stay out of trouble, some added guidance like a phone number, Web site, or special idea to make things easier, and some extra information you'll find interesting and helpful.

A word of caution: At press time Congress was considering a number of tax changes that would affect some of the ideas I've offered here. You will find explanations about any tax changes at both www.bwideas.com and www.jklasser.com. I also strongly suggest that you consult with a tax expert before implementing any of these ideas.

I'd like to thank the following people who helped me in the preparation of this book: Elliott Eiss, Esq., editor of *J. K. Lasser's Your Income Tax*, for his friendship and expert assistance with tax material; Gregory Lange, CLU, CHFC, of Cowan Financial Group, and Robert Liss, CLU, CHFC, of Liss Planning Associates, for their help with insurance information; my cousin David Goldstein, a family-business owner who shared his experiences and insights; and my editor, Bob Shuman, for his insightful suggestions, good humor, and continuing support in writing this book.

J.K. LASSER'S™

FINANCE & TAX FOR YOUR FAMILY BUSINESS

Starting a Family Business

CHAPTER 1

The Family Business

Before the industrial revolution, all businesses (with only minor exceptions) were family businesses. Farms stayed within a family for generations. Fathers taught sons their trades. Husbands and wives worked side by side—in the fields, in taverns, and in shops.

Today, despite all the technological developments and wholesale migration from the farms, a remarkable number of enterprises continue to be family businesses. Best estimates put the current number at about 20 million! It's been estimated that as much as 90 percent of all businesses in the United States today are family owned or controlled. In fact, about one-third of the Fortune 1000 companies are considered family businesses, with Wal-Mart, owned by the Walton family, in the number two spot. Ford, Marriott, DuPont—need we say more?

In this chapter you'll find out just what's meant by a family business. You'll see who fits within the various definitions used today. And you'll learn why it's essential for family businesses to make formal plans to guide day-to-day operations, assess performance, and move the company ahead.

> ### Example
>
> The X Corp. is owned equally by a mother and father. The business also employs their adult son and daughter as well as their daughter-in-law and son-in-law. The X Corp. is a family business.

What's a Family Business?

Generally the term "family business" refers to a business that's owned by two or more family members. These family members can be a husband and wife, a parent and child, siblings, or even relatives within an extended family. These businesses may also employ a number of relatives who do not have any ownership interests.

Some experts suggest that a one-owner business should also be considered a family business if other family members work for the business or if there is an intention to keep the business within the family even if there are no other relatives currently working for the company. For example, a mother may run a family business from home because she's using the services of her two teenagers even though she's the sole owner. Or a father may run a family business because he has visions of one day bringing his child into the business.

Family businesses don't have to be wholly owned by a family. Privately held companies may be considered family businesses where the family collectively owns more than half of the business, which is enough ownership to maintain control over it. Publicly held corporations are generally considered family businesses where the family owns more than 10 percent of the stock. Under this definition, Microsoft is considered to be a family-owned publicly held corporation because Bill Gates alone owns 15.8 percent of the stock (and his wife Melinda is also a shareholder in her own right).

A business may start out as a family business, or it may evolve into one. For instance, two siblings may found a business together, forming a family business from the outset. Or a business may operate for years as a nonfamily business and then suddenly become one. A father, for example, may operate a home contracting business as John Smith, with no thought to taking in partners or about passing on the business to his children. When his son is old enough and comes into the business, it may become John Smith and Son—a family business.

Look Who's in the Family-Business Way Today

The mom-and-pop grocery on the corner no longer represents the family-owned business in America. Because 90 percent of all U.S. businesses are considered family-owned, they now run the gamut from micro-companies operating from spare bedrooms to giant multinational corporations. One in three of the Fortune 500 companies, in fact, are family businesses. These companies alone account for about 55 percent of the U.S. gross national product.

It used to be that the family business was a two-generation affair, with the younger generation learning at the knee of the older one. Today, multigenerational businesses are the norm. Three generations all working for the same business are, in fact, common, and even four and five generations working together are no longer considered rare.

The change in the family business profile is due to one main factor: People are living longer and healthier lives. So the oldest generation is remaining in the business for a longer time. The founding generation, today into the over age 70 category, is still going strong and may continue to head the business. The next generation, middle-agers of 50 to 55, is poised to step into leadership positions. The third generation, late 20s to early 30s, is also committed to the business. This generation may already have a decade or more of experience within the company. And it's clear that the fourth generation is about to be launched—if the business remains healthy and survives changes in succession.

There's another phenomenon developing in this information age affecting family business. The younger generation, which may have shunned the business in the past, is now returning with a view toward using the family as a base for launching Internet-related commerce. One son may have shown little interest in his father's photography studio business. However, with digital photography now taking off, he joined the family business and expanded it to include digital imaging for Web sites.

Another reason for the return of the prodigal son or daughter is disillusionment with corporate America. Years of corporate downsizing have shown that there's no security, even in the most well-established multinational corporations. So where, just a decade ago, a family scion armed with an MBA would seek prestige and stock options in the halls of Fortune 500 companies, today those same well-educated children are putting their talents back in the family business. A young marketing maven who lost his corporate position after the economic downturn of the late 1980s sought his next opportunity in his mother's public relations firm. Using his MBA skills, he then success-fully diversified the firm into marketing areas.

Running a Business That's All in the Family

A business first and foremost, a family business secondarily happens to be a business owned by a family. This is an important distinction to remember. It means that the business must be run like any other—that is, in a businesslike way. You can't run a family business like a family, letting emotions and personal issues dominate decision making. This would not only lead to misunderstandings within the family, it would cause incalculable problems for the business.

CAUTION

Put everything in writing. The failure to do so can produce intrafamily disputes that may require resolution in court. Miscommunication within a family is common. Parties may hear what they want to hear. If it's specifically written down, there can be no misunderstanding.

To ensure that your family business achieves growth objectives and succeeds to the next generation, you must plan. If you're the company founder, don't just keep information in your head; you may just wind up taking it with you to your grave. Make sure you cover all the bases, and don't leave anything to chance.

To make your intentions clear to everyone involved in your business, it's a good idea to draft the following documents for your business:

- Business plan to get started and yearly strategic plan to monitor progress and implement changes.
- Operations manual.
- Succession plan.

In drafting these documents you and your family will need to speak frankly and resolve points of contention. The process of doing so is, perhaps, as valuable as the results produced.

Business Plan

Like any other business owner, you need to have a written business plan to serve as a road map for driving your company forward. A business plan is a report describing what your business is all about and where you see it going in the future. You need this plan to raise outside capital. But even if you're not seeking such financing, you need the plan to focus your business concept or your plans for expansion and avoid misunderstandings with other family members.

Having an initial plan isn't the end of the planning process. Each year you need to do strategic planning to monitor business progress and plan for changes. The contents of the business plan and how to write it as well as how to conduct annual strategic planning are discussed later in this chapter.

Operations Manual

You need to have an operations manual to govern the daily workings of your business. The policies and practices included in the manual must apply to both family and nonfamily employees. Having this manual from the start and updating it as the business matures will head off squabbles that can otherwise arise with respect to the management and decision making of the company, intentions about distributions of profits, and the nuts and bolts of hiring and firing.

The contents of an operations manual are discussed in Part 2 of this book.

Succession Plan

You need a succession plan to map out contingencies in case of death, disability, or simply retirement. The succession plan is a compilation of information contained in various documents:

- Wills
- Trusts
- Partnership or shareholder agreements
- Proxies
- Buy-sell agreements

The succession plan should address what happens to management and ownership of the business if an owner leaves the company for any reason. Who's going to lead the company? Who's going to acquire the ownership interest of a departing owner?

The plan should provide a mechanism for acquiring the interest of the outgoing owner. The plan should also take cognizance of tax issues that arise and address any tax cost by providing a funding mechanism. And the plan should include intentions on passing the mantle of leadership even in the absence of death or retirement.

TIP

According to some anecdotal information, it appears that having a written business plan can bring a family business greater respect—and dollars— when seeking financing from banks or outside investors. A family business may otherwise be dismissed as a small-time operation not worthy of commanding outside capital.

NOTE

According to statistics in a survey conducted by Arthur Andersen Consulting, 43 percent of family businesses in the United States are expected to change hands by 2002. The reason: Many company founders are now into their 70s and 80s. Unfortunately, about a third of these founders have not yet designated their successors.

Succession planning is discussed in Part 3 of this book.

Business Plan Essentials

Whether you're about to launch the next hot Internet IPO (initial public offering) or you're only starting up a local lawn service, you need a business plan. This is simply a written report detailing what your business consists of now, where you hope to be in, say, five years, how the business is organized, who runs it, and various items of financial information.

No matter how sophisticated or simple your plan, you need to cover certain basic information. This is so even with a family business where you may take some of this information for granted. The order of and emphasis on the information will, of course, vary with the purpose of the plan. What's included for a start-up business seeking financing is quite different from the information and order followed by an established company looking to expand or change direction.

Cover Sheet

The first thing the reader sees is the name of your business, its address, phone number, e-mail address, and, if applicable, Internet address. Like the rest of the plan, it must be typed and spell-checked to make a good first impression.

Purpose for the Plan

This one-page statement should explain why you wrote the plan. In a family business, this can be a mission statement of the purposes and objectives as they relate to your family (for example, your intention to create a business dynasty). Or your reason for writing this plan may be to raise seed money. If so, be specific about the amount of money you're looking to find (based on the financial information later in the plan).

Table of Contents

If your plan is intended for outsiders, then help them navigate through the material by including a table of contents. This will show the readers what each part of the plan is about as well as what type of supporting material is contained in the appendixes and where this can be found in the plan.

Part 1: Executive Summary

This is merely an introduction to what's in the rest of the plan. Provide a sentence or two about each of the other parts in your plan. While this summary description may seem redundant, it may be the only part that actually gets read. If there's nothing of interest, the readers will go no further. Well-written headline-like sentences describing the company, what you want, and why they should give it to you will keep your readers with you. It's helpful to write this summary *after* you've completed the other parts.

Part 2: Business Description

Include all the elements of a newspaper article in this part: the who, what, where, when, and why for your business:

- Company name and address (the same as on the cover page).
- The date on which your business was founded (or will be formed).
- The legal organization of the company (e.g., partnership, S corporation, etc., as explained in the next chapter).
- What your business does (the service it provides or the product it sells).

Part 3: Product or Service Description

You've already said what you do. Now tell the readers how you do it by detailing how your business operates. For example, if you're selling a product, explain whether you also manufacture it and, if so, where your plant is located.

Part 4: Marketing Plan

Why do you believe you'll be able to reach the targeted sales figures you'll include in your plan? By providing details about how you market your product or service—pricing, sales terms, the competition—you'll be able to support your projections.

If you don't write a full-blown business plan (because you don't need to raise money), at the very least you should have a written marketing plan. Too many family businesses are lax about their marketing strategies. They just try their hardest and hope for the best. They're probably doomed to failure, or at least a performance below what some thoughtful marketing strategies could have achieved.

Part 5: Operating Requirements

While this section may seem self-evident to you, it may come as news to readers. Describe your physical operations—where the company is run, what special equipment you use, and any other pertinent information about your day-to-day operations.

Part 6: Personnel

Like any business, yours is only as good as the people who run it. In family businesses, you may have both talented stars and deadwood carried for personal reasons. That's understandable. Just make sure to explain the talent—their skills and experience—and demonstrate how they've got all the bases covered (product development, marketing, finances, etc.).

In writing your personnel summary, you may find you don't provide coverage for all the necessary aspects of running a business. This is not a problem, as long as you recognize your shortcoming and provide a solution. You can certainly shore up your team with outside professionals. Maybe you will rely on an outside accountant for financial guidance. Maybe your board of directors includes outside people who offer advice. Or maybe you use consultants, such as management experts, to handle specific problems or areas. Just maybe you'll find that you need to hire key people to shore up your personnel gaps as your write.

Part 7: Financial Data

This is the heart of your plan where the numbers will tell the story of your business. They'll show what you have, what you need, and what you expect to earn in the near and distant future (three to five years down the road). If you're just starting out, some numbers are based on projections. Make them realistic so they'll be believable by potential investors or lenders. If, for example, you're projecting $1 million, or $10 million, or $100 million in annual revenue, your overall plan and other numbers must support these projections.

Financial data which needs to be included:

- Projected start-up costs (what you need to get the business off the ground and running for 6 to 12 months).
- Projected income statement (showing what you expect to earn during the start-up phase).
- Expected profit or loss (offsetting revenue against expenses to show whether the business is expected to make or lose money during the start-up phase).
- Projected monthly cash flow statement (which is the difference between money coming in and money going out).
- Personal financial statements (the owners' personal assets). This information is relevant only if the company is seeking outside financing, and the owners expect to be called upon to provide personal guarantees for loans to the business.

Financial data to be included for mature businesses is similar to the information for start-ups, but with refinements as to the type and time frame of the information:

- Balance sheet (showing the assets and liabilities of the business, including shareholder equity).
- Income statement for the past year.
- Expected profit or loss (on both a one-year basis, and a three- or five-year basis).
- Projected monthly cash flow statement for the next year.
- Personal financial statements if required for outside financing.

Appendixes: Supporting Documents

You've told readers all about your business, how good your product or service is, what you expect to earn, and more. Now back up your claims with supporting documents. Here are some common supporting documents to be included in appendixes to your business plan:

- Tax returns for the past three years (for mature businesses). Personal tax returns are also required if you've included personal financial information in Part 7 of your business plan.
- Resumes on each of your key management people and any outside management help.
- Copies of leases for space and equipment (or proposed leases).
- Copies of licenses, patents, and other proprietary items.
- Letters of intent from suppliers and manufacturers.
- Testimonials or scientific studies supporting your claims.

TIP

After you've drafted a business plan, it's a good idea to have it reviewed by experts. You can obtain free assistance through the Service Corps of Retired Executives (SCORE), an arm of the SBA. To find out about counseling in your area, call 800-634-0245 or click on www.score.org.

Don't let the task of writing a business plan overwhelm you. Take things step-by-step. For example, you can use an online tutorial from the Small Business Administration to guide you through writing your plan (www.sba.gov/starting/indexbus.plans.html).

Yearly Strategic Planning

Writing a business plan may be all that's needed to get started. But it may not be enough to carry you to the next stage of your business development. You need to review where the company stands and make plans to go forward. Like the business plan you use to get started, your strategic planning should be put on paper.

Strategic planning doesn't happen automatically. You have to make a deliberate effort. In a family business this serves as a wake-up call to see that everyone involved is on the same track. You may discover that one sibling wants to go in one direction while another is preparing to go in another.

The process of strategic planning can be formal or informal, depending on your situation. It can, for example, be conducted at board meetings or on company time. Or you may need to get away from the business atmosphere to address planning strategies.

CHAPTER 2

Organizing Your Business

Corporation? Partnership? How should you set up the legal structure of your business? The answer depends on your particular situation. There's no one solution for every family business. The type of structure you select depends not only on the nature of your business but also on whether you want to create equal or unequal ownership interests, tax rules, and other considerations.

In this chapter you'll learn about your choices for setting up a business. These include:

- Sole proprietorship
- Partnership
- Limited partnership
- Limited liability company
- S corporation
- C corporation

You'll find out what each type of organization means in terms of tax treatment and liability protection. You'll also see how to assess these choices in view of your particular family situation in terms of control issues (for example, whether certain owners should be given a say in business operations) and ease of transferring interests to other family members. Finally, you'll get some ideas on when you might want to adopt a new type of business organization as the business expands, as your family grows, or as other changes take place.

Entity Choices

How you set up the structure of your business is important for several reasons. Entity choice:

- Dictates the type of ownership interest each party will have.
- Affects the degree of control that each family member can exercise.
- Determines the tax treatment of business income, losses, fringe benefits, and more.
- Provides (or does not provide) protection from personal liability.
- Affords ease (or makes it difficult) to raise capital.

Thus, factors affecting your choice of entity include legal, tax, and personal ones. The final choice comes down to balancing these various factors.

Sole Proprietorships

If you are the only owner of a business and you don't take any formal steps to create a specific type of entity (such as a corporation), you're automatically a sole proprietorship. While this term connotes the solitary storekeeper, from a legal and tax perspective it applies to any one-owner business that's not a corporation or a limited liability company. Thus, a consultant, an independent contractor, or any other one-owner operation that has not defined itself otherwise is a sole proprietorship.

As a sole proprietor, you and the business are one and the same. This means that legally you are personally liable for the debts of the business. So if you sign a lease for business space and want to break the lease, your landlord can sue you personally and, if successful, look to your personal assets—your home and investments—to satisfy the lease terms. Or if a customer falls in your store and sues for personal injury, you may be on the hook for any damages above and beyond your liability coverage.

There are no legal steps required to form a sole proprietorship. Once you decide to be in business, you're considered to be in business. However, you may need to register your business with your city, town, or county to inform the government that you're operating under a specific business name. You simply file a "d/b/a" (doing business as) form that you can get from your local government and pay a small filing fee.

Registering your business, which may be mandated in your locality, protects your use of the business name. (And, of course, you can't take a name that's already in use in your area.) Registration also is necessary in order to open up your business bank account.

How Sole Proprietorships Are Taxed

Taxwise, as a sole proprietor, you're also one and the same as your business. You report your business income and expenses to the Internal Revenue Service (IRS) on Schedule C of Form 1040, Profit or Loss from Business (or in some cases a simplified version called Schedule C-EZ, Net Profit from Business) as part of your personal tax return (see Figure 2.1). Thus, the net profit (or loss) is added in with (or subtracted from) your other income and taxed directly to you.

A sole proprietorship may make sense as a starter for a one-owner business. It's simple to arrange and there are only minimal fees involved. Also, business losses, which are common during start-up years, are deductible so they generally can be used to offset other income on your personal return (such as a spouse's wages). Of course, losses may not be fully deductible because of certain limitations (for example, if the IRS proves you're in the business for personal enjoyment only and don't have a realistic profit motive). Or you may not have sufficient income to utilize the losses. You may, however, be able to treat the losses as net operating losses. These losses can be carried back two years and forward for up to 20 years and be used to offset income in those years.

However, as the business grows, this type of organization has limitations. You can't take advantage of certain fringe benefits for yourself such as tax-free medical coverage and dependent care assistance that the business may well be able to afford later on. At that time you may need to change your form of organization.

SELF-EMPLOYMENT TAX

As a sole proprietor, you don't receive any salary from the business. You're taxed on profits whether you take them out or leave them in the business. Since you don't have a salary, you don't have income tax withheld from a paycheck, and are not subject to FICA, an employment tax comprised of Social Security and Medicare taxes. However, you must satisfy your Social Security tax and Medicare tax obligations

SCHEDULE C (Form 1040)	**Profit or Loss From Business** (Sole Proprietorship)	OMB No. 1545-0074
Department of the Treasury Internal Revenue Service (99)	▶ Partnerships, joint ventures, etc., must file Form 1065 or Form 1065-B. ▶ Attach to Form 1040 or Form 1041. ▶ See Instructions for Schedule C (Form 1040).	2000 Attachment Sequence No. 09

Name of proprietor	Social security number (SSN)

A Principal business or profession, including product or service (see page C-1)   **B** Enter code from pages C-8 & 9 ▶

C Business name. If no separate business name, leave blank.   **D** Employer ID number (EIN), if any

E Business address (including suite or room no.) ▶ ....
City, town or post office, state, and ZIP code

F Accounting method: (1) ☐ Cash   (2) ☐ Accrual   (3) ☐ Other (specify) ▶ ....

G Did you "materially participate" in the operation of this business during 2000? If "No," see page C-2 for limit on losses   ☐ Yes ☐ No

H If you started or acquired this business during 2000, check here   .   .   .   .   ▶ ☐

Part I   Income

1	Gross receipts or sales. **Caution:** If this income was reported to you on Form W-2 and the "Statutory employee" box on that form was checked, see page C-2 and check here . . . . . . ▶ ☐	1	
2	Returns and allowances	2	
3	Subtract line 2 from line 1	3	
4	Cost of goods sold (from line 42 on page 2)	4	
5	**Gross profit.** Subtract line 4 from line 3	5	
6	Other income, including Federal and state gasoline or fuel tax credit or refund (see page C-3) . .	6	
7	**Gross income.** Add lines 5 and 6 . . . . ▶	7	

Part II   Expenses. Enter expenses for business use of your home **only** on line 30.

8	Advertising	8		19	Pension and profit-sharing plans	19	
9	Bad debts from sales or services (see page C-3) . .	9		20	Rent or lease (see page C-4):		
				a	Vehicles, machinery, and equipment .	20a	
10	Car and truck expenses (see page C-3)	10		b	Other business property . .	20b	
11	Commissions and fees . .	11		21	Repairs and maintenance . .	21	
12	Depletion	12		22	Supplies (not included in Part III) .	22	
13	Depreciation and section 179 expense deduction (not included in Part III) (see page C-3) .	13		23	Taxes and licenses . . .	23	
				24	Travel, meals, and entertainment:		
				a	Travel	24a	
14	Employee benefit programs (other than on line 19) . . .	14		b	Meals and entertainment .		
15	Insurance (other than health) .	15		c	Enter nondeductible amount included on line 24b (see page C-5) .		
16	Interest:						
a	Mortgage (paid to banks, etc.) .	16a		d	Subtract line 24c from line 24b .	24d	
b	Other	16b		25	Utilities	25	
17	Legal and professional services	17		26	Wages (less employment credits) .	26	
18	Office expense	18		27	Other expenses (from line 48 on page 2)	27	

28	**Total expenses** before expenses for business use of home. Add lines 8 through 27 in columns . ▶	28	
29	Tentative profit (loss). Subtract line 28 from line 7	29	
30	Expenses for business use of your home. Attach **Form 8829**	30	
31	**Net profit or (loss).** Subtract line 30 from line 29. • If a profit, enter on **Form 1040, line 12,** and **also** on **Schedule SE, line 2** (statutory employees, see page C-6). Estates and trusts, enter on Form 1041, line 3. • If a loss, you **must** go to line 32.	31	
32	If you have a loss, check the box that describes your investment in this activity (see page C-6). • If you checked 32a, enter the loss on **Form 1040, line 12,** and **also** on **Schedule SE, line 2** (statutory employees, see page C-6). Estates and trusts, enter on Form 1041, line 3. • If you checked 32b, you **must** attach Form 6198.	32a ☐ All investment is at risk. 32b ☐ Some investment is not at risk.	

For Paperwork Reduction Act Notice, see Form 1040 Instructions.   Cat. No. 11334P   Schedule C (Form 1040) 2000

FIGURE 2.1 Schedule C

Schedule C (Form 1040) 2000 Page 2

Part III **Cost of Goods Sold** (see page C-6)

33 Method(s) used to value closing inventory: a ☐ Cost b ☐ Lower of cost or market c ☐ Other (attach explanation)

34 Was there any change in determining quantities, costs, or valuations between opening and closing inventory? If "Yes," attach explanation . . . ☐ Yes ☐ No

35 Inventory at beginning of year. If different from last year's closing inventory, attach explanation	35	
36 Purchases less cost of items withdrawn for personal use	36	
37 Cost of labor. Do not include any amounts paid to yourself	37	
38 Materials and supplies	38	
39 Other costs	39	
40 Add lines 35 through 39	40	
41 Inventory at end of year	41	
42 **Cost of goods sold.** Subtract line 41 from line 40. Enter the result here and on page 1, line 4	42	

Part IV **Information on Your Vehicle.** Complete this part **only** if you are claiming car or truck expenses on line 10 and are not required to file Form 4562 for this business. See the instructions for line 13 on page C-3 to find out if you must file.

43 When did you place your vehicle in service for business purposes? (month, day, year) ▶ ..../........./.......

44 Of the total number of miles you drove your vehicle during 2000, enter the number of miles you used your vehicle for:

a Business .... b Commuting .... c Other ....

45 Do you (or your spouse) have another vehicle available for personal use? . . . ☐ Yes ☐ No

46 Was your vehicle available for use during off-duty hours? . . . ☐ Yes ☐ No

47a Do you have evidence to support your deduction? . . . ☐ Yes ☐ No

b If "Yes," is the evidence written? . . . ☐ Yes ☐ No

Part V **Other Expenses.** List below business expenses not included on lines 8–26 or line 30.

48 **Total other expenses.** Enter here and on page 1, line 27	48	

Schedule C (Form 1040) 2000

FIGURE 2.1 Continued

by paying self-employment tax. In 2001, the Social Security tax is 12.4 percent of your net earnings from self-employment (your profit) up to $80,400 (this will increase for later years), and the Medicare tax is 2.9 percent of all your net earnings from self-employment. Sole proprietors can deduct one-half of the self-employment tax they've paid as an adjustment to gross income on their personal income tax returns.

CAUTION

As a sole proprietor you need to set aside money to pay estimated taxes when due (April 15, June 15, September 15, and January 15 of the following year). If you lack the discipline to do this, then this is a factor mitigating against choosing sole proprietorship as your business entity.

ESTIMATED TAXES

Since there's no paycheck and no tax withholding, you must pay your anticipated taxes for the year through quarterly estimated tax payments. These payments must cover not only your business profits but also your self-employment tax. The failure to pay enough in estimated taxes can result in unnecessary interest and penalties.

Partnerships

If two or more family members own an interest in the business, then you can form a partnership to share the profits from the business. As owners of a partnership you're called partners. There's no limit on the number of partners in a partnership. And there's no limit on the type of people or entities that can be partners. For example, family members obviously can be partners. But trusts, corporations, and even other partnerships can also be partners.

TIP

Protection from personal liability for partners from lawsuits involving personal injury can be gained by carrying adequate liability insurance. Thus, while the partners remain potentially liable for claims, as a practical matter they don't have to be too concerned about personal exposure because of insurance protection.

There are two types of partnerships: general partnerships (which are usually referred to simply as partnerships) and limited partnerships. In a general partnership, all partners are personally liable for the debts of the business. This means that creditors can look to the personal assets of each partner to satisfy any money owed by the partnership. A creditor can include not only someone who lends money to the business but also someone with a claim against it, such as a person injured on the premises.

And each partner is "jointly and severally liable" for the partnership's debts. Creditors can look to any one partner to satisfy the entire debt. Then that partner can try to recoup his or her proportional share of the debt from the other partner or partners.

Example

Two sisters are equal partners in a business that incurs a debt of $20,000 (none of which is recourse). The creditor can look to either sister for the full $20,000 (or collect any amount from each for a total of $20,000). If the creditor collects the full amount from one sister, she can try to collect $10,000 from her sibling.

Partnerships are easy to set up and don't *require* any formal agreement or government action to come into existence. All that's necessary is that partners agree to form a business for the purpose of making a profit.

Recourse debt is a type of financing that allows a creditor to obtain the property acquired by the financing. For example, a mortgage on an office building is recourse debt because the lender can foreclose on the building if the mortgage is in default.

However, as a practical matter, it's a good idea to have a written partnership agreement. The agreement should detail how you'll split the business's income, deductions, gains, losses, and credits. Generally, each partner's share reflects his or her portion of ownership. For example, if two brothers put in equal amounts of capital, they would share profits equally. However, special allocations are allowed for tax purposes if certain conditions are met. In other words, one partner may be entitled to a greater share of losses if that partner contributed certain property to the business.

In addition to tax considerations, the partnership agreement can also be used to spell out what happens when one partner wants out, retires, becomes disabled, goes bankrupt, or dies. This is essential because legally a partnership automatically terminates when a single partner is no longer a partner for any reason. The partnership agreement can provide that in such a situation, the partnership will continue even though one partner has dropped out. The types of provisions that should be included in a partnership agreement to cover various contingencies to ensure that the partnership continues and that the partner (or his or her family) receives adequate compensation for leaving are explained in Part 3 of this book.

Besides having a partnership agreement, the entity may be required to file with county or local government indicating that it is a partnership doing business as (d/b/a) the name indicated. For example, cousins form the CC Partnership to perform consulting services under the name of Cousins Consulting Associates. The d/b/a allows the partnership to have a bank account, collect sales taxes, and perform other necessary business tasks under the proper name.

How Partnerships Are Taxed

Partnerships aren't taxed. Only partners are taxed on their share of partnership items. A partnership is *never* a taxpayer for income tax purposes. Instead it's called a "pass-through" entity because income, deductions, gains, losses, and tax credits pass through to partners and are reported on their personal income tax returns.

Even though a partnership doesn't pay tax, it's required to file a tax return called Form 1065, U.S. Partnership Return of Income (see Figure 2.2). It acts as an information return, telling the IRS and the partners exactly what the partnership earned (or lost). The partnership also completes Schedule K-1 of Form 1065 to apportion partnership items to each partner according to his or her partnership interest (or as required by the partnership agreement). A partner's share of partnership items is called his or her "distributive share." A copy of Schedule K-1 must be furnished by the partnership to each partner. As you can see from the sample Form 1065 and the Schedule K-1, items receive parallel listings. For example, the first section of Form 1065 covers total income (or loss). It is this amount, as allocated to the partner, that is reported on the first line of Schedule K-1.

Items passing through to partners fall into two categories: trade or business income (or loss) and separately stated items. Trade or business income (or loss) is the net amount of most ordinary income and deductions of the business. A partnership's ordinary income would include fees it charges for services rendered and net sales of goods (gross receipts less cost of goods sold). Ordinary deductions include compensation paid to employees, rent, interest, repairs, and so on. Payments to partners may or may not be deductible, depending on how they're characterized. Guaranteed payments are deducted from business income. Draws (advances against profits) that are not considered guaranteed payments are not deductible.

Separately stated items are those subject to special limitations on

> **CAUTION**
>
> A partner must report items on his or her personal return as they are reported on the Schedule K-1. If a partner wants to take an inconsistent position and report an item differently than it was reported on the K-1, then Form 8082, Notice of Inconsistent Treatment or Amended Return, must be attached to the partner's return. This is a sure audit flag, so inconsistent treatment should be used only in unusual circumstances.

Form **1065**		**U.S. Return of Partnership Income**		OMB No. 1545-0099
Department of the Treasury Internal Revenue Service		For calendar year 2000, or tax year beginning .... , 2000, and ending .... , 20..... . ▶ See separate instructions.		2000

A Principal business activity	Use the IRS label. Other- wise, please print or type.	Name of partnership	D Employer identification number
B Principal product or service		Number, street, and room or suite no. If a P.O. box, see page 12 of the instructions.	E Date business started
C Business code number		City or town, state, and ZIP code	F Total assets (see page 12 of the instructions) $

G   Check applicable boxes: **(1)** ☐ Initial return   **(2)** ☐ Final return   **(3)** ☐ Change in address   **(4)** ☐ Amended return

H   Check accounting method: **(1)** ☐ Cash   **(2)** ☐ Accrual   **(3)** ☐ Other (specify) ▶ ....

I   Number of Schedules K-1. Attach one for each person who was a partner at any time during the tax year ▶ ....

Caution: *Include* only *trade or business income and expenses on lines 1a through 22 below. See the instructions for more information.*

Income

1a Gross receipts or sales		**1a**		
b Less returns and allowances.		**1b**	**1c**	
2 Cost of goods sold (Schedule A, line 8)			**2**	
3 Gross profit. Subtract line 2 from line 1c.			**3**	
4 Ordinary income (loss) from other partnerships, estates, and trusts *(attach schedule)* . . .			**4**	
5 Net farm profit (loss) *(attach Schedule F (Form 1040))*			**5**	
6 Net gain (loss) from Form 4797, Part II, line 18.			**6**	
7 Other income (loss) *(attach schedule)*			**7**	
8 **Total income (loss).** Combine lines 3 through 7			**8**	

Deductions (see page 14 of the instructions for limitations)

9 Salaries and wages (other than to partners) (less employment credits)		**9**	
10 Guaranteed payments to partners		**10**	
11 Repairs and maintenance		**11**	
12 Bad debts		**12**	
13 Rent		**13**	
14 Taxes and licenses		**14**	
15 Interest		**15**	
16a Depreciation (if required, attach Form 4562)	**16a**		
b Less depreciation reported on Schedule A and elsewhere on return	**16b**	**16c**	
17 Depletion **(Do not deduct oil and gas depletion.)**		**17**	
18 Retirement plans, etc.		**18**	
19 Employee benefit programs		**19**	
20 Other deductions *(attach schedule)*		**20**	
21 **Total deductions.** Add the amounts shown in the far right column for lines 9 through 20 .		**21**	

22 **Ordinary income (loss)** from trade or business activities. Subtract line 21 from line 8 . .		**22**	

Please Sign Here

Under penalties of perjury, I declare that I have examined this return, including accompanying schedules and statements, and to the best of my knowledge and belief, it is true, correct, and complete. Declaration of preparer (other than general partner or limited liability company member) is based on all information of which preparer has any knowledge.

▶ _____   ▶ _____
Signature of general partner or limited liability company member   Date

Paid Preparer's Use Only

Preparer's signature ▶		Date	Check if self-employed ▶ ☐	Preparer's SSN or PTIN
Firm's name (or yours if self-employed), address, and ZIP code	▶		EIN ▶	
			Phone no.	( )

For Paperwork Reduction Act Notice, see separate instructions.   Cat. No. 11390Z   Form **1065** (2000)

FIGURE 2.2   Form 1065 and Schedule K-1

SCHEDULE K-1	**Partner's Share of Income, Credits, Deductions, etc.**	OMB No. 1545-0099
(Form 1065)	▶ See separate instructions.	**2000**
Department of the Treasury Internal Revenue Service	For calendar year 2000 or tax year beginning _____ , 2000, and ending _____ , 20 ___	

Partner's identifying number ▶	Partnership's identifying number ▶
Partner's name, address, and ZIP code	Partnership's name, address, and ZIP code

A This partner is a ☐ general partner   ☐ limited partner
    ☐ limited liability company member
B What type of entity is this partner? ▶ ....
C Is this partner a ☐ domestic or a ☐ foreign partner?
D Enter partner's percentage of: **(i)** Before change or termination   **(ii)** End of year
    Profit sharing . . . . % .... %
    Loss sharing . . . . % .... %
    Ownership of capital . . . . % .... %
E IRS Center where partnership filed return:

F Partner's share of liabilities (see instructions):
    Nonrecourse . . . .) $ ....
    Qualified nonrecourse financing . $ ....
    Other . . . . $ ....
G Tax shelter registration number . ▶ ....
H Check here if this partnership is a publicly traded partnership as defined in section 469(k)(2) . . . . . ☐
I Check applicable boxes: **(1)** ☐ Final K-1 **(2)** ☐ Amended K-1

J **Analysis of partner's capital account:**

(a) Capital account at beginning of year	**(b)** Capital contributed during year	**(c)** Partner's share of lines 3, 4, and 7, Form 1065, Schedule M-2	**(d)** Withdrawals and distributions	**(e)** Capital account at end of year (combine columns (a) through (d))
		(	)	

(a) Distributive share item			**(b)** Amount	**(c)** 1040 filers enter the amount in column (b) on:
	1	Ordinary income (loss) from trade or business activities . . .	**1**	See page 6 of Partner's Instructions for Schedule K-1 (Form 1065).
	2	Net income (loss) from rental real estate activities	**2**	
	3	Net income (loss) from other rental activities	**3**	
	4	Portfolio income (loss):		
	a	Interest	**4a**	Sch. B, Part I, line 1
Income (Loss)	**b**	Ordinary dividends	**4b**	Sch. B, Part II, line 5
	c	Royalties	**4c**	Sch. E, Part I, line 4
	d	Net short-term capital gain (loss)	**4d**	Sch. D, line 5, col. (f)
	e	Net long-term capital gain (loss):		
		(1) 28% rate gain (loss)	**e(1)**	Sch. D, line 12, col. (g)
		(2) Total for year.	**e(2)**	Sch. D, line 12, col. (f)
	f	Other portfolio income (loss) *(attach schedule)*	**4f**	Enter on applicable line of your return.
	5	Guaranteed payments to partner	**5**	See page 6 of Partner's Instructions for Schedule K-1 (Form 1065).
	6	Net section 1231 gain (loss) (other than due to casualty or theft) .	**6**	
	7	Other income (loss) *(attach schedule)*	**7**	Enter on applicable line of your return.
Deduc- tions	**8**	Charitable contributions (see instructions) *(attach schedule)* . .	**8**	Sch. A, line 15 or 16
	9	Section 179 expense deduction.	**9**	See pages 7 and 8 of Partner's Instructions for Schedule K-1 (Form 1065).
	10	Deductions related to portfolio income *(attach schedule)* . . .	**10**	
	11	Other deductions *(attach schedule)*.	**11**	
	12a	Low-income housing credit:		
		(1) From section 42(j)(5) partnerships for property placed in service before 1990	**a(1)**	
		(2) Other than on line 12a(1) for property placed in service before 1990	**a(2)**	Form 8586, line 5
Credits		**(3)** From section 42(j)(5) partnerships for property placed in service after 1989	**a(3)**	
		(4) Other than on line 12a(3) for property placed in service after 1989	**a(4)**	
	b	Qualified rehabilitation expenditures related to rental real estate activities	**12b**	
	c	Credits (other than credits shown on lines 12a and 12b) related to rental real estate activities.	**12c**	See page 8 of Partner's Instructions for Schedule K-1 (Form 1065).
	d	Credits related to other rental activities	**12d**	
	13	Other credits	**13**	

For Paperwork Reduction Act Notice, see Instructions for Form 1065.   Cat. No. 11394R   Schedule K-1 (Form 1065) 2000

FIGURE 2.2 Continued

Schedule K-1 (Form 1065) 2000 — Page **2**

(a) Distributive share item	(b) Amount	(c) 1040 filers enter the amount in column (b) on:
Investment Interest		
14a Interest expense on investment debts **14a**		Form 4952, line 1
b (1) Investment income included on lines 4a, 4b, 4c, and 4f . . **b(1)**		See page 9 of Partner's Instructions for Schedule K-1 (Form 1065).
(2) Investment expenses included on line 10 . . . . . . **b(2)**		
Self-employment		
15a Net earnings (loss) from self-employment **15a**		Sch. SE, Section A or B
b Gross farming or fishing income. **15b**		See page 9 of Partner's Instructions for Schedule K-1 (Form 1065).
c Gross nonfarm income. **15c**		
Adjustments and Tax Preference Items		
16a Depreciation adjustment on property placed in service after 1986 **16a**		
b Adjusted gain or loss **16b**		See page 9 of Partner's Instructions for Schedule K-1 (Form 1065) and Instructions for Form 6251.
c Depletion (other than oil and gas) **16c**		
d (1) Gross income from oil, gas, and geothermal properties . . **d(1)**		
(2) Deductions allocable to oil, gas, and geothermal properties **d(2)**		
e Other adjustments and tax preference items (attach schedule) **16e**		
Foreign Taxes		
17a Name of foreign country or U.S. possession ▶ ------------------		
b Total gross income sourced at partner level **17b**		
c Total gross income sourced at partnership level (attach schedule):		
(1) U.S. source and listed categories . . . . **17c(1)**		
(2) Passive . . . . **17c(2)**		
(3) General limitation . . . . **17c(3)**		
d Deductions allocated and apportioned at partner level:		Form 1116, Part I
(1) Interest expense . . . . **17d(1)**		
(2) Other . . . . **17d(2)**		
e Deductions allocated and apportioned at partnership level (attach schedule):		
(1) U.S. source and listed categories . . . . **17e(1)**		
(2) Passive . . . . **17e(2)**		
(3) General limitation . . . . **17e(3)**		
f Total foreign taxes (check one): ▶ ☐ Paid ☐ Accrued . . . **17f**		Form 1116, Part II
g Reduction in taxes available for credit (attach schedule) . . . **17g**		Form 1116, Part III and Instructions for Form 1116.
Other		
18 Section 59(e)(2) expenditures: a Type ▶ ------------------------		See page 9 of Partner's Instructions for Schedule K-1 (Form 1065).
b Amount **18b**		
19 Tax-exempt interest income **19**		Form 1040, line 8b
20 Other tax-exempt income. **20**		
21 Nondeductible expenses **21**		See pages 9 and 10 of Partner's Instructions for Schedule K-1 (Form 1065).
22 Distributions of money (cash and marketable securities) . . . **22**		
23 Distributions of property other than money **23**		
24 Recapture of low-income housing credit:		
a From section 42(j)(5) partnerships **24a**		Form 8611, line 8
b Other than on line 24a. **24b**		

25 Supplemental information required to be reported separately to each partner (attach additional schedules if more space is needed):

Supplemental Information

Schedule K-1 (Form 1065) 2000

FIGURE 2.2 **Continued**

a partner's individual tax return and so need to be segregated from ordinary income and deductions. They are considered stand-alone items. Examples of separately stated items include:

- Charitable contributions by the partnership, since they are subject to adjusted gross income limits on an individual's return (or a 10 percent taxable income limit if a partner happens to be a corporation).
- First-year expense deduction (called the Section 179 deduction) for equipment purchases. This deduction is subject to a dollar limit at *both* the partnership and partner levels.
- Capital gains (and losses) since these must be netted against an individual's other gains and losses to determine taxation of capital gains.
- Tax credits, such as employment-related tax credits. These are claimed against a partner's tax liability (a partnership has no liability since it doesn't pay any tax and so would be unable to use tax credits).

Fringe benefits provided to partners generally are taxable to them (even though such benefits may be tax-free to the partnership's employees). For example, if the partnership provides health insurance, partners are treated as receiving income. Then, they can claim a deduction for health coverage on their personal returns (in 2000 and 2001, 60 percent is deductible as an adjustment to gross income although the percentage may be increased by Congress).

Payments to Partners

Partners can *never* receive a salary from the business since they can't be considered employees. They are self-employed persons working for their business. Payments to them can come in a variety of ways—draws (advances against a share of partnership profits), guaranteed payments, fringe benefits paid by the business, and loans from the business. These payments aren't reported on a W-2 form as is the case for payments to employees. Nor are they reported on a Form 1099, as is the case for payments to independent contractors (self-employed individuals) who work for the partnership. Instead, they're taken into account in the Schedule K-1. Since partners pay tax on their distributive share of partnership interest, draws generally have no impact on this tax reporting. However, guaranteed payments are reported separately.

Partners pay self-employment tax on both their distributive share of partnership income *and* any guaranteed payments to them. As explained earlier, self-employment tax covers both the employer and employee share of the Social Security and Medicare taxes for self-employed individuals. Thus, in 2001, the Social Security tax portion of the self-employment tax is 12.4 percent on net earnings from self-employment up to $80,400. The Medicare portion is 2.9 percent on all net earnings from self-employment.

Partners can deduct one-half of the self-employment tax they've paid as an adjustment to gross income on their personal income tax returns.

Loss Limitations

Businesses, particularly in start-up years, may experience losses in their operations. Partnership losses pass through to partners and are claimed on the partners' returns. However, losses cannot exceed a partner's basis in the partnership interest. Basis is the amount of cash and property (based on the fair market value, which is the cash that could be realized on the sale of the property in an arm's-length transaction) that the partner contributed to the partnership.

Basis can be increased by a partner's share of partnership debt. However, in a general partnership, basis is not increased by nonrecourse liability. Also, basis is not increased by accrued partnership liabilities such as accounts payable.

Another limitation on claiming losses is the passive activity loss limitation rules, called PAL rules for short. Partners who are mere investors and who don't perform sufficient services for the business to be considered "material participants"

> **TIP**
>
> Self-employed individuals do not pay the Social Security portion of self-employment tax to the extent they receive a salary from another business that is subject to FICA. This is because no more than a dollar limit—$80,400 in 2001—in employee compensation and self-employment income is taken into account in figuring this tax. Thus, for example, if they are full-time employees of a corporation and are paid $80,400 or more in 2001, then their distributive share of partnership income from a partnership in which they've invested does not cause them to pay any additional Social Security tax.

Example

You and your spouse each contribute $5,000 to start the HW Partnership. In 2000, as the partnership is just getting started, it shows an operating loss of $12,000. Your share of the loss is $6,000. However, since your basis is only $5,000, your loss deduction for 2000 is limited to that amount. The unused loss of $1,000 is carried forward and can be used when there is additional basis to offset it.

can't deduct losses in excess of income from their involvement. These highly complex rules are explained in IRS Publication 925, "Passive Activity and At-Risk Rules."

Limited Partnerships

A limited partnership is a form of business organization comprised of at least one general partner—a party with personal liability for partnership debts—and one limited partner—a party who, as the name implies, has no personal liability. For example, a parent may be the general partner and a child the limited partner in a limited partnership.

Being a limited partner means lacking the ability to participate in the management of the business. Only general partners can dictate day-to-day activities and determine whether profits should be distributed or withheld for expansion purposes or otherwise. By law, limited partners have a right to only a fixed share of partnership income or other items as specified in the partnership agreement and a share of assets upon the sale or liquidation of the business.

Being a limited partner also means having limited liability with respect to partnership debt. The most that a limited partner can lose is the amount of money invested in the partnership (or promised to be invested).

A limited partnership must be organized in accordance with state law. This requires the partnership to have a limited partnership agreement that meets state law requirements, which generally includes a recitation of who is a general partner and who is a limited partner and what right each partner has in partnership profits.

Note

Family limited partnerships, or FLPs, are commonly used today not only as an organizational structure for running a business but also for holding investments. They allow parents to transfer ownership interests to children and grandchildren at greatly discounted values from those of the underlying assets in the partnership. The reason: Since the parents retain control over the assets of the partnership—running the business or making investment decisions—the limited partnership interests must be discounted to reflect their limited role. Family limited partnerships as an estate-planning device are explained in Part 3.

Example

Two sisters are partners in a business that incurs a debt of $20,000. The older sister is the general partner and the younger sister is the limited partner. The creditor can look only to the older sister for the full $20,000. The older sister can't collect money from the younger sister to pay the debt (unless that sister hasn't yet made the full contribution initially promised to the partnership).

Taxation of Limited Partnerships

A limited partnership is taxed exactly the same way as a general partnership. The limited partnership files the same Form 1065 and the same Schedule K-1 as a general partnership. Income and other items pass through to partners and are reported on the partners' individual returns according to the partners' distributive shares.

However, limited partners are *not* subject to self-employment tax on their distributive share of partnership income. Since, by definition, they don't work for the partnership, the law excuses them from self-employment tax. Of course, a general partner in a limited partnership is still subject to self-employment tax.

The basis rules for limited partnerships are the same as for general partnerships, with one difference. If the general partner assumes the liability (i.e., the debt is recourse), then the general partner can increase basis. If the debt is nonrecourse, then all partners, including limited partners, increase basis by their share of the debt.

Limited Liability Companies

Limited liability companies, or LLCs, now recognized in all states, are a relatively new type of business organization. They must be organized according to state law in much the same way as corporations. Owners of LLCs are called members.

These companies can be run by all of the members. In effect, each member has a say in the business to the extent of his or her LLC interest. Alternatively, the members can designate managers to run the business. In this case, members who are not managers are more akin to silent partners, enjoying the profits from the business but prevented from having a say in management and other business decisions.

Limited liability companies try to combine the best aspects of partnerships and corporations. As in a partnership, income and other items pass through to owners. Like a corporation, however, LLCs allow owners to enjoy protection from personal liability. Creditors can satisfy debts only from LLC assets and cannot look to members' personal assets.

While most of the tax rules are the same for LLCs as they are for partnerships, there are some points of difference. For basis purposes, the treatment of liabilities is not clear. Since a member's liability for the LLC's debt is limited to the amount of his or her contribution (i.e., the member is *not* personally liable for the LLC debt), it would seem that all LLC debt should be treated as nonrecourse for basis purposes and should *not* be used to increase a member's basis. However, there is no case or ruling on this point.

The tax treatment of members for purposes of self-employment tax is also unclear. The IRS had been prohibited from implementing regulations that would have defined when a member is considered a limited partner exempt from self-employment tax or a general partner subject to it. However, that ban has long since expired. Still, no guidance has yet been issued on this question.

S Corporations

From a legal point of view S corporations are regular corporations, which are artificial persons created under state law. They must be

Note

A corporation can be set up in any state even though it may do business in another state. It is common for publicly traded corporations to be organized in states such as Delaware and Nevada, states with laws friendly to corporate management. The laws in these states make it more difficult for shareholders to contest the actions of management. For closely held corporations—family businesses—there's no compelling reason to incorporate out of state. Tax-wise, out-of-state corporations are still subject to the tax laws of the state in which they do business and may, in fact, incur additional tax costs by an out-of-state incorporation.

organized according to state law. Owners of corporations are called shareholders or stockholders.

Corporate owners do not have any liability for the debts of the business. Creditors can look only to the assets of the business to satisfy their claims. However, as a practical matter, it's virtually impossible for small corporations to raise capital without shareholders personally guaranteeing corporate debt. For example, if a bank loans the business $100,000, shareholders must give their personal guarantee that the loan will be repaid. Thus, in effect, they can become personally liable for the corporation's debt.

Corporate stock of an S corporation must be restricted to common stock. This is because an S corporation cannot have more than one class of stock. However, differences in voting rights do not create a second class of stock. Thus, owners of family corporations who want to limit control in the business for certain members whom they wish to receive only income from the business can use nonvoting stock for these relatives. Nonvoting stock does not entitle the holder to any say in most corporate actions, including day-to-day operations.

CAUTION

Shareholders can become 100 percent personally liable for their corporation's trust fund taxes. These are income taxes withheld from employee wages and the employee share of FICA. If the corporation doesn't pay up this debt, the IRS may look to "responsible persons" who include shareholders with certain decision-making authority.

Who Can Be Shareholders

Tax laws limit who can own shares in an S corporation. First, there can be no more than 75 shareholders. A husband and wife are counted as one shareholder regardless of whether the stock is owned individually or jointly. In the case of a trust holding stock, each beneficiary is counted as a shareholder.

NOTE

Over half of all S corporations have only one shareholder. More than 90 percent of all S corporations have three or fewer shareholders.

While the 75-shareholder limit may seem like a restriction, for family businesses this is of little consequence. Family members owning shares in the corporation are not likely to total more than the limit. The only time this shareholder limit becomes a problem is if the family business decides to go public. At that time, the corporation must terminate its S status.

Another restriction on shareholders is the type of entities that are eligible. Individuals can be shareholders, regardless of age. However, no nonresident aliens are permitted as shareholders.

Tax-exempt organizations are permitted as S corporation shareholders. Thus, individuals can place their S stock in a charitable remainder trust for transfer tax savings without harming the tax status of the business. The use of charitable remainder trusts in family-business planning is explained in Part 3 of this book.

Partnerships, limited liability companies, and corporations (other than tax-exempt organizations) cannot be S corporation shareholders under any circumstances. If they become shareholders, S status is terminated automatically.

Only certain trusts are permitted as shareholders. These include:

- *Grantor trusts.* These are trusts in which the grantor—the person who sets up the trust—is treated as the owner of the trust so that income earned by the trust is taxed directly to the grantor and not to the trust. Grantor trusts can be eligible shareholders for the life of the grantor and for up to two years following the grantor's death.

- *Voting trusts.* These are trusts formed by eligible shareholders to vote their stock as a block.

- *Testamentary trusts.* These are trusts created under the terms of a shareholder's will.

- *Qualified subchapter S trusts (QSSTs).* These are trusts in which there is only one income beneficiary at a time. The income must be distributed to the current income beneficiary (the trustee cannot exercise discretion about whether to distribute current income).

- *Electing small business trusts (ESBTs).*

TIP

Qualified subchapter S trusts (QSSTs) can be used, for example, solely for the purpose of shifting income to a child or other family member without permitting any participation in the business. The trust can hold nonvoting stock.

ELECTING SMALL BUSINESS TRUSTS (ESBTS)

These are trusts that elect to be treated as such and meet certain requirements. They can have more than one current income beneficiary (but each current income beneficiary is taken into account for purposes of the 75-shareholder limit). If a current income beneficiary is also a direct shareholder in the S corporation, he or she is not counted twice. A current income beneficiary for ESBT purposes is any beneficiary who is entitled to, or at the discretion of any person may receive, a distribution from income or principal from the trust. Interests in an ESBT must be acquired through gift, inheritance, or some other nonpurchase acquisition. However, the trust itself can ac-

TIP

In family businesses, ESBTs can serve a useful purpose by allowing the trustee of the trust to determine which beneficiary, and to what extent that beneficiary, should receive income from the trust.

quire S corporation stock by purchase without disqualifying the trust. The trustee of an ESBT can distribute income ("spray income") to any one or more beneficiaries on a discretionary basis. Also, a beneficiary of an ESBT can be a nonresident alien.

Special tax rules apply to an ESBT. The portion of the ESBT that consists of stock in one or more S corporations is treated as a separate trust. The trust's taxable income attributable to the S stock is taxed at the highest rate imposed on trusts and estates (currently 39.6 percent for ordinary income and 20 percent for capital gains). Taxable income includes the following items:

- Items of income, loss, or deduction allocated to the trust as an S corporation shareholder under the general rules for S corporations.
- Gain or loss from the sale of S corporation stock.
- State or local income taxes and administrative expenses of the trust properly allocable to the S corporation stock.

The ESBT may deduct capital losses only to the extent of capital gains. Beneficiaries cannot deduct capital losses against $3,000 of ordinary income. No income deduction is allowed for this portion of the trust. But when the trust terminates, any unused carryovers or excess deductions are taken into account by the entire trust. The ESBT must compute alternative minimum tax with respect to the portion of the trust holding the S stock, but no AMT exemption is allowed.

Taxation of S Corporations

S corporations aren't born into that status; they're elected to it. First a corporation is formed, then the shareholders agree to be taxed as an S corporation. Being taxed as an S corporation means that generally only the shareholders, and not the corporation, pay income tax on company profits, thereby eliminating the "double tax" that would otherwise apply (tax on the corporation and again on the shareholders when profits are distributed to them in the form of dividends). The

CAUTION

Check on the income tax treatment of an S corporation under your state's law. Some states follow the federal treatment, while others impose a separate tax on them.

election process is discussed later in this chapter. Assuming an effective S election has been filed, here's what it means for federal tax purposes.

While S corporation status provides protection from personal liability, from an income tax standpoint S corporations are taxed in much the same way as partnerships. They are considered pass-through entities. The S corporation return is Form 1120-S, U.S. Income Tax Return for S Corporations. Shareholders receive a Schedule K-1 of Form 1120-S to report their share of S corporation items.

S corporation income, deductions, gains and losses, and tax credits, collectively referred to as S corporation "items," are allocated to shareholders on a per-share per-day basis. Thus, shareholders who come into (or leave) the corporation mid-year do not receive a full allocation of each item; it's prorated for the number of days they were shareholders.

However, there are certain differences between the tax treatment of partnerships and S corporations. While partnerships can *never* be taxpayers, S corporations can become taxpayers in limited situations. All of these situations, however, relate to an S corporation that had been a C corporation before making the S election.

> **CAUTION**
>
> S corporation shareholders may be reluctant to take a salary, thinking that they can avoid FICA. The IRS looks closely at these situations, and courts have required that shareholders receive a reasonable salary for services they perform for the business.

Shareholders are not self-employed individuals and so are not subject to self-employment tax. They (and the corporation) pay FICA only on salary they receive. Thus, unlike partners who pay self-employment tax on their share of business profits, S corporation shareholders pay FICA only on actual salary payments to them.

Like partnerships, S corporation shareholders owning more than 2 percent of stock cannot receive certain fringe benefits tax free. For example, company-paid health insurance becomes taxable to such owners who can then claim a deduction on their personal return (in 2000 and 2001, 60 percent as an adjustment to gross income on page one of Form 1040 and not as an itemized deduction although the percentage may be increased by Congress).

Losses passed through to shareholders are deductible to the extent of basis in both stock and loans to the corporation. However, al-

> **Example**
>
> Roslyn is a 50 percent shareholder in an S corporation for just 100 days in 2001 (she became a shareholder on September 23, 2001). The S corporation's income for the year is $100,000. Her share of the corporation's income is $13,699 ($100,000 × 50% × 100/365 days).

though the percentage may be increased by Congress mere guarantees by a shareholder of corporate debt to third parties do not increase a shareholder's basis.

S corporation shareholders are also subject to the passive activity loss limitation rules (PAL rules). Shareholders who are mere investors and who don't perform sufficient services for the business to be considered "material participants" can't deduct losses in excess of income from their involvement. These highly complex rules for S corporation shareholders are explained in IRS Publication 925, "Passive Activity and At-Risk Rules."

Making the S Election

The election to be taxed as an S corporation for federal income tax purposes is made by filing with the IRS its Form 2553, Election by Small Business Corporations to Tax Corporate Income Directly to Shareholders. This election must be made no later than the 15th day of the third month of the corporation's tax year. If the election is made after this date, then it is automatically effective for the following year.

If the corporation is formed during the year and wants immediate S status, then the election must be made by the 15th day of the third month after the month the corporation began. For example, if a business is incorporated on May 1, 2001, it must file the S election by August 15, 2001, for the election to be effective for the corporation's first year.

You can't make the election *before* the corporation is set up. Then, at that time, the corporation's board of directors must agree to the S election and reflect the vote in the minutes of the corporation's board of directors meeting.

CAUTION

Where the law in your state recognizes S corporation status, the corporation must make a separate S election for federal and state tax purposes.

CAUTION

States have their own laws regarding S corporations. Some states tax them separately while others follow the federal rules and exempt S corporations from state income tax. Be sure to make a separate tax election for S status if necessary.

Example

A corporation using a calendar year wants to elect S status for 2001. It must file the election no later than March 15, 2001. (It can file the election at any time during 2000.) If it files after March 15, 2001, then the election takes effect in 2002.

MAKING THE QSST ELECTION

The election to be treated as a qualified subchapter S trust is made in Part III of Form 2553 (the form used to make the S election) or a statement containing the same information found in Part III, which you send to the IRS if the corporate stock has been transferred to the trust on or before the date on which the S election is to be effective. If a corporation is already an S corporation, then a QSST election is *not* made on Form 2553 but on a separate statement containing the information required in Part III of Form 2553, which is then sent to the IRS.

MAKING THE ESBT ELECTION

The ESBT election for a trust to be treated as an electing small business trust is made by the trustee (not the beneficiaries or the S corporation). The trustee makes the election simply by signing and filing with the IRS a statement containing certain information (such as the name, address, and taxpayer identification number of all potential current beneficiaries, the trust, and the corporation) and by identifying the election as being made under Tax Code Section 1361(e)(3). The election must also specify the date on which the election is to be effective but no earlier than 15 days and two months before the date on which the election is filed. The election must be made within the 16-day and two-month period beginning on the day the S stock is transferred to the trust. For a newly electing S corporation, the statement can be made by attaching a required statement to the S election made on Form 2553. However, there is no separate space on this form for making the election.

C Corporations

C corporations are separate entities apart from their shareholders. They have their own legal existence. For example, they can sue and be sued. From a legal standpoint, they're no different from S corporations. But from a tax standpoint, they're a world apart.

C corporations offer certain advantages that S corporations lack. C corporations can have an infinite number of shareholders (S corporations are limited to 75), so they can offer shares to the public (only C corporations are traded on stock exchanges). And if the company does business in a number of states, being a C corporation simplifies matters because only the corporation must file tax returns and pay income taxes to those states. In contrast, an S corporation operating a multistate business would not only have to file returns (and may be liable for certain taxes) in all those states, but the owners would have to file income tax returns in all those states as well to report their shares of the company's profits.

Taxation of C Corporations

C corporations are separate taxpayers. They file their own tax returns (Form 1120, Corporate Income Tax Return) to report income and losses. Certain small C corporations (those with gross receipts under $500,000) can file a simplified tax return, Form 1120-A, U.S. Corporations Short-Form Income Tax Return.

The corporation reports its own income and deductions. Shareholders do not report any income of the corporation. However, shareholders do report items paid out to them, such as salary, taxable benefits, and dividends.

C corporations potentially create a double-tax situation. This arises where the corporation first pays tax on its income. Then, when it distributes a dividend to shareholders, they pay tax again on that same income. The corporation cannot deduct dividend payments it makes. However, the double-tax situation is avoided when earnings can be paid out to shareholders in some tax-deductible manner, such as salary, bonuses, or fringe benefits.

C corporations are subject to tax rules that may differ from the rules applied to individuals. For example, corporations have their own graduated tax rates as shown in Figure 2.3.

Personal service corporations (PSCs) are subject to a flat 35 percent tax rate on all taxable income. Family businesses can be PSCs only if all the owners are eligible to be principals of the business. For example, in an architectural firm all shareholders must be licensed architects.

FIGURE 2.3 Corporate Tax Rates

Taxable Income Over . . .	But Not Over . . .	Tax Is . . .	Of the Amount Over . . .
$0	$50,000	15%	$0
$50,000	$75,000	$7,500 + 25%	$50,000
$75,000	$100,000	$13,750 + 34%	$75,000
$100,000	$335,000	$22,250 + 39%	$100,000
$335,000	$10,000,000	$113,900 + 34%	$335,000
$10,000,000	$15,000,000	$3,400,000 + 35%	$10,000,000
$15,000,000	$18,333,333	$5,150,000 + 38%	$15,000,000
$18,333,333	—	35%	$0

Personal service corporations (PSCs) are C corporations that perform services in the fields of health, law, accounting, engineering, architecture, actuarial science, performing arts, or consulting and meet certain ownership and service tests.

Personal service corporations are also subject to a number of other rules that distinguish them from ordinary C corporations:

- PSCs generally are required to use the same tax year as that of their owners. Since individuals typically use a calendar year, their PSC must also use a calendar year. If the PSC wants to use a fiscal year, it must make a special election and pay a special tax (that effectively defeats any tax-deferral benefit otherwise gained from using a fiscal year).

- PSCs can use the cash method of accounting even though other C corporations may be required to use the accrual method.

- PSCs are subject to the passive loss rules (while other C corporations generally are not).

- PSCs are subject to a more limited exemption from the accumulated earnings penalty. While most C corporations can accumulate up to $250,000 in the corporation without any special reason and be free from penalty, PSCs have only a $150,000 exemption.

- PSCs may have their income and deductions reallocated by the IRS between them and their shareholders if reallocation more closely reflects the economics of the situation.

C corporations do not get any tax break for capital gains. Capital gains are taxed at the same rate as ordinary income. And capital losses can be used only to offset capital gains (unlike individuals, who can deduct up to $3,000 of capital losses in excess of capital gains).

C corporations can provide employees (including owner-employees) with an array of fringe benefits. These include such benefit plans as:

- Health insurance
- Group term life insurance
- Adoption assistance
- Education assistance
- Dependent care assistance

C corporations may be subject to the alternative minimum tax (AMT), designed to ensure that they pay at least some income tax.

The corporate AMT rate is 20 percent. However, C corporations with average gross receipts of $5 million or less for the three previous tax years are exempt from AMT.

Tax-Free Incorporations

Generally, you can form a corporation without any immediate tax consequences. You contribute money, property, and/or services to the corporation in exchange for stock. As long as the incorporating group controls at least 80 percent of the corporate stock immediately after contributing to the corporation, then it's considered a tax-free incorporation.

There are, however, certain areas that can trip you up in trying to have a tax-free incorporation.

- *Receiving "boot."* If you get back money or property other than corporate stock, you've received what's called "boot," which can be taxed upon receipt. This can happen, for example, when two people want to contribute equal amounts but the properties they each put in are of unequal value. Obviously, one person must get back a certain amount to maintain the balance, and the value of the property received can be taxable (depending on what was contributed and other factors).

- *Contributing liabilities.* If the corporation agrees to take on a liability of yours (for example, you contribute equipment being paid for in installments), the incorporation generally is still treated as tax-free. However, if the liabilities exceed your basis in the property contributed, then you must recognize this excess as gain.

Choosing a Form of Business for Your Family Situation

Understanding how each form of business operates is only half the process in determining which type of organization is best suited for your situation. Consider what you want to accomplish by working with your relatives.

- Equal or unequal ownership rights
- Income-shifting to minors
- Opportunity for gifting and other estate-planning measures

General partnerships are suitable for family businesses where owners want equal say and are not concerned with personal liability. For example, a husband-wife team running a local shop may opt for partnership treatment. However, equality of ownership can be

accomplished with other types of entities (for example, equal interests in LLCs or equal shares owned in a corporation).

Limited partnerships are suitable for family businesses where some
owners wish to limit participation by others. For example, a limited
partnership can be used to allow parents to act as general partners
and run the business while children are limited partners entitled to receive a share of the business income. In this way, income is shifted
from the parents to the children with the intention that the family will
save tax overall. Income-shifting can also be accomplished with other
types of ownership arrangements, such as LLCs and corporations.

Today, LLCs are being used by many new businesses as the organization of choice. It affords both personal liability protection and the
ease of partnership taxation. It also allows management decisions to
be controlled by a select few (managers designated for this purpose). The downside to using LLCs is a function of their newness.
The laws on LLC taxation and treatment from state to state are unclear in several instances.

TIP

There may be multiple
types of business
organization used for
different purposes. For
example, the family may
wish to own the building
in which the business
operates by using an LLC
to hold title to the
property. The business
itself may be a C or S
corporation. The reason
for separate ownership
of property: to facilitate
a sale of that property
without possible double
taxation.

S corporations continue to be popular vehicles
for family businesses. Newly liberalized rules allowing for ESBTs and QSSTs as well as tax-exempt
organizations provide greater flexibility for S corporations than was previously possible.

C corporations are the optimum choice of business organization in a number of situations:

- When the business is profitable and can
  afford to provide owners with fringe benefits.

- When the business wants to take in a diverse
  group of investors, such as other corporations.

- When the business intends to make a public
  offering of stock.

The bottom line in choosing a form of business organization for your family business is to
familiarize yourself with your options. Then review your choice with a tax professional who
can evaluate that choice in light of your particular circumstances.

Changing Your Form of Business

You may have already set up your business and been operating under a particular legal structure. However, this structure is not carved

in stone. You can make changes whenever you want. Changes may in fact be warranted when:

- *The business grows.* Prosperity may mean that you need to become a C corporation in order to take advantage of certain fringe benefit opportunities such as tax-free medical coverage for owners. It may also mean changing to a C corporation to facilitate taking the company public or selling out to venture capitalists.

- *The family grows.* As family members enter the business, you may want to simplify things by using stock rather than partnership interests.

- *The family ages.* You may have been operating as a partnership. However, you may want to become a limited partnership in order to more easily transfer interests to younger family members at reduced transfer tax cost without losing your control over the business.

- *There's a complete change of ownership.* When the business passes from one generation to another, the old form of organization may no longer suit the new owners. A change may be warranted simply because of the number of new owners involved.

Changing from One Type of Format to Another

In deciding whether to change the type of business organization you already have, take into account any possible current tax cost for your action. Changing your type of business format may or may not be a taxable event.

PARTNERSHIP TO LLC

If your partnership converts to an LLC in order to gain personal liability protection for owners, no gain or loss is recognized by the partners on the conversion. It's as if the partners contribute their interests to the LLC in exchange for interests in that new entity. Since

---

Example

Sam, who operated his plumbing business as a sole proprietorship, has retired, and his two sons have taken over the business. Obviously it can no longer be run as a sole proprietorship, because there are now two owners. They can choose to run it as a partnership or organize it as a limited liability company, S corporation, or C corporation.

the business does not cease after the conversion, there is no termination of the partnership because there is no sale or exchange resulting from the conversion; hence there is no current taxation.

C OR S CORPORATION TO PARTNERSHIP OR LLC

In general, this is treated as a liquidation of the corporation, which is a taxable transaction. Both the corporation and the shareholders may realize taxable income as a result of the conversion. This result applies even if the corporation is merged into the partnership or the LLC. There are three ways to handle the conversion:

1. An asset exchange where the corporation transfers its assets in exchange for partnership/LLC interests, which are then distributed to shareholders.

2. A liquidation of the corporation where assets are distributed to shareholders, who then contribute those assets to the partnership or LLC in exchange for partnership/LLC interests.

3. A merger in which the corporation merges into the partnership or LLC and the shareholders exchange their stock for partnership/LLC interests.

LLCS OR PARTNERSHIPS TO C OR S CORPORATIONS

Incorporation of an existing business can be handled in a tax-free manner as explained earlier in this chapter.

Recapitalizations

A business may not want to change its legal format but only provide for different ownership interests than it has at present. For example, a C corporation capitalized solely with common stock may wish to recapitalize in order to create a class of preferred stock. This preferred stock can be held by older family members who are no longer participating in the business and are more interested in receiving a steady income flow than gambling on possible stock appreciation.

Preferred stock is a class of stock that entitles the holder to receive annual dividends at a fixed rate *before* any dividends are paid to those owning common stock.

Generally, a recapitalization can be accomplished on a tax-free basis. Recapitalizations are explained in further detail in Part 3 as an estate-planning strategy.

CHAPTER 3

Your Management Team

Who's minding the store? As with any business, no matter what its product or service, success is largely in the hands of those who run the company. Whether it's a small company headed by a husband and wife or a large company governed by a board of directors and corporate officers, the management team is the core of the business. In a family business, however, leadership can be a problem area for several reasons. Ownership interests can dictate who holds management positions without regard to ability or the needs of the business. Personalities and past family history can get in the way of effective decision making.

In this chapter you'll see the types of positions you need to fill in order to run your company effectively and who should fill them. You'll learn about the pros and cons of shared leadership. You'll see what it means to turn to nonfamily outsiders for leadership and how to keep them happy. And you'll get some ideas about grooming the next generation to assume leadership positions in the future.

Who's Needed on Your Team?

The components of your management team depend in part on the size and nature of your company. In a mom-and-pop type operation, a single leader can probably handle day-to-day operations as well as planning for future growth, with co-owners or others responsible for other aspects of the business. For example, an electrical contractor heads up the business started by his grandfather more than 70 years ago, providing electrical contracting services as well as company leadership. But he's not alone in the company. His wife, who is a co-owner, handles many of the administrative chores, such as scheduling jobs, ordering supplies, figuring payroll, and keeping the company books.

However, for larger companies, a number of people are needed for effective management. Generally, there's a CEO—chief executive officer—who heads up the team. He or she usually is the final arbiter in decision making at the highest level. This position may be labeled "president" or have some other designation, but the responsibilities are the same. The buck stops here. In some companies, there may be a CEO *and* a president. The CEO is the head of the company, while the president typically heads up a division or simply assumes what is essentially the number two position for the entire company, reporting to the CEO.

Another important member of the management team is the CFO—chief financial officer. This is the "numbers" person who oversees cash flow, debt servicing, collections, and other financial aspects of the business. In smaller companies, there may not be an inside person monitoring the money. The company may rely on an outside accountant or consultant to provide this type of guidance. But as a company grows, and certainly when it's sizable, such an inside position becomes imperative.

Depending on the size of the company and the departments or divisions it may have, managers are needed to head up these divisions. For example, there may be a need for a head of marketing, human resources, research and development, and customer service, to name a few.

In addition to officers and managers who conduct the day-to day affairs of the business, a corporation is required by law to have a board of directors. The board has the rights and responsibilities granted under state law as well as in the corporation's bylaws. These rights include such actions as amending the bylaws or certificate of incorporation, electing S corporation status, adopting fringe benefit plans, and making plans for retained earnings.

The board can be comprised of the same people involved in the daily operations of the company—the CEO and other insiders. In smaller family businesses this is often the case. Or the board can be comprised of both inside directors and outside directors. These outside directors can bring to the table special expertise or experience in corporate management.

A *board of directors* is the governing body of a corporation. The minimum number of directors (typically three) and who is eligible to serve in this capacity are dictated by state law. A corporation's certificate of incorporation or bylaws can impose additional requirements for directors and prescribe terms of office.

While business enterprises other than corporations are not required to have a board of directors, they may want to use advisory boards to provide the same objective guidance routinely used by corporations. The same considerations that operate in selecting corporate board members apply with equal force to advisory board members.

Choosing Leadership in a Family Business

In family businesses, who should assume the leadership and other roles in the business may or may not be clear. Nepotism may be a key factor in determining whether someone works for the business, but it shouldn't dictate what position the relative assumes. In the ideal situation, each relative involved in the business would take the role that he or she is best suited for. Assignments should be based on skills, past experience, and natural abilities rather than merely on percentage of owner-ship and longevity with the company.

TIP

In small companies, there may not be enough people to handle all the jobs that need to be done. It may be helpful, and less costly, to rely on outside consultants to resolve specific issues, such as devising marketing strategies or formulating cash flow solutions.

Where there's a founder, such as a father or mother, typically that person heads up the busi-ness (at least initially). Other family members who work for the business may be assigned to various positions. The best guidance that any family business can follow in filling leadership jobs is to use the same criteria that would be used for nonfamily em-ployees. This means assessing what the job requires and then match-ing that up with each person's talents, skills, and temperament.

Nepotism means giving positions in an organization based on blood or marital relationships. While the practice has a negative connotation because some inept individuals have obtained positions solely because of their familial connections, there's no law against it. And, in a family business, nepotism is a primary consideration.

Where siblings or spouses cofound a company, job assignment can be problematic. In fortunate situations, there's a natural leader among the group and the rest are willing to accept this arrangement. In one apparel company started by two brothers, it was clear from the start that only one had the business savvy to take the helm. The other brother, who was more artistic, was content to limit his supervisory control to the design department. In this company, personal skills and personality of the owners meshed well and provided the type of leadership necessary for success.

However, this is not always the case. Siblings or other relatives may vie for the head position. Some may not be satisfied with secondary roles. To resolve this issue and ensure that the business fills its management team with the most capable individuals, compromise may be in order. Here are some alternatives to consider:

- *Alternating leadership.* Where two relatives each want to head up the business, agree to "term limits" where one takes the lead for a certain number of years and then the other takes control. The positive aspect to this solution is to keep everyone happy, at least for some period of time. The negative aspects may be that one may be a better leader than the other, and the company may suffer from a lack of continuity in leadership.

- *Sharing leadership.* Two individuals can comanage the company. Both may share the title of CEO or other primary position. According to one survey cosponsored by the Arthur Andersen Center for Family Business and MassMutual's Family Business Enterprise, about 10 percent of family businesses are already using co-CEOs and another 42 percent have coleadership under consideration for the next generation. This arrangement may be particularly appealing to a founder stepping aside who wants to give equal treatment to children. As the numbers demonstrate, this arrangement can clearly work in the right circumstances.

TIP

To make any shared leadership arrangement work, it's necessary to have a conflict resolution plan in place. A third party such as a parent or the board of directors can be used to break a deadlock on key issues.

- *Splitting leadership.* Where it's essential that there be only one CEO, a secondary role can be assumed by another relative without being too unequal. For example, in one small manufacturing business, there were two children about to assume control over a company. In this instance, one sibling functioned as the CEO while the other became its president. Each enjoyed equal ownership interests and identical compensation packages.

In a family business it's important to recognize that unless special arrangements are made, it should be assumed that the person in control will probably stay in control for a long time. It's been said that the average tenure of the business founder serving as CEO in a family business is about 25 years. This compares with just seven years in public nonfamily businesses.

Titles Tell It All

What's in a name? In a family business, the title given to a position can mean a little or it can mean a lot. Titles may be bestowed for show to include family members within the business. There may be little correlation between the title and the job description or responsibility. Titles may, for example, be doled out in an effort to give at least the facade of equal treatment to children.

To ensure that titles alone don't create family disharmony or undermine the workings of the business, it's helpful to follow certain business practices in assigning designations:

- Create a job description for a position before assigning someone to it. This will ensure that the skills and expertise required for the job are filled.
- Require job performance. Don't let a title be in name only. Demand that the person with the title does what's required for the job.

CAUTION

Don't assign titles in the belief that it will keep family harmony. The result may be not only disharmony within the family but dissatisfaction (and disaffection) by nonfamily employees and by those who may be doing the job that someone else holds the title to. In the end, it can be a detriment to the business.

Putting Immediate Family on the Payroll

Hiring a spouse and/or children can provide not only valuable services for the company but also economic and tax benefits for your family. Your immediate family need not be included in management to achieve these benefits.

Whether immediate family—your spouse or children—is part of your management team depends on the situation. For example, if your children are teenagers, it may be premature to give them any decision-making roles. If your spouse wants to work only part-time, he or she may not need a position of authority.

The economic and tax benefits of putting immediate family on the payroll are discussed in Chapter 5.

Integrating In-Laws into the Business

Who's considered to be in the family? Does the family include in-laws who are relatives solely by marriage? Many may feel the old adage to be true that blood is thicker than water. There's good reason for this belief. In-laws may come and go while blood relations remain. Nearly one-quarter of those in family businesses have experienced at least one divorce within the past five years. The dissolution of a marriage can, in some cases, lead to the dissolution of a business. Of course, divorce may split a family but may not necessarily separate an in-law from the business. One successful realty company continues to be headed up by the founder's son-in-law even though he's divorced from the daughter. Founder and son-in-law continue to get along well even though the exes are barely on speaking terms, proving perhaps that money is thicker than blood.

Some experts counsel against hiring in-laws as a matter of policy. However, there may be good business or personal reasons for doing so:

- Hiring in-laws raises the opportunity for a wider pool of related employees for a growing business. They may bring to the company new talents needed by the business.

- Hiring in-laws may keep family members from moving away. For example, if a founder's daughter doesn't work for the company, hiring her husband may be a way to keep the daughter from relocating for another job opportunity that her husband might want or need to pursue.

TIP

Bringing in-laws into the business not only provides a benefit for the business from their talents and skills. It also can lead to greater closeness within the family.

In-laws can be well used if openness and trust exist among participants. For successful integration within the business, in-laws need to receive information so they can do their jobs properly. Family secrets are out of place in a family business.

It's important to head off potential problems—for the business and for the in-laws.

- *Dangerous precedent.* There may be a dangerous precedent set by taking in-laws into the business. While the early entries may be qualified for the positions they assume, later marriages may produce less able in-laws who feel entitled to join in because of the established pattern of in-law employment by the business.

- *Rank.* There may be problems of rank. In-laws may be given lower positions than their spouses. In fact, in-laws may never achieve the equality they believe they should have with blood relations working for the company.

- *Ouster.* Problems can obviously arise if marriages break up. In-laws may be asked to sign prenuptial or postnuptial agreements (explained in Part 2 of this book), which may cut them out of any connection with the business in case of divorce. Thus, in-laws need to recognize that they may, in a sense, always remain second-class citizens within the business.

Family Board Members

There's no legal limit to the number of seats on a board of directors. However, as a matter of practicality, the board should be only as large as circumstances dictate. Too many members make it difficult to get a quorum and engage in productive meetings. Typically, smaller companies have about five or six board members and larger companies have about a dozen seats.

Where there are more family members than there are seats on the board, special care must be used in selecting which relatives sit on the board.

Don't assign seats primarily to:

- Reward or punish someone for loyalty alone. Using selection as a stick for keeping a relative in line doesn't produce independent thinkers who can generate creative ideas for the company.

- Avoid bad blood among certain individuals. Certain hard feelings in seat selection can carry over into performance on the board.

- Maintain a status quo. For example, just because an older relative has held a seat is no reason that it should later be passed on to that relative's offspring.

Do assign seats to:

- Provide expertise to the board. Select those relatives with the most experience and knowledge to provide ideas for the company.

- Create consensus. Select those relatives who can work well with others to sculpt strategies for the business.

Rotate service on the board to allow each family member to have a say. Typically, board members serve in that capacity for two to three years. Terms of members generally are staggered so that the board always has old and new members on it. This ensures continuity (from the old members) and fresh input (from the new members).

CAUTION

Board members should understand the extent of their liability. They can be sued for their actions, for example, mismangement or corporate waste, although statistics show such actions against board members in privately held corporations are rare. Liability protection is available through insurance; directors' and officers' insurance (called D&O) indemnifies board members for any lawsuits brought against them.

Turning to Outsiders

In some family businesses, relatives control all key roles, from inside management to seats on the board of directors. However, not every company has the right pool of talent to fill all positions. This is especially so as the business expands, creating new positions. In such a case, it's necessary to look outside the family. Bringing in those outside doesn't spell the end of the family business. It's merely a new incarnation.

To avoid conflicts between family members and avoid bad feelings by outsiders it's helpful, however, to have clear policies on nepotism. Obviously, since these are family businesses, the policy is not a ban on nepotism, but rather guidelines on hiring relatives. Family pressures shouldn't force the hiring of a bungling brother-in-law in the place of a qualified outsider. And children shouldn't assume their entry positions will be at an executive level when outsiders with abilities equal to the children's must start at a lower rung on the corporate ladder. As mentioned earlier, the best policy is to put qualifications first and blood second.

Compensation and incentive packages for nonrelatives are discussed in Part 2 of this book.

Outside CEOs

There may come a time in the life of your company when there's no qualified relative to assume the helm. This can happen, for example, when a founder dies and children are too young or too inexperienced to run the company. Or it can happen when the younger generation is more interested in being passive investors than active participants.

At such time, it's necessary to look outside the family for leadership. The nonfamily CEO can be someone who has worked within the company for some time or may be someone brought in specifically to assume the top position.

KEEPING OUTSIDE CEOS HAPPY

For a nonrelative to succeed in the position of CEO of a family-owned business, there needs to be support from the family. The emphasis must be on the business rather than on the family.

The CEO must have the authority that comes with the job. In nonfamily businesses this goes without saying. In family businesses, however, there's still a question of control since ownership lies elsewhere. The CEO cannot do the job if he or she is subject to constant second-guessing and veto by family members. The family must give up control, at least over daily operations, if an outside CEO arrangement is to work.

The CEO must have complete access to all financial information. Some families have a natural reluctance to share what they consider to be personal money matters. However, this reluctance must be overcome so that the CEO is playing with a full hand.

In addition to financial information, the CEO should also be informed about personal issues within the family relevant to the business, such as marital discord that could disrupt current ownership arrangements.

The CEO must also have the unqualified backing of the board, whether it's entirely family or comprised of both family and nonfamily members. Without such support, the company can become a train with two engines pulling in opposite directions.

Outside Managers

Just like an outside CEO, nonfamily members who serve as managers of departments or divisions in a family business must be given the authority and assistance to fulfill their job descriptions. Obviously, an outside manager is selected primarily on ability (as opposed to family members who have nepotism on their side). But it's essential that they be treated the same as family members in terms of their decision-making authority. For example, rules on nepotism should be spelled out so that outside managers know when they're within their rights to hire or fire relatives.

Nonfamily managers must be included in the company's vision for the future. It can't just be about the family's wealth opportunity. The vision must include what the company stands for and hopes to accomplish.

Nonfamily managers must recognize, however, that no matter what contribution they make to the company and no matter how valued they are as employees, they will never be family. There may be a family feeling to the workplace, but nonrelatives aren't blood. Expectations on advancement must be realistic. No matter how great a job a nonfamily manager might do, if the business remains privately held, then ownership potential probably isn't there.

All companies have difficulties in some interpersonal relationships. Family businesses, though, have special problems. Ongoing family feuds can spill over into the workplace. To keep outside managers satisfied, it's important to keep those personal issues separate from work and not involve those managers in family affairs.

Outside Board Members

Many small operations rely on family owners to provide the leadership and direction for the business. But larger companies, and sophisticated small ones, typically turn to outside directors. Outside directors can bring to the boardroom objectivity that may otherwise be lacking within the family. To make effective use of outside directors, it's important to take these five steps:

1. *Get the right people.* Select outside directors who can add expertise and objectivity to your board. For example, maybe there's a retired executive in your industry who can add maturity to your start-up business.

2. *Provide adequate compensation.* While family members may be willing to attend board meetings occasionally gratis, outside board members require payment. What you pay depends on what you ask the members to do (frequency of meetings, size of your company, etc.). Typical compensation for outside board members ranges from $1,000 per meeting to $15,000 for annual assistance.

3. *Define the job of the board.* Make it clear from the start what the board is supposed to do. Maybe you need help in strategic planning. Or maybe you need to resolve management difficulties. Or perhaps you're at the point of succession planning and need guidance. Whatever your intentions, make them clear so the board can serve your needs.

4. *Share information.* You can't expect valuable advice if board members aren't given all the facts. Provide board members with updated financial information. Let them see your operations. Discuss issues of importance to you (such as succession planning). You don't have to limit this information sharing to scheduled meetings. You can keep members informed as the situation warrants it.

5. *Listen to the board.* To retain the advice of experienced outside board members, you have to pay attention to their advice. Failure to take them seriously can lead to defection.

Want the benefits of outside board members without giving them a say in your business? You can turn to advisory services to provide a forum for brainstorming and problem-solving advice. For example, TEC Worldwide (www.teconline.com) has an international network of CEOs to offer guidance. TEC Worldwide has membership programs for emerging companies ($1 million to $5 million in sales) and for established companies ($3 million to $5 million in sales). Members participate in monthly sessions that address specific company problems in a confidential manner. The cost of this assistance is an annual membership fee that can range up to $10,000.

Employment Practices

Most businesses have employment policies dictating behavior and expectations required on the job. In family businesses, it's *essential* that these policies be clearly spelled out and that they be applied to both family and nonfamily individuals with equal force at all levels within the company.

- *Hiring.* Job openings should be filled by the most qualified applicant. Obviously, an eager family member may be given preference over an outsider where the qualifications of both applicants are about equal. When filling openings with family members, make sure they have the experience, training, and skills to handle the position. Some family businesses require relatives to obtain outside work experience before joining the family enterprise.

- *Work schedules.* If part time or flextime is an option for family members, then it should also be available to nonfamily employees.

- *Punctuality and absences.* Company policy toward lateness and days off must apply equally to all employees, regardless of familial connection. Giving greater leeway to family members will create poor morale among the rest of the staff.

- *Performance reviews.* It's customary to schedule formal annual job reviews for most positions. Some companies also use semi-annual reviews. In a family business, relatives should be subjected to the same scrutiny as nonfamily employees. They should receive the same rewards for good reviews and the same consequences for bad performance.

- *Firing.* It must be clear that poor performance can result in termination, regardless of ownership interest in the business or familial relationship to the head of the company. Keeping an inept relative on the payroll may ease family tensions, but it can undermine the success of the business. If it's a question of money, find another way to shift income to the relative outside of the work relationship (for example, pay dividends).

In addition to what can be put in writing, it's important to make the intangibles just as clear. Relatives must be encouraged to display respect and courtesy to all company workers. They must use the chain of command to register complaints or grievances instead of running to mommy or daddy.

Even if the company is comprised entirely of family members, it's still important to fix employment policies. Set expectations in writing so there are no misunderstandings. This can be done through a nonlegal document, such as a charter, worked out through intrafamily communications.

What does each family member expect from the business for himself or herself? What does each family member hope to achieve for the business? By going through the process of working out expectations and objectives, it is hoped that potential conflicts will be resolved before they can ripen into problems.

Making Changes

The leadership team isn't static. While the head of the company may be stable for many years, there's always turnover in other positions. And even in the head position, change will certainly come—sooner or later. This may be when the owner decides to retire or dies. Or it may be when the company reaches another level of growth beyond the abilities of the founder (if he or she is wise enough to step aside at this point). Statistics show that about 42 percent of current family businesses may have a change in leadership within five years.

Change isn't necessarily a bad thing. It does, however, take preparation and planning. Grooming the next generation to take over the business is discussed next. Other aspects of succession planning are discussed in Part 3 of this book.

Note

One study cosponsored by the Arthur Andersen Center for Family Business and Mass-Mutual's Family Business Enterprise shows that the concept of primogeniture (where the oldest male succeeds his father) is virtually dead. While only 9 percent of family-owned businesses are currently headed up by women, about 30 percent of businesses expect that to change with the next CEO. More than 40 percent of family businesses have at least one full-time female employee, and 10 percent have two females so there is a potential pool of female leaders. For many, gender is really a nonissue when it comes to choosing a company leader.

Grooming the Next Generation

Good genes may not be enough to ensure ability to run the business when the current leader steps down. It takes something more—education, skills, experience, and maturity.

Some children are fortunate to learn the family business from the ground up. They literally grow up within the company. As young children they may have done menial tasks about an office after school. As teenagers they spent summer vacations on the job. Instead of "take a daughter to work day" once a year, these children of family business owners learned the ropes at their parents' elbows. Over the years, at one local ethnic restaurant you could watch the owner's son go from delivery boy to waiter to maître d'.

In other family businesses, children may have little or no involvement with the company. They may start other careers and work for other companies before returning as prodigal children to the family business. Here, the learning curve is different. These children may have the education and outside expertise. They only need to learn the unique aspects of their family's enterprise and can be up to speed in a short time.

If you have a business that you plan to bring your children into and they want to be brought in, then you need to establish ground rules early on. It's up to you to make clear your expectations for their education and participation in the business. Do you want your children to join the company immediately upon completion of a college degree? Do you expect them to attain a graduate degree? Or gain work experience at another company first?

Once your children are working for the company, don't expect them to automatically assume leadership positions as a birthright. They need to be ready for such authority and responsibility. As with any individual, mentoring can provide the personal guidance necessary for your children to grow into leadership positions. This guidance can range from the nuts and bolts of describing where to find the best subcontractors to more subtle help in managing difficult employees.

Mentoring is a process of providing guidance and friendship by experienced individuals to typically younger, less experienced individuals.

Who Should Be a Mentor?

In a family business, the parent often is the mentor for the child. The parent teaches the ropes by example as well as by direct information.

However, the line between mentoring and parenting can often be blurred. Founders wishing to impart their knowledge to their children may be acting more as a parent than as a business teacher. They may wish or even demand that things be done as they have done them for years. Children may perceive this guidance more as criticism than help and resist making needed changes in their actions.

In some cases, mentoring is better left to nonfamily members. Nonfamily mentors can offer some things a parent or other relative cannot:

- *Fresh perspective.* A parent's view on how to do things may be outdated. A nonfamily mentor may bring a new approach to handling problems.

- *Nonjudgmental guidance.* Because of the relationship, a parent may treat the son or daughter as simply a child rather than as a mature company employee. A nonfamily member can look at the young person with an objective view that's not colored by family issues.

There are a number of alternatives for finding nonfamily members to serve as mentors. One option is to use an executive within the company. An inside mentor can provide special insight into how things work: which employees may be difficult to handle, which company processes may be tricky, and so on. The mentoring process can be overt, where this person is assigned the job of mentoring. Or it can be more casual, with guidance offered on an as-needed basis.

If there isn't any nonfamily member willing or able to serve as a mentor, then guidance for the next generation may be found outside the company. There are several avenues of outside help to consider.

- *Family business institutes* provide training programs to groom the younger generation to assume leadership positions. A listing of university-based family business institutes may be found in Appendix A.

- *Paid coaches* who are consultants working on an hourly or per-job basis to provide guidance in the areas of leadership training and financial and business operations training. Key: Find consultants who specialize in family businesses and are familiar with the dynamics of these enterprises.

- *Roundtables* to obtain peer guidance. Typically these groups meet on a monthly basis and provide give-and-take on issues raised by participants.

CHAPTER 4

Raising Money

Whether you're just starting out or already into expansion, you need money to see you through this phase of operations. The start-up phase typically lasts anywhere from three to six months. Expansion can take even longer. *Not* having sufficient cash to meet your expenses while the business gets up and running or tries to expand can spell disaster. Undercapitalization, the lack of funds in a business, is the number one reason why businesses fail.

In family businesses, the same need for capital exists as with nonfamily enterprises. However, there are certain opportunities for raising capital available within the family that may not exist for other businesses.

In this chapter you'll learn about projecting your capital requirements so you'll be able to raise adequate financing. You'll also learn about the two main types of financing to consider: equity and debt. You'll find out about the ordinary ways to seek each type of financing. And you'll see what unique money opportunities exist within the family.

Determining Your Capital Requirements

How much money is enough to get started in business or expand? There's no single dollar amount. Each business has different needs, and it's up to you to project those needs so your financing efforts will raise sufficient capital.

Generally, capitalization needs are a part of every business plan. If you've made a business plan (as explained in Chapter 1), then you've already determined what you anticipate your cash needs to be. If you haven't yet written a comprehensive business plan, then you can use the following information to guide you in projecting your cash requirements. You can then incorporate this information in your business plan when you do write it.

If you're just starting out, you need to figure how much cash is required to open your doors and keep you going until business revenue makes the company self-sustaining. While some businesses may start making money from day one, most businesses take time to establish themselves, bring in customers or clients, and start to realize a regular cash flow. It's best to figure on your capital needs for a period of six months. Should the company do better than expected, you can always put that extra capital to good use!

The worksheet in Figure 4.1 provides a guideline to the type of expenses encountered in starting a business. After reading the information on the following pages, you can then fill in your own numbers to arrive at your anticipated need for start-up capital.

Occupancy Costs

These are amounts you'll spend to ready your premises for business. Whether it's a storefront, an office, or a factory, you'll need to pay for space and customize it for your use. You'll probably have to pay for:

- Lease deposits, typically first and last month rentals, but there may be some other arrangement.
- Utilities deposits (for electricity, telephone service, etc.).
- Remodeling costs, such as wiring, walls, painting, and carpeting. You may need to install special lighting fixtures, air-conditioning, or other fixtures required for your business.

Of course, if you're running a business from your home, you won't incur any additional occupancy costs other than some remodeling you may want to have done to customize your work space.

Professional Fees

You'll probably use the services of an attorney and an accountant to get you started. The amount of fees, which could be several hundred dollars or more, depends on the services you require. For example, if

FIGURE 4.1   Estimate of Your Start-up Costs

Item	Estimated Cost
Occupancy costs*	$
Lease deposit	
Utilities deposit	
Remodeling expenses to ready the premises	
Professional fees	$
Legal fees (for incorporation, etc.)	
Accounting fees (to set up books and accounts)	
Licenses and permits	$
Equipment	$
Office furniture and fixtures	
Technology items (computer, telephone, copier, fax)	
Machinery (for manufacturing)	
Inventory	$
Supplies	$
Office supplies	
Stationery, business cards, business forms	
Cleaning supplies	
Insurance	$
Fire and liability on premises/products	
Workers' compensation	
Disability insurance	
Medical (optional)	
Initial operating costs	$
Debt servicing on loans	
Payroll (wages and employment taxes)	
Advertising	
Utilities	
Miscellaneous expenses	$

*If you're starting a home-based business, you can skip these expenses since you're already paying them.

you incorporate, figure on about $500 for the process. The same amount usually is required for forming a limited liability company. You can self-incorporate, but the modest professional fee may be well worth the cost to make sure you do it right.

If you do your own books and accounts, you'll save on accounting fees. For example, you may want to use computer software, such as Quick Books and Quick Pro, for this purpose. Just factor in the cost of the software in lieu of accounting fees.

Licenses and Permits

Depending on the type of business, you may be required to obtain certain licenses and permits to operate.

If you plan to sell a product, be sure to obtain a manufacturer's ID code from the Uniform Code Council. This code identifies your company and enables merchants to scan the Universal Product Code (UPC) bar code of your product, track shipments of your goods worldwide, and facilitate e-commerce. You can find details about obtaining your ID code at 513-435-3870 or www.uc-council.org.

Equipment

Whether you go with used furniture or the deluxe desk and credenza, you'll need some furnishings for an office. Usually you'll buy office furniture, but you can rent it instead. Either way, there's a cost to consider.

You'll also need various technology-related items to let the business function:

- Computers (and peripherals, such as printers, modems, and scanners)
- Copier machines
- Faxes
- Telephones, cellular phones if necessary, pagers, and other communication devices

If you're opening a retail establishment, you'll need counters, racks, cash registers, and other equipment to ready your store.

If you're starting a manufacturing business, you'll need machinery and other special equipment.

If you're in a trade, you'll need tools of that trade. Make sure to have enough tools for the number of employees you anticipate using initially.

Inventory

Unless the business is one based on providing personal services, you'll need to stock items for sale. So, for example, if you have a store, use a mail order catalog, or sell on the Web, you'll need to have sufficient inventory to meet anticipated demand. But you don't want to tie up too much capital in inventory that may take a long time to sell. On the other hand, in ordering inventory, consider any cost savings you can command if you place quantity orders. To strike a balance between ordering too little or too much, you need to understand what your cash flow cycle will be.

Cash flow cycle is the time over which inventory is manufactured by you or ordered from a supplier, you pay for the inventory, it's sold to customers, and you receive payment.

Supplies

Regardless of the nature of your business, you'll surely need some supplies to get started. Office supplies, from stationery and business cards to paper clips, are needed even if you don't have an office-type business.

Your business may require special supplies. For example, if you have a cleaning service, you'll need to stock up on cleaners, paper towels, and sponges. A gift basket business requires ribbons, tissue paper, and baskets.

Insurance

All businesses need some types of insurance. As a start, be sure to have adequate coverage for liability in the event of personal injury or damage to property on your premises. Insurance is always the first line of defense for any business owner in protecting against claims from those who may have suffered an injury related to your business. If you operate from a home office, you may even have to adjust your homeowner's coverage to include business protection or buy a separate policy for this purpose.

TIP

Don't overstock your supplies, even if there's a cost savings for bulk orders. The savings may be small compared with the money wasted if the type of supplies you need should change. For example, business cards used to get you started may have to be changed as you add a fax line, Web page, or cellular phone.

CAUTION

If your business is a sole proprietorship or partnership without personal liability protection for owners, it's essential to maintain adequate liability insurance. Failure to do so can expose your personal assets, even your home, to claims from creditors (which include people who may have been injured on your premises).

CAUTION

People serving on the company's board of directors aren't employees of the company in their capacity as board members. They aren't covered by the company's errors and omissions coverage; they need directors' and officers' liability insurance (D&O).

Having employees (including yourself if you're on the payroll) requires the business to carry certain types of coverage:

- *Workers' compensation and disability insurance.* The amount of coverage is dictated by the nature of your business, the number of employ-ees, and your business revenues (the insurance company tells you the coverage you must carry).
- *Unemployment insurance.* This is state-mandated coverage for workers.
- *Medical coverage.* You're not required to provide it, but you may choose to do so, especially if it's needed by you and your family.

Other types of insurance you may want or need to carry:

- *Errors and omissions coverage.* This provides protection for doing or failing to do something for the business. Accountants, architects, attorneys, doctors, and other professionals need professional liability coverage (commonly called *malpractice insurance*) for the same purpose.
- *Employer practices liability coverage.* This insures against claims from employees for age discrimination, sexual harassment, wrongful termination, and other work-related claims.
- *Business interruption insurance.* This policy covers operating expenses if the business temporarily closes because of a fire, storm, or other natural disaster or unexpected event. The policy will pay your rent, payroll, and other operating expenses.
- *Key person life insurance.* If the business relies heavily on the talents of you or other owners and key employees, you'll want to carry life insurance. With the policy payable to the business, you can then use the proceeds to look for a replacement and tide the business over until the new person is up to speed.
- *Performance bonds.* Also called *surety bonds*, these ensure that the business completes performance on its contracts.

- *Fidelity bonds.* These protect clients, customers, and other third parties against theft or embezzlement by your employees.
- *Product liability insurance.* You may be required to carry this by stores stocking your product that want protection against any claims their customers may make because of your product.
- *Credit insurance.* This provides payment to the business should creditors fail to meet their obligations.
- *Cyber coverage.* If you maintain a Web site, this relatively new type of insurance provides protection against claims relating to misinformation you may post as well as copyright and trademark infringement you may inadvertently commit.

It's advisable to work with a knowledgeable insurance agent or broker who can advise on the type and extent of coverage you need. Make sure this person is versed in business coverage. Don't rely on the agent who sold you a life insurance policy to reliably advise on business insurance needs.

Initial Operating Costs

Once you have everything in place to open your doors—your space is ready, your equipment purchased, your insurance in place—you still need more capital to see you through the next several months. It usually takes this long before you can enjoy a steady revenue stream to cover your ongoing expenses, such as rent, utilities, and payroll.

To figure what you need to cover your initial operating costs, make a list of your fixed monthly expenses (rent, utilities, payroll, etc.). Then multiply that figure by the number of months you expect it will take you to become established. No guess? Then base a rough estimate of your capital needs on a six-month period.

Miscellaneous Expenses

No matter how well you plan out your capital needs, something unexpected always arises. Dues to the chamber of commerce you may have overlooked. A computer breaks, can't be repaired, and must be replaced. Be sure to build in some cushion to get you over the hump. How big a cushion? It depends on the nature of your business and how confident you are about how quickly you'll be able to generate revenue.

Types of Capital

Now that you know *what* you need, you want to focus on deciding *how* to get it. There are two main types of financing to consider in raising capital: equity and debt. Established companies can also use retained earnings, discussed later in this chapter, as a source for financing equipment purchases or business expansion, and as reserves for a rainy day.

Equity Financing

Equity is an ownership interest in a business acquired in exchange for contributing cash, property, services, or a combination of these things to the business. It's investment capital. The person putting in the funds and receiving an interest in the business becomes an owner.

In a corporation, this ownership interest is evidenced by a stock certificate spelling out the number of shares owned. In a partnership, there's no separate piece of paper denoting an ownership interest. It's simply called a partnership interest (the percentage of profits to which your ownership interest entitles you). The same is true of a limited liability company.

Equity means there's an ongoing relationship with the business and the other owners. That interest runs indefinitely. The equity interest need never be paid back.

> **CAUTION**
>
> Don't be too quick to part with large interests in your business, no matter how much you need the capital. This is a mistake all too common with inexperienced business owners. Try to negotiate for smaller interests or seek to convert those capital contributions to mere loans that you'll pay back.

Equity doesn't mean equal. Owners can have differing equity interests in the business. The 100 percent of business ownership can be divided in any way the parties desire. Example: A business is owned by a parent and two children. The parent owns 60 percent of the business, while each child owns 20 percent.

Keep in mind that as you give away equity interests in the business in exchange for capital contributions, you dilute your own interest. Example: You own 100 percent of a business. You want your two siblings to come into the business. If they each acquire 25 percent of the business, you've effectively given away control (you now only own just 50 percent and you need *more than* 50 percent for control).

Equity financing usually is brought in when the business is formed as a means to get it started. However, it can also be used when a business is successful and sells stock to the public as a means of raising large amounts of capital for further expansion. When a corporation goes from being privately owned to offering shares for sale to the public, it's called "going public," or an initial public offering (IPO).

Note

There's another type of financing—grant money—but it's very limited. This is the best type of financing of all because it's free money. It's given to the business by tax-exempt organizations that acquire nothing in return. The grant never has to be repaid. For a listing of grants, see the annual *Awards, Honors and Prizes* (Gale Research) found in local libraries. However, grants are very rare for most business enterprises, so you should focus primarily on equity and debt.

Debt Financing

Debt is a loan that must be repaid. It's borrowing. The lender (also called a creditor) has a temporary relationship with the business. Once the loan is repaid, the lender is no longer involved in the business. The loan must be repaid regardless of how well, or poorly, the business is performing.

Deciding between Equity and Debt

You don't have to make a choice between the two. You can use a combination of equity and debt to raise the capital you need. Just understand the pluses and minuses of each alternative. To repeat, with equity financing you share ownership of the business with others. But the business does not have to make any repayments, so it needs less operating capital to run. With debt financing your relationship with the lender lasts only as long as the loan. But the business must be able to pay back the money with interest. However, the business can deduct its debt servicing, thereby reducing the out-of-pocket cost of repayment.

Generally, the debt-equity ratio of a family business should reflect the ratio norm for the industry in which the business operates. But

Caution

When owners also become creditors of their own business, there's a risk that what is called debt is really only equity in disguise. If the business is thinly capitalized (there's a greatly disproportionate amount of debt to equity), the IRS may recharacterize interest deductions on debt repayment as nondeductible dividends to owners. What's too thin? Despite authorization more than 20 years ago for the IRS to provide guidelines on an acceptable debt-equity ratio, no such guideline currently exists.

also consider your own comfort level with debt and equity investments. Remember that having too much debt places a burden on the business and limits your flexibility in additional financing options.

In a family business, active members generally are owners in the company. They contribute cash or property in exchange for their interests, or they receive their interests as gifts from some other family members. However, relatives may wish to help your enterprise by *lending* you money, their only concern in your business being to be paid back with interest.

Your Own Resources

Generally, it's a good idea if possible to find the capital you need from your own resources (with each of your co-owners doing the same). In this way, you maximize your ownership interest and minimize the say that others can have in how you do things. If you must bring in outside funding, look to your family first, as explained in the next section.

If you want to raise as much of the money as possible from your own resources, your personal savings should be the first place to look. Instead of investing in the stock market or keeping your money in the bank, you'll be investing in yourself. Hopefully, your business will prosper and you'll be able to replace those savings in the future.

If you don't have a nest egg to call upon, then you may be able to borrow on your personal resources to raise the cash. There are a number of places to look:

- *Home equity loan.* If you own your home and it has appreciated and/or you've paid down your mortgage, you may be able to borrow against the equity in the home (what you'd realize if you sold the home and paid off any existing mortgage). You can arrange this loan as a second mortgage (a fixed amount with predetermined repayments) or as a line of credit you can draw upon as needed. Just remember that if the business fails and you can't repay the home equity loan, you may face possible foreclosure unless you find some other means of repayment.

- *Margin loan.* If you have a portfolio at an investment firm, you may be able to borrow using your stocks, bonds, and mutual funds as security for the loan. Generally, you can borrow up to 50 percent of the value of your portfolio (90 percent in the case of U.S. Treasury obligations). Interest fluctuates on this type of loan, and you pay back only what you want when you want (although interest continues to accrue on the outstanding balance). The danger in this type of loan is that the value of the portfolio could drop and you may have to sell securities at distressed prices to satisfy margin requirements.

- *Life insurance.* If you have a whole-life policy that has built up sizable cash surrender value, you can arrange a quick loan against the policy at attractive interest rates. The danger here is that should you die, the outstanding balance is subtracted from the proceeds that will be payable to your beneficiaries, leaving them with less than you had planned.

- *Retirement plan benefits.* You can't borrow from your individual retirement account (IRA). You can, however, use the funds once a year on a tax-free basis if you replace them within 60 days. If you have money in a company plan, you may be permitted to borrow as much as 50 percent of your accrued benefits under favorable loan terms. The loan must be repaid in level payments within five years. The reason why this source of borrowing isn't very favorable is that you deplete the funds that are building up on a tax-advantaged basis.

- *Credit cards.* While interest on most credit cards runs high, you may need to tap into your borrowing power in certain situations. It may make sense to use your credit card when buying a piece of equipment for the business. It probably doesn't make sense to use the funds for advertising or other ongoing costs.

> **NOTE**
>
> A startlingly high percentage of businesses get started with credit card borrowing, even though interest rates run annually to 18 percent or more. According to one source, while credit card borrowing for business purposes was only 24 percent in 1996, it was up to 47 percent in 1998 (the last year for which statistics are available).

Deducting Interest on Your Personal Borrowing

Is the interest you pay on what you borrow to invest in your business deductible? It depends on the source of the borrowing and your relationship with your business. Generally, personal or consumer interest (other than home mortgage interest) isn't deductible. But just because you borrow from your personal resources doesn't make the loan a personal one. The deductibility of interest usually depends on what you use the money for. If it's for business or investment, then some or all of the interest you pay may be deductible.

- *Business loans.* Interest paid on business loans (business interest) is fully deductible. Business loans are those made to protect a trade or business. This includes being an employee of your own business. Thus, interest you pay on a loan made to protect the salary you receive from the business is treated as fully deductible business interest. If this salary is the only or primary source of your income, then the loan is considered a business loan.

- *Investment loans.* Interest you pay on an investment loan is deductible up to the amount of investment income (dividends, interest, etc.). Usually, loans taken to *start* a business are treated as investment loans. The reason: You don't yet have a salary from the business that's worth protecting in comparison to the cash investment you're making. But loans to expand a business or keep it afloat once it's going may then become business loans, with interest fully deductible.

- *Passive activity loans.* Interest on these loans is deductible only to the extent of passive income from all passive activities. Passive activities are businesses in which people do not materially participate on a day-to-day basis; instead, they're only silent partners. So, for example, you start a business and your uncle, who lives across the country, invests but doesn't help out in any other way. He's subject to this limitation on deducting the interest he pays if he later borrows from the business.

- *Retirement plan loans.* The source of the financing—a loan from a qualified retirement plan—isn't determinative. You usually look to the three categories just listed to classify the interest. However, if you're considered a key employee in that retirement plan, then you can't deduct interest no matter what you use the money for.

If the business itself borrows money, interest on the loan to the business is fully deductible. There are no limitations on interest deductions claimed by a business.

Turning to Your Family

Your name doesn't have to be Rockefeller or Ford to have a family that's in a position to help you out. If a relative believes in you, that may be all that's needed to get the capital required. One enterprising baker starting up a pie company raised small sums from dozens of relatives who were sold on his business concept.

In turning to family members when raising capital, be sure to consider the usual upside and downside to the equity and debt alternatives.

Relatives as Investors

If your relative becomes an investor in your business, good communication is essential to maintaining harmony and avoiding misunderstanding. You need to consider how much say that person will have in your daily operations. You may have one idea but your relative has another. Also, can you get along with your relative if there's to be an ongoing working relationship?

You also need fully to understand the expectations of your relative about receiving payments from the business. Is your investor in it for the long haul or is he or she seeking a quick return on investment? You may wish to reinvest any profits in the business to see it grow. Your investor may want them paid out as dividends. While you may have control and be in a position to determine the outcome, you could create bad feelings because things weren't clear from the start.

Relatives as Creditors

If, instead of giving away an interest in the business, you take a personal loan from a relative so you'll have the funds to invest in the business, or if that relative lends funds directly to the business, make sure you formalize the arrangement. Don't be casual about the loan just because it's from a relative. The chief reason for observing formalities is protection for your benefactor. Should the loan go unpaid, you want to make sure that your relative can claim a bad debt deduction and write off his or her loss. Without formalities, the IRS, which looks closely at family transactions, may claim the loan was merely a gift from a relative.

> **CAUTION**
>
> Before you borrow from a relative, make sure that person can afford to lose that money. If you or the business can't repay the loan, you don't want to create hard feelings within the family. And you don't want to impose any economic hardship on your goodwilled kin.

- Put the loan in writing.
- Specify the rate of interest.
- Detail the loan repayment schedule and other terms of the loan.

Taking Business Loans

Most businesses, at least at some time in their lives, must borrow from outside sources to meet ongoing expenses or underwrite expansion plans. Most small business owners turn to Small Business Administration (SBA) loans to meet their capital needs.

The SBA doesn't make loans itself. It does, however, provide certain guarantees to commercial lenders to encourage them to make loans to small businesses. There are a variety of SBA loan programs.

Some are intended for start-up capital, while others provide funding only for established companies. The details of SBA loan programs may be found at the Web site www.sba.gov/financing/index.html. These loan programs change with some frequency. Here's a rundown of the current SBA loan programs to consider.

7(a) Loan Guarantee Program

This is one of the main lending programs intended to help small businesses that can't obtain financing on reasonable terms through normal lending channels. (What constitutes a "small business" eligible for this program depends on the industry in which the business operates.) These loans are made by banks that can receive an SBA guarantee of 75 percent of the total loan amount (for a maximum guarantee of $750,000). Owners of 20 percent or more of the business must provide their personal guarantees. The loan can be used to purchase real estate from which the business operates; acquire furniture, machinery, and equity; purchase inventory; and provide working capital. The maximum loan maturity is 25 years for real estate and equipment purchases and 7 years for working capital. The maximum interest rate for this loan program for loans over $50,000 is 2.25 percent above the prime rate for maturities up to 7 years, or 2.75 percent for longer maturities. However, if the loan is under $25,000, the top rates are prime plus 4.25 percent and 4.75 percent respectively. For loans between $25,000 and $50,000, the maximum rates are prime plus 3.25 percent and 3.75 percent respectively.

SBA LowDoc Loan Program

This program is intended to secure an SBA guarantee within 36 hours so the bank can provide quick loan approval. The loan process is a simple application. The SBA guarantees 80 percent for loans up to $100,000, and 75 percent for loans between $100,000 and $150,000, the maximum loan under this program. These loans can be used to start or grow a business. The maximum maturity is 5 to 10 years (25 years for loans for office buildings, plants, and other fixed assets). The top interest rates charged are prime plus 2.25 percent for maturities under 7 years, and 2.75 percent for loans of 7 years or longer. Higher rates may be imposed for loans under $50,000. Personal guarantees of company owners are required.

> **NOTE**
>
> The parameters of the LowDoc loan program are provided under a pilot program set to expire on September 30, 2001. After that date, unless the pilot program is renewed, the old LowDoc parameters, which were less favorable, would then apply.

SBAExpress

This loan program enables lenders to use their own application forms while obtaining up to a 50 percent guarantee from the SBA within 36 hours for amounts up to $150,000. Generally loans must be fully secured, but unsecured lines of credit up to $25,000 may be given. The program is designed to help small businesses start and grow. Again, what constitutes a small business depends on the industry involved. Loan maturity is 5 to 10 years (25 years for fixed-asset loans). Maximum interest rates are 2.25 percent over prime for loans less than 7 years and 2.75 percent over prime for loans of 7 years or longer.

Community Express

This program works in collaboration with the National Community Reinvestment Coalition (NCRC) and is similar to the SBA*Express* program. It's intended to help small businesses in low- and moderate-income areas by providing loans up to $250,000. Unsecured loans up to $25,000 can be approved. The same interest rates for SBA*Express* loans apply here, but higher rates may be charged on loans under $50,000.

CAIP Loan Program

The U.S. Community Adjustment and Investment Program (CAIP) is intended to help businesses in communities that suffer economic losses due to the North American Free Trade Agreement (NAFTA). The loans are intended to help businesses with the hope of creating new jobs or preserving old ones. The maximum loan guarantee is 75 percent of loans up to $1 million. Maturity for working capital loans is 7 years and for real estate loans it's up to 25 years. The same maximum interest rates apply to CAIP loans as to 7(a) loans.

CDC-504 Loan Program

The 504 Certified Development Company program is intended to help established businesses obtain long-term fixed-rate financing for buildings, realty improvements, and other so-called long-term asset acquisitions. The maximum loan generally is $750,000 ($1 million in certain cases). Interest rates are pegged to 5-year and 10-year U.S. Treasuries, and maturity can range from 10 to 20 years.

CapLines

This loan program is intended to provide short-term working capital for eligible small businesses. The SBA can guarantee $750,000 (75 percent of loans up to $1 million). Generally, the loan maturity is up to five years, and interest, which can be negotiated, usually is 2.25 percent over prime.

International Trade Loans and Export Working Cap Loans

These loan programs encourage eligible small businesses to engage in international trade by providing sizable fixed-asset and working capital loans.

Delta Program

The Defense Loan and Technical Assistance (DELTA) program, a joint program with the Department of Defense, is intended to help small businesses adversely affected by defense reductions. Loans are available for working capital, inventory, and asset acquisitions.

Prequal Pilot

The Prequalification Pilot loan program enables intermediaries to provide help to borrowers at no charge in completing loan application packages before submission. The SBA will provide approval within three days for loans up to $250,000. The maximum guarantee is 80 percent for loans up to $100,000, and 75 percent for larger loans. The program is limited to moderate-income, new-market customers; disabled, new, and emerging businesses; veterans; exporters; rural industries; and certain specialized industries. Loans for working capital can run 7 years; fixed-asset loans, up to 25 years. The same interest rates applicable to 7(a) loans apply here. Owners of at least 20 percent of the business must give their personal guarantee.

Qualified Employee Trusts Loan Program

This program provides help to employee stock ownership plans (ESOPs) and company-created benefit plans, so they can relend money to the business by buying qualified employer securities or by purchasing a controlling interest in the company. The maximum guarantee is 80 percent for loans up to $100,000, and 75 percent for larger loans up to $1 million. Loans for working capital can run 7 years; fixed-asset loans, up to 25 years. The same interest rates applicable to 7(a) loans apply here. Owners of at least 20 percent of the business must give their personal guarantee.

Microloan Program

This program is intended to encourage lenders to make very small loans (something commercial lenders generally would not otherwise do). The SBA makes funds available to nonprofit organizations that, in turn, lend the money to eligible small businesses. The maximum loan under this program is $25,000, but loans typically average $10,000. The term and interest rate depends on the size of the loan, the use of the funds, and other factors.

Figure 4.2 can be used to determine the type of loan best suited for your business purposes.

Taking In Outside Investors

If you don't want the burden of having to repay borrowed money with interest, then you'll need to find investors willing to gamble on your business. If you've already looked within the family and come up short, then look to outsiders.

How much of an ownership interest should you be willing to part with in exchange for an investment in the business? There's no easy answer. It's something to be negotiated with a potential investor. Factors affecting the amount of ownership interest given away:

- *The size of the investment.* Obviously, someone adding just a few thousand dollars to your business, no matter how helpful that may be, can't command a sizable piece of the business. On the other hand, a large infusion of cash may require a similarly large ownership interest.
- *Your level of desperation.* If you're on the ropes and the funds to be received will make or break the business, then you may

FIGURE 4.2 Main Types of Small Business Administration Loans

SBA Loan Program	Dollar Limits	Working Capital	Fixed Assets
7(a) loan guarantee	$1 million	Yes	Yes
SBA LowDoc	$150,000	Yes	Yes
SBA*Express*	$150,000	Yes	Yes
Community Express	$250,000	Yes	Yes
CAIP	$1 million	Yes	Yes
CDC-504 loans	Usually $750,000	No	Yes
CapLines	$1 million	Yes	No
Prequal Pilot	$250,000	Yes	Yes
Microloans	$25,000	Yes	Yes

be more inclined to part with a larger ownership share than if you believe you'll find the money elsewhere for a smaller share. Remember that you can only split the pie in so many ways. The larger the slice to the outside investor, the less remaining for you and your family.

Silent Partners

Getting investments from outsiders is generally no different than with relatives. Before you accept money from outside investors, make sure you and the investor understand what the relationship will be. How involved does the investor expect to be in the operations of the business? You can limit this role in various ways. As long as you stay in control (more than 50 percent ownership), the investor can't dictate whether the business makes dividend distributions or other terms and conditions.

Of course, as a practical matter, the investor can make your life unpleasant with constant suggestions and demands. If you want to take in silent partners who can't have any input in the business, you don't want to use a general partnership. Each general partner can have a say in how things work (though limited to the extent of his or her partnership interest).

Consider the following strategies, depending on the type of business organization involved:

- *Limited partnerships.* Limit outside investors to limited partnership interests. By definition, limited partners cannot exercise control.

- *Limited liability companies.* Here, articles of organization can provide for management only by designated managers rather than by each member having a say. Again, limit outside investors to general member status.

- *S corporations.* To qualify for S status, the corporation can have only one class of stock. However, differences in voting rights do not create a second class of stock. Thus, capitalize the business with voting and nonvoting shares, and limit outside investors to nonvoting shares.

- *C corporations.* This type of entity affords the most flexibility in limiting participation by outside investors. There can be any number of classes of stock desired, with restricted stock given to outsiders. Also, preferred stock (that pays dividends) can be used to provide outsiders with some return on investment without participation in daily business activities.

Note

You can find venture capitalists through *Pratt's Guide to Venture Capital Sources 2000* (24th edition, edited by Stanley E. Pratt and published by Venture Economics), available in local libraries. Venture capitalists are also easily found on the Web. However, don't approach venture capital firms directly, or your business plan is apt to get lost among other submissions. Instead, use an intermediary—accountant, attorney, or banker—who has a relationship with the venture capitalists and can see that you receive the consideration you deserve.

Venture Capitalists

In today's high-tech marketplace, there's a lot of talk about venture capitalists willing and eager to put funds into a business. For the most part, venture capitalists are interested in companies that can be expected to produce high returns in a relatively short time. This usually means having a hot product or new technology to sell. While family businesses aren't precluded from attracting venture capital, it's important to recognize that if you fit the traditional mom-and-pop profile of a family business, then you probably won't fit the demands of venture capitalists. What's more, venture capitalists generally take a sizable share of the business in exchange for their money—something you, as a family business owner, may be unwilling to part with.

However, according to some sources, the availability of venture capital for family businesses appears to be growing. Private investors, flush with cash from stock market gains in the past several years, are willing to gamble on family companies for a piece of the action.

Going Public

It's hard to open a newspaper today without learning about a company just starting out that's gone public—sold shares to the general public—and made the original owners wealthy beyond their wildest dreams. Millions of dollars have been made this way, and with the economy continuing to be strong, millions more will be made in the future.

Is this for you? You can sell shares in your company to the public and still keep control. This is accomplished by using different classes of stock. For example, the Sulzberger family still controls the New York Times Company, which is a public company listed on the

New York Stock Exchange. Thus, the company can remain primarily a family-owned business even though there are thousands of outside owners.

In order to go public, consider certain factors. The business must be one of interest to the public. Today, Internet and telecommunications companies are hot. Who knows where the interest will lie tomorrow? Also, the company must be organized as a C corporation in order to facilitate public stock sales. No other type of business organization can be used for this purpose.

Using Retained Earnings

Once your company is established and profits roll in, you may not want or need to distribute all those funds to owners. You can keep the money in the business. In a corporation this is referred to as retained earnings, but the same principle applies to any type of business enterprise. Retained earnings can be viewed as "free money" because there's no downside. Unlike borrowing from a bank or elsewhere, they do not have to be repaid; and unlike raising additional equity, using retained earnings doesn't dilute your ownership share.

Retained earnings can be used for:

- *Working capital.* Retained earnings can be put back into the business as needed to purchase equipment, provide benefits packages, or be used in any other way necessary.

- *Financial cushion.* Almost every business goes through cycles of good times and bad times. Retained earnings can be used to carry you through those hard periods when cash flow is inadequate to meet your company needs.

- *Expansion.* Instead of borrowing to build a new facility or start a new division, use retained earnings for this purpose.

Of course, it's difficult for most businesses to retain earnings. There always seems to be an expense to be met. However, to the extent you can save earnings by not spending them immediately, they will be a ready source of funding for the future.

PART 2

Running a Family Business

CHAPTER 5

Compensation Planning

Owners in family businesses hope to make money from their enterprises in two ways. First, in the long term they want their business to prosper so that its value will appreciate. Then they can capitalize on this appreciation by either borrowing against the value of the business, selling the company, taking it public, or in other ways. Second, however, in the short term they want their business to pay their ongoing personal expenses. Owners of small family businesses usually need to receive some steady payments from the business for this purpose. It's on this aspect of compensation that this chapter focuses.

How to design compensation packages in a family business becomes a complex matter. It includes not only the same financial considerations facing every company—what the company can afford to pay and the tax rules governing the treatment of payments—but also personal issues unique to a family business.

In this chapter you'll acquire a general introduction to compensation from a tax perspective. You'll learn about compensation options to consider for family business owners. You'll examine how to provide compensation to nonfamily members to attract and keep good talent for the business. And you'll find out about employment taxes for both family and nonfamily members.

Components of Compensation Packages

Businesses typically have certain core benefits included in their compensation packages: salary, medical coverage, and a retirement plan. This chapter focuses on salary (or similar compensation). Medical coverage, use of a company car, and other fringe benefits are discussed in Chapter 6. Retirement plans are discussed in Chapter 7.

The type of compensation to be provided for each company worker, whether a family member or not, obviously depends on the nature of the business and on the worker's level of participation in the business. Top management positions at fair-sized companies are at the highest rung of the salary scale, while rank-and-file employees of smaller businesses generally receive much less compensation.

The types of compensation provided also depend on the type of business organization in use. For example, if you have an S corporation or a C corporation, then owners who work for the business receive salary in addition to any other compensation provided. If you have a sole proprietorship, partnership, or limited liability company, you are not an employee of your business. You're considered self-employed. You may take a draw or other regular payments from the business, but these payments aren't salary.

If you act as a corporate officer as well as a director, only payments made for being an officer are treated as compensation for tax purposes. Director's fees are separate payments. Directors treat these payments as self-employment income separate from any salary they may receive in their executive capacity with the corporation.

Tax Rules for Compensation

Compensation isn't limited to a weekly or monthly paycheck. It includes salary, wages, commissions, bonuses, sick pay, vacation pay, and other payments for personal services performed by an employee. It also includes deferred compensation—amounts earned currently but to be received in later years (such as in retirement). So, if you're an owner in a corporation, whether an S or a C corporation, you receive compensation for your services in the form of salary or other such payments. These payments are, of course, taxable to you as ordinary income.

In order for compensation paid to employees—family members and nonfamily members—to be deductible by the business, two

Note

If you're an owner of a sole proprietorship, partnership, or limited liability company, you're never an employee. You're automatically taxed on your share of business profits, whether or not you take any distributions from the business. Typically, if you're in this type of enterprise, you'll take regular or periodic payments from the company to cover your personal expenses. These payments may be called "draws." They're not salary. They're not deductible by the business. Figuring your draw, however, is very similar to setting compensation if you're an employee. It depends on the work you do and what the business can afford to pay.

main conditions must be met. First, the compensation must be an ordinary and necessary business expense. This means it must be directly connected to the conduct of your business and necessary for you to carry on your business. This first condition is easy to satisfy and usually presents no problem.

Second, the compensation must be reasonable. Reasonableness applies to the whole package—salary, bonuses, and other payments—not just the weekly paycheck. And reasonableness is tested on a per-employee basis. Just because your total payroll is reasonable in view of the number of employees you have doesn't make compensation to certain owner-employees reasonable.

CAUTION

If compensation is found by the IRS to be *unreasonable*, then amounts paid to owners under the label of compensation will be treated as disguised dividends. Result: The company loses its tax deduction for the payment, but the owners must still report the income.

While public companies generally are limited to an annual deduction for compensation up to $1 million for certain executives (regardless of what's actually paid), there's no dollar limit on what's reasonable in closely held corporations. It depends on the facts and circumstances of your situation.

The corporate deduction for compensation is a write-off frequently under attack during IRS audits. In family businesses, be prepared for the fact that the IRS may use greater scrutiny on the question of reasonableness because of the opportunity for owner-employees to influence corporate decision making on salary payments. Here are some factors that the IRS has used to determine whether compensation is reasonable that you should apply in fixing your compensation:

- The employee's qualifications.
- The nature, extent, and scope of the employee's work. For example, where an owner wears many hats, functioning in effect as president, marketing director, and chief financial officer, it may be reasonable for compensation to reflect all these jobs.
- The employee's direct contribution to the corporation's profits.
- The size and complexity of the business.
- Comparison of salaries with the gross income and net income of the business.
- Prevailing economic conditions within the area (cost of living).
- Industry practices in fixing compensation. For example, formula-based compensation, such as a percentage of sales, may be reasonable if it's used within the industry.
- Comparison of salaries with distributions made to shareholders (dividend payments).
- Salaries paid by competitors.
- Salary policy of the company with respect to all employees.
- The amount of compensation paid (or not paid) in prior years. In small businesses it's common for owners to forgo compensation in the lean years and take make-up payments in the profitable years.

To find out what your competitors are paying for similar work in a similar business, you can check out statistics available through the U.S. Department of Labor Web site at www.dol.gov.

Courts have also recognized another standard used in determining reasonableness: whether a hypothetical independent investor would approve the compensation in light of his or her return on investment. Would the compensation paid to you and other owner-employees still leave such an investor with something to show for his or her investment in the business? If the answer is yes, then compensation may be viewed as reasonable.

Some family businesses may be overly generous in fixing compensation. To test whether your compensation levels are reasonable, ask yourself whether other businesses would pay the same amount if they were in your circumstances.

Generally, it's presumed that compensation voted on by the board of directors is reasonable. However, the fact that compensation has received board approval does not always make it reasonable, and the IRS may still contest what it considers to be unreasonable payments. Stipulating the amount of compensation in an employment contract can be helpful in showing that such amount is fixed in an arm's-length transaction (at least where the employee is not a controlling owner when the contract is signed).

Another requirement for deducting compensation is that it must be paid for services actually performed. For nonfamily employees this isn't an issue, because you wouldn't pay for work that isn't done. But in family businesses, some members may be on the payroll as a way of providing them with income even though they don't do any work for the business.

To deduct compensation paid to family members, make sure the compensation is geared to work actually performed. If spouses, children, parents, or other relatives are on your payroll, make sure that work they do is well documented. Keep time sheets or other records to prove the time spent and work performed for the business. One family business that employed a child as young as seven years old was able to prove compensation paid to him was reasonable under the circumstances (the child helped with cleanup and was paid a modest sum for the time he worked).

Assuming compensation is deductible, then you must determine *when* to take the deduction. Usually deductibility depends on the company's method of accounting. But for businesses on the accrual basis of accounting, there is a special rule governing year-end bonuses paid to "related parties" after the close of the year. The deduction cannot be accrued in the year the bonus is declared (year-end); it's deductible when paid. Related parties that come under this rule include the following relationships:

- Members of your immediate family (spouse, children, brothers and sisters of whole or half blood, grandchildren, and grandparents). It doesn't include in-laws.
- An individual and an S corporation in which he or she owns *any* of the corporation's outstanding stock.
- An individual and a C corporation (other than a personal service corporation) in which he or she owns more than 50 percent of the value of the corporation's outstanding stock.
- A personal service corporation and an owner-employee (regardless of the amount of stock ownership).

Year-end payments to nonrelated parties can be accrued if payment is made within two and a half months after the close of the year.

> **CAUTION**
>
> Don't include a clause in the employment contract requiring repayment of any compensation the IRS determines to be unreasonable. Courts have found this type of clause to be evidence that the business knew such compensation was unreasonable from the start.

> ### Example
>
> You wholly own an accrual-basis C corporation that reports on a calendar year ending December 31. The corporation employs your child. On December 15, 2000, the corporation declares a bonus to your child of $10,000. The corporation cannot accrue the expense until the bonus is paid to your child. An equal bonus is payable to your manager, who is unrelated to you. As long as it's paid by March 15, 2001, the company can accrue the expense and claim a deduction in 2000.

If compensation is deferred beyond the two and a half months, the business can deduct it only when it's paid out to the employee (and included in his or her income). This rule applies whether the business is on the cash or accrual method of reporting its income and expenses. Deferred compensation for both related and nonrelated parties is discussed in Chapter 8.

Special Compensation Arrangements

A weekly paycheck isn't the only means of paying compensation. Owners may receive payments from the business in a variety of ways. Fringe benefits and retirement plans are discussed in chapters that follow. But here are some additional means of compensation of particular interest to family business owners.

Salary Continuation Plans

The company may wish to continue paying salaries to owner-employees who become disabled. To ensure that the company can deduct the payments, it's advisable to set up a salary continuation plan. Without such a plan, the IRS may charge that payments are dividends or withdrawals of capital, neither of which are deductible by the business.

Interest-Free or Below-Market Loans

The company may make loans to owners and other key employees on advantageous loan terms. There may be no interest required or only a modest rate of interest charged. Loans may be made only to certain individuals and not to others.

In the past, loans were used to extract money from the business on a tax-advantaged basis. Since the funds borrowed from the business were only loans, the borrower did not report the loans as income. The tax law tried to close this loophole, but only went so far.

> **Caution**
>
> For S corporation owners, there's a danger in making interest-free or low-interest loans on an individual basis. The IRS can charge that this arrangement is really a disguised dividend. This would result in the S corporation having two classes of stock (one that paid the disguised dividend and one that did not). Since an S corporation cannot have two classes of stock, it would lose its S status if the IRS charge was successful. Thus, in S corporations it may be advisable to make identical loans to owners to avoid this potential pitfall.

Thus, it's still possible to use loans to provide an important benefit without serious adverse tax consequences. The owner has the use of the funds at little or no tax cost.

If the loan is no more than $10,000, it can still be made on an interest-free basis without triggering any tax consequences for the company or the borrower. The key is to make certain the loan is not principally for tax avoidance purposes. For example, a modest interest-free loan to an owner-employee to help relocate to another city when opening a new facility there would not trigger tax consequences because such a loan isn't motivated by tax avoidance purposes.

If the loan is more than $10,000 (or in any amount if made principally for tax avoidance) and the amount of interest charged on the loan is less than what the IRS says it should be (called the applicable federal interest rate—AFR—for the particular term of the loan or for a loan payable on demand), then the interest *not* charged is treated as taxable compensation to owner-employees. (The AFR is fixed monthly and is posted on the IRS Web site at www.irs.gov.) The company can, of course, deduct the compensation. But if the loan is to an owner who is *not* an employee (such as an owner who is a mere investor), then the interest not charged gives rise to a nondeductible dividend from the corporation.

Loans should be put in writing. Specify all the terms of the loan—interest rate, repayment schedule, and consequences of nonrepayment. In addition to a promissory note or other loan document, it's advisable to include the loan in the corporate minutes. And, of course, it's necessary to carry the loan on the corporate books.

Using Employment Contracts

While many companies routinely use employment contracts to spell out the terms and conditions of employment, their role in family businesses is especially important. The contract is a means of conveying expectations by both parties to the agreement.

For the company, an employment contract can:

- *Protect confidential information.* An employment contract prohibits a relative from revealing trade secrets and other sensitive information in the event there's a dispute and that relative leaves the business.
- *Avoid misunderstandings.* When multiple family members work for the business, one may assume he or she has a greater say than the business intends. Spelling things out avoids conflicts between family members on who has authority to do what.
- *Demonstrate fairness to nonfamily employees.* Holding family members to job descriptions in employment contracts shows outsiders that the business will treat each employee fairly regardless of family relationship.
- *Make discharge easier.* Not every family member turns out to be a stellar employee. There may come a time when the business would be better off without such a person. While pushing a relative out the door is never easy in a family business, having a contract makes it a little easier if that relative doesn't perform according to the terms of the agreement or otherwise breaches it.

For relatives, having an employment contract can:

- *Define the job.* The job description and the responsibilities that come with the job can be detailed in the agreement. This clarification can avoid misunderstandings about authority and expectations.
- *Provide security.* Relatives who are seduced into joining the family enterprise may want some guarantee. This is especially so if they leave higher-paying jobs for potential within the family business.
- *Outline potential.* Promises of future ownership or leadership positions in the business should be in writing so there is no confusion about expectations.

Using Independent Contractors

Payments to independent contractors for work performed for the business are not considered wages. Whether workers are employees or independent contractors is an important issue to be resolved by the business for two good reasons:

1. There are significant dollars at stake. If workers are employees, then the company is responsible for employment taxes and must include such workers in its benefit plans.

2. The IRS looks closely at this issue because of the tax dollars involved. It's easier for the government to collect employment taxes from a company than to follow up on individual workers. The IRS now routinely reviews worker classification whenever it conducts business audits.

Determining Employment Status

Whether a worker is an employee or an independent contractor is measured by the degree of control exercised by the company and the relationship of the parties.

- *Behavioral control.* If the business tells the worker when, where, and how to perform the job, and provides the supplies necessary for the work, this is a strong indication that the worker is an employee. Obviously, the amount of instruction depends on the job. So even where a business doesn't have to provide instructions because the worker is highly skilled, the worker may still be an employee if the timing and other conditions are present.

- *Financial control.* The extent of a worker's risk of loss and investment in the job affects worker status. If the company bears the risk of loss and has made a financial investment (e.g., put money into facilities), then this indicates employee status. If the reverse is true and the worker has risk and the opportunity to make a profit, then this shows independent contractor status. The method of payment is some indication of this risk. A regular paycheck is typical of employment status, whereas payment by the contract or upon job completion shows independent contractor status. Also, the ability to work for others in the marketplace is relevant.

- *Relationship of the parties.* How the company and worker view the relationship is critical. This view should be described in a written contract. The permanency of the relationship (for the job or ongoing) and the provision of employee benefits are other factors showing worker status.

Can a relative be an independent contractor to a family-owned business? Sure, in certain circumstances. For example, when a founder retires, he or she may continue to provide counsel and advice to the business through a consulting arrangement (discussed in greater detail in Part 3 of this book). In this way, the retired owner can continue to receive a regular payment from the business without the nine-to-five (plus) grind of an employee relationship. And the business continues to benefit from his or her experience and knowledge.

Both the company and the retired relative generally prefer to have the relationship viewed as one of an independent contractor rather than an employee. To ensure that the independent contractor relationship will be respected by the IRS, it's advisable to put the agreement in writing. Reserve to the consultant the right to provide services to other companies (whether or not such action is taken).

Can a current employee also be an independent contractor for the business? Theoretically it's possible (for example, where such person is providing different services as a contractor than he or she is providing as an employee). However, this arrangement is sure to raise an IRS eyebrow.

Establishing Compensation Policies

Setting compensation for relatives and nonfamily members is certainly a difficult task. However, if the business sets compensation policies, it becomes a little easier. Determining compensation policies in advance allows family members to have an opportunity to offer their opinions on what those policies should be.

Here are some suggestions for compensation policies to be used in family businesses to create an atmosphere of fairness for all concerned.

- *Pay the job, not the person.* Set the compensation based on the job requirements, not on who is filling the position. This will ensure that outsiders receive the same compensation if they do the same work as family members.

- *Be competitive.* The compensation paid for your company's jobs must measure up to what's being paid by other companies in your industry. This is the only way to attract and keep good employees, an especially critical consideration in today's tight job market.

- *Pay what the business can afford.* How many mouths can one company feed? This is a hard question for some family business owners to answer. When pop started the hardware store on the corner, his compensation fed his immediate family—mom and two young sons. When the store expanded and the two grown boys—each with a wife and two children of his own—joined the business, the mouths to feed now included the boys' families.

The same business that used to feed four people is now being asked to feed 10 people. Can it be done? Obviously, the answer depends on the individual company.

- *Do performance reviews.* Hold family members to the same periodic reviews as outsiders. Criticism should be objective, and relatives should face the same consequences as nonfamily members, including demotion, no pay raise, or even termination. It's difficult for a relative to judge the performance of another relative, but, as a matter of policy, it provides a framework in which a family business can function. Obviously, there's an added degree of tact needed when reviewing a relative's performance. It may be easier to have the review performed by a manager or even an outside adviser who is not related.

- *Review compensation by the board of directors.* In fixing pay packages for top employees, have them reviewed and agreed to by the board of directors. This is especially helpful where there are outside directors who are completely objective and devoid of family involvement.

Setting Pay for Family Members

Fixing a dollar amount to compensation for yourself and your family members who work for the business is a difficult undertaking. Of course, you need to bear tax rules in mind so that compensation is reasonable and thus deductible by the business. However, in a family-business context, emotional or personal issues come into play. It's sometimes difficult to be objective. Compensation is often the most problematic area for family businesses, creating conflicts and jealousy that can undermine the best interests of the company.

TIP

If you don't know whether salary levels you've established are reasonable or how to determine compensation for particular individuals, it's best to consult with experts. Ask business and financial people (accountants, business advisers, and others) to give you an unbiased perspective.

The fact is that some family businesses overpay relatives while others underpay them (and overwork them). Parents who control the business may set pay for children based on love and good wishes rather than sound management decisions. For example, in one company the founder wanted to give equal compensation to his two sons so that neither would be jealous of the other. But one son was a hard worker who put in long hours for the business and held a top management position. The other son was somewhat of a deadbeat, coming in late, leaving early and generally not giving his all. Both sons knew the score and, contrary to the father's intentions, the hard-working son did indeed grow jealous of the slacker, while the dead-beat felt guilty about what he was taking from the business. What was purported to be fair turned out to be unfair to everyone. In addition to bad feelings, the risk here is that the hardworking son may leave the family business and go to another company that will pay him what he's really worth.

Some family owners use compensation as a means of control over other family members. Parent may control child, or even vice versa, through numbers on a paycheck. One patriarch of a family restaurant in which his two adult daughters worked would not agree to pay them a fair wage. His old-world beliefs about family relations governed his business decisions in this case. The daughters felt trapped between their desire to please their father and receive their inheritance—ownership of the business—and their current need to earn a living wage. This created bad feelings all around. In another business a father used the promise of added compensation to get his son to side with him in disputes with other owners.

Aside from fairness, another consideration is whether equal compensation is deductible in certain situations. There have been several cases in which spouses each took equal paychecks from the business even though one spouse was a professional (such as a doctor or engineer) and the other functioned in a clerical capacity. The compensation arrangement did not hold up to IRS scrutiny. Obviously, the job performance by the professional commanded a greater salary than that paid for clerical assistance.

The key is to pay relatives for the work they do rather than for their relationship to the owner or their ownership interest. This becomes particularly important if the company goes through difficult financial periods and must cut back on compensation. If it's based on fair pay for work performed, then relatives won't (hopefully) take it personally when there are salary reductions. In fixing compensation, keep these parameters in mind:

- *The company isn't a welfare state.* Don't use the company to put unproductive relatives on the dole. If you need to provide them with funds, it's better for the business that you make personal gifts to them outside of the business framework. True, the gifts aren't deductible, but you'll avoid conflicts with other relatives working for the business.

- *The company isn't a slave state.* Don't use relatives as cheap labor. Pay them fairly for the work they do. Don't hold out the carrot of future ownership instead of giving them their current due.

- *The company isn't the place to play out family feuds.* Don't use compensation as a means for punishing, controlling, or lording it over relatives. Again, pay relatives fairly for the work they do.

Be prepared to adjust compensation levels as the roles of family members change over time. For example, children may start out in menial roles. But as they progress through management positions, their compensation should be adjusted accordingly. By the same token, founders who eventually accept a less prominent role in running the company should expect to have compensation reduced.

Setting Pay for Nonfamily Members

For a family business to attract and retain top nonfamily employees—from senior executives to rank-and-file workers—you need to apply fairness and creativity. Compensation must, of course, be commensurate with the job. The same criteria used for determining fairness to family workers also apply to nonfamily workers.

But owners need to recognize that top executives working for a family business may need something more. These outsiders recognize that they will probably never have an ownership interest in the family business—a right reserved for relatives. And even if they do receive some stock in the company, it will never amount to more than a minority interest, devoid of any real control. Unlike public corporations that can use a variety of stock option plans to compensate executives, family businesses need to provide other forms of compensation. These forms of compensation, which may be performance incentives, can be tailored in any way that's best for the company. They can be limited to certain employees or can be open to rank-and-file workers as you see fit.

Bonuses

Outsiders can be provided with incentive to perform by rewarding them with bonuses. These bonuses should be tied to company performance (such as increased sales, net profits, etc.). There need not be any ceiling to this potential (other than the bounds of reasonableness). Remember that an accrual-basis company can deduct bonuses in the current year only if they are actually paid within two and a half months of the following year.

Phantom Stock

Instead of giving actual ownership interests in the company, cash payments can be made in lieu of what would otherwise be stock.

Since no actual shares are used, the term "phantom stock" best describes this equity appreciation plan. The value of the phantom stock should be tied to some valuation formula. For example, in service businesses, value can be pegged to gross revenues, while in manufacturing or other businesses with large capital investments, value can be pegged to capitalization rates of net earnings (e.g., three or five times earnings before interest and taxes). This allows the executive to receive a monetary benefit, but doesn't entail any downside (even if the company's value declines, the executive loses nothing).

Stock Appreciation Rights (SARs)

This is a type of cash bonus linked to the price of company stock. The holder of the rights can receive the bonus when the value of the stock exceeds the stock's value on the date the rights are given. Since there's no market to determine value for privately held corporations, the SARs should spell out how value is fixed (e.g., book value). There's usually a time limit to exercise the rights (such as five years). If the stock hasn't appreciated within that time and the rights aren't exercised, they simply expire. From the employee perspective, the rights aren't taxable until the cash bonus is paid pursuant to the exercise of the rights.

Deferred Compensation Arrangements

Provide added compensation that will be paid when the nonfamily employee leaves the company. This compensation can have strings attached (for example, it will be paid only if the employee has completed a certain number of years of employment with the company). Deferred compensation is discussed in Chapter 8.

Creating a Human Resources Department

In very small businesses, company heads typically fix compensation down the line. However, as a business grows, it may be helpful to

---

Tip

In creating valuation formulas used for phantom stock or stock appreciation rights, be aware that you are creating an obligation for the company. Should the business grow substantially, a valuation formula may impose a sizable liability on the company. So it may be helpful to impose some limit on the valuation formula, such as a cap of 5 percent or 10 percent of profits annually. This will keep debt manageable.

shift this decision making to a human resources (HR) department. The HR managers are professionals who can handle all aspects of compensation planning.

The HR manager can implement the employment policies fixed by you and your board. The HR manager can function in an independent, objective manner, treating relatives who work for the company the same as nonrelated employees.

When does it make sense to bring in HR people? There's no cut-and-dried size that a business should be in order to justify making this change. One consulting firm has estimated that family businesses typically make the move when revenues approach $10 million for service businesses and $15 million for manufacturing. But smaller companies may benefit from expert assistance if they can support the compensation to the HR manager.

Of course, in order for the HR manager to be successful in the family business environment, the CEO must be able to give up this aspect of control. Founders who have years of practice in doling out compensation to family members may prefer to retain this control. However, from a business standpoint, it's probably better for the company head to be spending time and effort on growing the business rather than on holding onto the purse strings.

Employment Taxes and Compensation

It's important to understand how payments to owners in a family business are treated for employment tax purposes. Employment taxes include Social Security and Medicare taxes, collectively called FICA (Federal Insurance Contributions Act) tax, and federal unemployment taxes, called FUTA (Federal Unemployment Tax Act) tax.

Employment tax rules are discussed in IRS Publication 15, Circular E, "Employer's Tax Guide," available through the IRS Web site at www.irs.gov.

For FICA tax purposes, the same tax is levied on both the employer and the employee. The tax rate for the Social Security portion

Example

You take a salary of $100,000 from your C corporation. In 2001, you and the corporation each pay $6,434.80 ([$80,400 × 6.2% = $4,984.80] + [$100,000 × 1.45% = $1,450]). The total employee and employer tax amounts to $12,869.60.

Caution

S corporation owners are subject to FICA tax only on salary payments to them (in contrast to partners, who pay self-employment tax on their share of profits). But if you're an owner of an S corporation, you can't avoid FICA tax by characterizing payments to yourself as something other than salary. Courts have required that S corporation owners take reasonable compensation for services performed for their business so that FICA tax gets paid.

of FICA is 6.2 percent of wages up to $80,400 in 2001 (the wage ceiling subject to Social Security tax is adjusted annually for inflation). The tax rate for the Medicare portion of FICA is 1.45 percent of all wages (there's no ceiling).

The employee portion of FICA tax, along with income tax withheld from pay, is considered a "trust fund obligation." If the company fails to pay over this amount to the federal government as required by law, the IRS can hold owners and other "responsible persons" within the company 100 percent personally liable for these taxes. This is true regardless of how the business is organized (i.e., you don't enjoy personal liability protection for failure to pay over trust fund obligations).

Self-employed individuals, who do not receive a salary and so are not subject to FICA tax on payments to them, pay self-employment tax to cover their Social Security and Medicare tax obligations. Self-employment tax equals both the employer and employee share. Thus, the Social Security portion of the self-employment tax is 12.4 percent of net earnings from self-employment up to $80,400 in 2001. The Medicare portion of the self-employment tax is 2.9 percent of all net earnings from self-employment. However, self-employed individuals can deduct one-half of their self-employment tax (the equivalent to the employer share) on their personal returns as an adjustment to gross income.

Example

You're a sole proprietor showing a net profit in 2001 of $100,000. Your self-employment tax is $12,869.60 ([12.4% of $80,400 = $9,969.60] + [2.9% of $100,000 = $2,900]). However, $6,434.80 of this tax is deductible on your personal return.

FUTA tax applies only to the first $7,000 of compensation for each employee. The FUTA tax rate is 0.8 percent of taxable wages. This tax is paid entirely by the employer. In addition, the employer may owe state unemployment taxes.

Owners in unincorporated businesses may function as silent partners, owning the business or a share of it but not performing any services. Here's how such owners figure self-employment tax:

- *Sole proprietors* are subject to self-employment tax on net income from the business. Self-employment tax is not dependent on what sole proprietors take out of their business, but only on profits.

- *General partners* are subject to self-employment tax on their distributive share of net earnings from the business plus any guaranteed payments to them. Self-employment tax is not dependent on what these partners take out of the business.

- *Limited partners* are generally exempt from self-employment tax.

- *Members in limited liability companies* may or may not be subject to self-employment tax on their distributive share of net earnings from the business. The answer isn't clear. Members have limited liability just like limited partners. But they may or may not perform services for their business like general partners. So how should they be treated for self-employment tax purposes? The IRS had been precluded from implementing regulations on this issue to July 1, 1998. That date has long passed but there has been no IRS guidance on this point.

Directors' Fees

Directors' fees are considered self-employment income. They're subject to self-employment tax (separate and apart from FICA tax that may be levied on compensation paid for being a corporate officer).

Example

As company president you receive a salary of $100,000. You also receive $5,000 a year as a member of the board of directors. For self-employment tax purposes, you pay only the Medicare portion of the FICA tax, which is $145 (2.9 percent of $5,000). You satisfied your Social Security taxes through FICA tax on your salary. Had your salary been only $78,000, you would have also paid the Social Security portion of self-employment tax on $2,400 (the difference between the ceiling of $80,400 and your salary of $78,000).

> ### Example
>
> In 2001, your salary is $125,000, and you agree to defer $25,000 to retirement. Since your salary (without regard to the deferred amount) is already above the ceiling of $80,400, there are no additional Social Security taxes imposed on the deferred amount. (The Medicare portion of FICA tax is imposed on the full $125,000 since there is no ceiling for this tax.) Say you retire in 2010 and receive the $25,000. Since it was already subject to FICA tax (even though there was no Social Security tax on it), there is no further employment tax obligation.

However, the Social Security portion of the self-employment tax is not imposed if Social Security taxes have already been paid on the ceiling amount ($80,400 in 2001).

Deferred Compensation

Employment taxes are due when the compensation is earned, not when it's paid (even though the company cannot deduct the compensation until it's paid). Thus, for example, if you agree to defer $25,000 of your compensation until retirement, FICA and FUTA taxes are figured in the year of deferral, not the year of retirement. This can produce tax savings for you and the corporation.

Employing Young Children in a Family Business

There are some compelling reasons—financial and otherwise—for hiring your own children while they're still young.

- They learn good job ethics—hard work and responsibility (showing up on time, completing tasks, following instructions, etc.).

- They learn the ropes of the business. They get to observe you at work, watch how you operate, and see what it takes to run a business. And they'll get hands-on training with whatever area you assign them to.

- They earn their money instead of simply getting it for free. Instead of an allowance with no strings attached, you can pay your children for work they've done. It's hoped that in this way the money means more to them and, in turn, they'll spend it wisely.

- They have a basis for saving for the future. Their earnings up to $2,000 can be invested in a Roth IRA to build up a tax-free retirement fund. There's no minimum age for starting a Roth IRA;

all that's required is earned income. Even if they spend what they earn, you can gift them the $2,000 to put into a Roth IRA (assuming they earned at least $2,000). By starting young, their savings potential through this tax vehicle is huge.

- Income-shifting to them through salary payments results in over-all tax savings for the family. Earnings up to the standard deduction for single taxpayers are exempt from federal income tax. So, for example, in 2001, a dependent child can earn up to $4,550 and owe no income tax. You still retain the right to claim your child as your dependent. Had you simply earned this money yourself, you'd have only $2,912 after tax if you're in the 36 percent bracket ($4,550 less $1,638 federal income tax at 36 percent).

- The business can deduct payments to them. Compensation paid to a child is deductible as long as it is reasonable compensation for work actually performed.

> **CAUTION**
>
> There's no exemption from the federal minimum wage laws or child labor laws for hiring your own children. If you're unsure about these legal rules, check with your state employment office.

Employment Taxes

If you're a sole proprietor and employ your child, there's no FICA tax on compensation paid to the child as long as he or she is under the age of 18. This results in a tax savings for both you and your child. For example, if your teenager, age 16, works for your business and earns $3,000 during the summer, you and your child *each* save $230 (7.65% × $3,000).

Your child's wages are exempt from FUTA tax until he or she reaches the age of 21.

> **CAUTION**
>
> There's no FICA or FUTA tax exemption for wages paid to a spouse, parent, or other relative, regardless of whether your business is incorporated.

CHAPTER 6

Fringe Benefits

Company owners often view their businesses as their personal pocketbooks. They use their companies to pay for certain personal expenses—health coverage, a car—on a tax-advantaged basis. Unfortunately, some family business owners may even take this a step further, using their businesses to pay for a wider range of personal expenses. While other shareholders may not object because they're all related, the IRS may vigorously oppose efforts to claim tax write-offs for these personal payments. Leona Helmsley's real estate business paid for her lingerie among other personal expenses and she went to jail because of it. Certainly, owners have some leeway in the types of expenses the business can pay for on their behalf, but deductions for these expenses must conform to tax law requirements.

In this chapter you'll see the types of fringe benefits typically available for small business owners, their spouses and dependents, and their employees. You'll learn what benefits must be provided to rank-and-file employees if owners want to enjoy those benefits as well. And you'll find out about strategies for maximizing benefits for owners and for providing benefits at no cost to the company. A prime fringe benefit—a retirement plan—is discussed in the next chapter.

Overview of Fringe Benefits

The tax law contains a number of personal expenses that can be provided by a company on a tax-advantaged basis. The term "tax-advantaged" means the company can deduct the expense and the owner is not taxed on the benefit or is taxed at less than the actual cost of the benefit. To qualify for this tax treatment, the benefit usually has to be provided on a nondiscriminatory basis. This means that if higher-paid employees receive the benefit, then rank-and-file workers must also be entitled to it. If the benefit is limited to owners and other highly paid employees, generally the benefit becomes taxable to the recipient (or at least to owners and highly paid employees who receive it).

In most cases, benefits can be provided only to employees. Thus, owners of C corporations who work for their companies can receive a wide range of fringe benefits without incurring personal income as a result. On the other hand, self-employed individuals (including partners and members in LLCs) and S corporation shareholders owning more than 2 percent of the stock cannot enjoy these benefits on a tax-free basis. Throughout this chapter, however, opportunities for self-employed individuals and these S corporation owners to receive fringe benefits are pointed out.

In considering various fringe benefits, take into account not only the income tax consequences to the company and recipient, but also employment taxes. Some benefits are not subject to employment taxes, while other benefits may be subject to employment taxes (even if exempt from income tax withholding). Where benefits are exempt from employment taxes, the company can save significant tax dollars. Bear in mind that the FICA tax cost can run up to 7.65 percent of every dollar in benefits.

> **NOTE**
>
> According to the U.S. Chamber of Commerce, fringe benefits nationwide account for more than 40 percent of payroll costs.

Medical Coverage

Businesses are not required to provide medical coverage or pay any part of the cost. But if they choose to do so, coverage must be made available on a nondiscriminatory basis. Medical insurance provided by a company for employees, their spouses, and their dependents is a tax-free fringe benefit that's fully deductible by the business. Medical coverage includes not only health insurance but also long-term care insurance (the type of policy that covers a nursing home stay).

> **Tip**
>
> If an owner is about 55 or older, it may be advisable to offer long-term care insurance as part of health coverage for employees. This long-term care insurance can be viewed as inheritance protection. The reason: There's about a 40 percent chance of a nursing-home stay during one's lifetime and the average annual cost of care is over $40,000, with such cost running in excess of $100,000 in some locations. So, if long-term care is needed, having a long-term care policy means the insurance company pays the bill, leaving one's assets available for heirs.

Strategies for Sole Proprietors, Partners, and S Corporation Owners

Self-employed individuals and S corporation shareholders owning more than 2 percent of the stock cannot receive company-paid health insurance on a tax-free basis. If the company pays for their coverage, then the following treatment applies:

- *Sole proprietors.* Coverage for the owner is *not* a deductible business expense. The owner may claim a deduction for the expense within the limits explained later in this section.

- *Partners.* Coverage may be treated as guaranteed payments to partners (deductible by the partnership and taxable to partners). Alternatively, distributions to partners can be reduced by coverage provided for them (which is not deductible by the partnership). Again, partners may claim a deduction for the expense as explained later.

- *S corporation shareholders.* Coverage is treated as compensation to shareholders (and fully deductible by the corporation). However, premiums are not treated as wages for purposes of FICA tax.

Sole proprietors, partners, and S corporation shareholders can deduct a percentage of the premium as an adjustment to gross income on their personal returns. This includes the premiums for any long-term care policies. The balance of the premium can be treated as an itemized medical expense deduction (assuming that the total of this portion of the premium plus other unreimbursed medical expenses exceeds 7.5 percent of adjusted gross income). Figure 6.1 shows the deductible percentages.

There have been bills in Congress to accelerate the 100 percent deduction before 2003. These bills have been vigorously supported

FIGURE 6.1 Percentage of Premium Deductible
by Self-Employeds

Year	Deductible Percentage
2000–2001	60%
2002	70%
2003 and later	100%

by many small business interest groups and trade associations. It remains to be seen if and when such a measure is enacted.

But regardless of possible congressional action, self-employed individuals now can enjoy full tax-free coverage if their spouses (who are not owners) work for the business. In that case, health coverage provided to employees and their spouses would cover self-employed individuals because they are spouses of employees. So if you own an unincorporated business, putting your spouse on the payroll will enable you to receive company-paid health coverage at no tax cost to you.

Strategies for Reducing the Cost of Coverage

Medical insurance is an ever-increasing expense that can be burdensome for some businesses. In small businesses, there's a desire to provide coverage as a means of competing with larger companies in attracting and keeping valuable workers. But there's also a need to keep costs down.

A key way to keep costs down is to shop around for the coverage at the most advantageous price. Costs and coverage vary greatly from carrier to carrier. Check coverage available through trade associations and professional organizations, which can extend to small businesses the same favorable group rates usually enjoyed by large businesses.

Example

The AB Partnership provides health coverage for employees, spouses, and dependents. Sue Adams, a 50 percent partner, and George, her spouse, work for the business. If the health policy covers employees (George) and their spouses (Sue), then Sue receives tax-free medical insurance by virtue of being an employee's spouse even though she's self-employed.

In addition to finding low-cost coverage, there are other ways to reduce the company's burden by shifting the cost of medical coverage to employees. Here are some alternatives to consider.

SHARE PREMIUM COSTS

Instead of having the business pick up the entire cost of coverage, shift some of the cost to employees. For example, pay the cost for singles, but require married employees to pay the additional cost of family coverage for spouses and dependents if they want this added protection.

USE CAFETERIA PLANS

A cafeteria plan is a written plan that allows employees to choose among two or more benefits consisting of cash and nontaxable benefits (such as health coverage). The company pays the entire cost of benefits under the plan. But it lets each employee decide whether to select health coverage. This can produce a savings where married employees who are receiving coverage through a spouse's plan forgo health coverage under your cafeteria plan. As long as the plan is nondiscriminatory, then the selection of health coverage is a tax-free benefit. If the plan is discriminatory, the highly paid employees and owners receiving the health coverage are taxed on this benefit.

USE PREMIUM-ONLY CAFETERIA PLANS

These plans let employees choose between receiving cash or using the cash to pay for medical coverage on a pretax basis. Employees who want medical coverage agree to salary reductions that are then used to pay premiums. The salary reductions are not subject to income tax if used to pay premiums (they're taxable if cash is taken instead). For example, if both spouses work for the company, only one needs to opt for the health insurance (which will cover the other spouse as well). The other spouse can receive the salary.

> ### Note
>
> Salary reductions under premium-only plans are *not* treated as wages for purposes of FICA tax. This means that both the company and the employee save on FICA tax if medical coverage is chosen. Say coverage runs $500 a month and an employee agrees to a monthly salary reduction in this amount. This results in an annual FICA tax savings of $459 for both the business and the employee ($500 per month × 12 months × 7.65 percent FICA tax rate).

USE FLEXIBLE SPENDING ACCOUNTS (FSAS)

These are arrangements that employees pay for medical expenses not covered by insurance on a pretax basis. Like premium-only plans, employees agree to salary reduction contributions to the FSAs. Then funds can be used to pay for eyeglasses, out-of-pocket costs for prescription drugs, and other expenses not paid by insurance. Since employees are picking up out-of-pocket costs, the company can provide a more limited type of coverage, producing a cost savings.

From the employees' perspective, an FSA is a use-it-or-lose-it arrangement. They commit themselves to a regular salary reduction contribution and can't recoup contributed amounts that aren't used for medical expenses.

From the company perspective, there's a potential risk of loss in FSAs. Employees are entitled to reimbursement for their full commitment even before all salary reduction contributions have been made. So, in the example, in January you would be entitled to reimbursement of $2,400 even though you had made only a $200 salary reduction contribution. If employees leave the company before making full contributions but after having submitted claims for reimbursement, the company is out the money. Of course, the company keeps any salary reductions not fully used by employees; so, at least in theory, potential losses can be offset by this potential windfall.

USE MEDICAL SAVINGS ACCOUNTS (MSAS)

Small businesses that regularly employ 50 or fewer employees and self-employed individuals can use MSAs to cut insurance costs. If they provide "high deductible" insurance coverage, then the business can contribute to medical savings accounts on behalf of employees (or let employees make their own contributions). Contributions to MSAs are tax deductible. The deduction is 75 percent of the deductible in the

Example

You're an employee of your C corporation and agree to a monthly $200 salary reduction contribution to the company's medical FSA. You'd need to submit receipts for reimbursement from the plan of $2,400 in medical costs during the year in order to fully utilize your contributions. If you submit receipts for only $2,000, then you've lost $400 that you could have received in income had you not made that salary reduction agreement.

FIGURE 6.2   Limits for Medical Savings Accounts

Type of Coverage	Deductible at Least . . .	Deductible No More Than . . .	Limit on Out-of-Pocket Costs . . .
Family coverage	$3,100	$4,650	$5,700
Self-only coverage	$1,550	$2,350	$3,100

case of family coverage and 65 percent of the deductible for self-only coverage (or a proratable portion if coverage is for less than the full year). Income earned on MSAs is not currently taxable.

"High deductible" plans are plans that have an annual deductible and limit on out-of-pocket expenses within certain ranges. Figure 6.2 shows the ranges that apply for 2000.

Withdrawals from these IRA-type accounts that are used to pay uninsured medical expenses are not taxed. Withdrawals for any other purpose are taxed and subject to a 15 percent penalty (although the penalty does not apply to withdrawals after age 65).

Medical savings accounts are explained in greater detail in IRS Publication 969, "Medical Savings Accounts," available through the IRS Web site at www.irs.gov.

Medical Reimbursement Plans

Companies may wish to subsidize employee health costs by picking up amounts not paid by insurance. They can do so on a tax-advantaged basis by setting up a medical reimbursement plan. Employees are not taxed on the coverage, while the company deducts in full any payments it makes under the plan.

Typically, a medical reimbursement plan covers dental expenses, vision care, hearing aids, and other uninsured health costs. The plan sets a dollar limit on annual coverage (say $5,000). The plan must be approved by the corporation's board of directors and the motion entered in the corporate minutes.

Caution

Medical savings accounts are run under a four-year pilot program set to expire at the end of 2000. Only a limited number of participants can use MSAs. However, this limit has not been reached. Congress is considering an extension of MSAs beyond 2000 and expansion of the deduction to 100 percent of the deductible.

Medical reimbursement plans are self-insured (there's no insurance policy from an outside carrier). The company must pay liabilities under the plan from its own coffers.

Medical reimbursement plans are limited to employees, including owners of C corporations who work for their business (but not S corporation owners). However, like health coverage discussed earlier, medical reimbursement plans can be used in non–C corporation family businesses to cover owners if spouses who are not owners work for the business. Again, coverage is provided to employees (the spouses) and their spouses (the owners) to cover out-of-pocket expenses. The only limitation for medical reimbursement plans: The coverage must be provided to employees on a nondiscriminatory basis.

CAUTION

Set a dollar limit that won't expose the business to extensive payments if claims turn out to be higher than anticipated. Figure on the worst-case scenario (all covered employees submit maximum claims). Then work backward to fix a dollar limit the company can live with.

In small companies where a significant number of employees are family members, a medical reimbursement plan can provide a cushion against sizable out-of-pocket expenses. This is especially helpful since employees may not be able to deduct these uninsured costs on their personal returns. Only unreimbursed medical expenses in excess of 7.5 percent of adjusted gross income (AGI) are deductible as an itemized medical deduction, so high AGI will preclude or severely limit any write-off.

Before adopting a medical reimbursement plan, consider the administrative burden of administering the plan. If the company is small, this may be minimal. But if the company has numerous employees, a medical reimbursement plan can become an administrative nightmare.

Other Rules for Health Insurance

Once you decide to provide health coverage, understand your obligation to continue coverage for departing workers. You may be required to offer coverage under certain circumstances.

CONTINUING COVERAGE FOR RETIREES

The company isn't required to provide health coverage for workers who retire (other than COBRA, discussed next). However, it can choose to do so and may want to if retiring individuals happen to be owners who want this benefit. Such coverage may be continued indefinitely or end when the retiree reaches 65, the age he or she becomes entitled to Medicare coverage. The company can, of course, deduct the cost of medical insurance for retirees.

But the company should protect itself from a continuing liability for retiree health coverage that it may want or need to end in the future by reserving the right to terminate this obligation. Note this reservation in any plan or agreement made with employees to provide such coverage (such as offers of inducement for early retirement).

COBRA COVERAGE

If the company provides health coverage and it regularly employs 20 or more workers, then it must offer to terminated employees and certain other individuals continued health coverage, called COBRA coverage (after the Consolidated Omnibus Budget Reconciliation Act that created it). This law gives departing workers the opportunity to pick up health coverage for up to 18 months (longer in certain situations). There's no cost to the company for doing so. The former employee pays the full cost of coverage, plus a fee of up to 2 percent to cover administrative expenses.

CAUTION

Companies that are required to offer COBRA coverage and fail to do so may be subject to penalty taxes.

Typically, larger companies providing COBRA coverage use outside companies to administer their programs. Smaller companies with only a limited number of COBRA participants usually continue to administer their programs in-house.

TIP

Unlike many other fringe benefits, providing company-owned cars to owners and not to other employees is permissible. This fringe benefit need not be provided on a nondiscriminatory basis.

Company Cars

It is a common fringe benefit for a company to provide owners who work for the business and other top management with company cars or to reimburse them for use of their personal cars. In family-owned businesses, company cars are key benefits almost universally provided. C corporations, S corporations, or other business entities may choose to own the cars or help owners pay for business use of their personal cars. Who owns or leases the car and how reimbursements of expenses are made will control the tax treatment for both the company and the employees enjoying the benefit.

Business-Owned Cars

By having the corporation own or lease the car, the business can deduct car expenses (subject to certain limitations). Where there is more than one company car, the business may be able to command favorable purchase or lease terms and insurance discounts not otherwise available to individuals with one or two cars. What's more, corporate ownership of the car provides an added measure of liability protection to owners if there's an accident (the business rather than the owner would be the party to sue).

Owners who work for their companies and are given the use of company cars for personal purposes are taxed on this benefit. The corporation has a choice of how to report this taxable benefit on employee W-2 forms.

METHOD 1

Include 100 percent of the value of the use of the car in the employee's income (personal and any business use). Value can be determined in several ways. It can be the cost of leasing a comparable car at a comparable price for a comparable period of time. The cost of the vehicle can be its fair market value if the car was purchased in an arm's-length transaction. There is a safe harbor rule using the manufacturer's invoice price (including all options), plus 4 percent. Another valuation method—the cents-per-mile method—can be used if the car is used regularly for business (defined as being used at least 50 percent for business or for driving at least three employees to and from work in a carpool) or driven at least 10,000 miles a year. The cents-per-mile rate is the IRS's standard mileage rate—32.5 cents per mile in 2000. And there's a valuation method based on the car's annual lease value (ALV), which may be found in Figure 6.3.

Whichever valuation method is selected, the company reports the employee's use of the car. Then the employee can deduct the business use as an itemized deduction on his or her personal return. However, as a practical matter the employee may receive little or no benefit from this write-off since unreimbursed employee business expenses such as business use of a company car included on the W-2 form are deductible only to the extent they exceed 2 percent of adjusted gross income.

Example

Assume a company car's fair market value on January 1, 2000, is $20,000 and an employee uses the car half for business and half for personal purposes (based on mileage). The ALV (from Figure 6.3) is $5,600. The amount included in the employee's income is $2,800 ($5,600 × 50%). If the car was used by the employee only from May 1 through September 30, the $2,800 is prorated for 153 days of personal use. In this case the amount included in the employee's income is $2,340.98 ($5,600 × 153/366).

FIGURE 6.3   Table of Annual Lease Values

Car's Fair Market Value	Annual Lease Value
$ 0 to $ 999	$ 600
1,000 to 1,999	850
2,000 to 2,999	1,100
3,000 to 3,999	1,350
4,000 to 4,999	1,600
5,000 to 5,999	1,850
6,000 to 6,999	2,100
7,000 to 7,999	2,350
8,000 to 8,999	2,600
9,000 to 9,999	2,850
10,000 to 10,999	3,100
11,000 to 11,999	3,350
12,000 to 12,999	3,600
13,000 to 13,999	3,850
14,000 to 14,999	4,100
15,000 to 15,999	4,350
16,000 to 16,999	4,600
17,000 to 17,999	4,850
18,000 to 18,999	5,100
19,000 to 19,999	5,350
20,000 to 20,999	5,600
21,000 to 21,999	5,850
22,000 to 22,999	6,100
23,000 to 23,999	6,350
24,000 to 24,999	6,600
25,000 to 25,999	6,850
26,000 to 27,999	7,250
28,000 to 29,999	7,750
30,000 to 31,999	8,250
32,000 to 33,999	8,750
34,000 to 35,999	9,250
36,000 to 37,999	9,750
38,000 to 39,999	10,250

FIGURE 6.3 Continued

Car's Fair Market Value	Annual Lease Value
40,000 to 41,999	10,750
42,000 to 43,999	11,250
44,000 to 45,999	11,750
46,000 to 47,999	12,250
48,000 to 49,999	12,750
50,000 to 51,999	13,250
52,000 to 53,999	13,750
54,000 to 55,999	14,250
56,000 to 57,999	14,750
58,000 to 59,999*	15,250

*For cars over $59,999, figure the ALV as follows: Multiply the fair market value of the car by 25 percent and add $500.

METHOD 2

Include only the value of the personal use using the valuation methods previously discussed. If the car is used for less than the entire year (but at least 30 days for personal purposes), then prorate the value of personal use.

The ALV figures apply for a four-year period starting with the year of the ALV election. After this period, the car's actual fair market value is used for figuring income. The ALV method takes into account maintenance and insurance but not fuel costs. If gas is charged to a company credit card, then the actual charges must be used to figure personal use to be included in the employee's income. If gas is not paid by credit card, then it can be figured at fair market value or 5.5 cents per mile.

How to figure the taxable benefit of using a company car is explained in IRS Publication 15A, "Supplemental Employer's Tax Guide," available from the IRS Web site at www.irs.gov.

SELECTING THE BETTER METHOD

Method 1 is easy for the business since it merely has to report the full value of the use of the car. There is no record keeping or administrative burden on the company. However, from the employee's perspective, this arrangement can result in a fully taxable benefit. While business use is theoretically deductible, as a practical matter the employee's adjusted gross income may be too high to permit a full or even partial deduction.

TIP

If the company wants to report only personal use of a company car, it should set up a record-keeping procedure to enable it to figure this personal use. Weekly expense reports or other records can be used for this purpose.

CAUTION

Providing a company car to an owner's relative for personal use is a benefit that will be taxed to the owner as income. However, it may well be considered a nondeductible dividend from the company perspective.

Method 2 is more complicated for the business to figure since it requires record keeping of personal and business use of each car by the employee. However, it means less income for the employee to report. And it saves employment taxes for both the employer and employee (only the personal use portion is subject to FICA tax).

Whichever method is selected, it can be seen that a company car is still less costly to the employee than paying for one personally. In our example, 50 percent personal use of a $20,000 car resulted in income of only $5,600. Even in the top tax bracket of 39.6 percent, this results in a tax cost of only $2,218.

Personally Owned Cars

If the business reimburses employees for business use of their personally owned cars, the arrangement under which reimbursement is made controls the tax treatment of the payments for employees.

ACCOUNTABLE PLANS

No income results from reimbursement made to employees for business use of their cars if the arrangement is an accountable plan. An accountable plan requires employees to substantiate business expenses to the company and repay within a reasonable time of any excess reimbursement. The advance or reimbursement is not included in the employee's W-2 form. Of course, the employee cannot deduct any business use of the car (it's been reimbursed on a tax-free basis).

NONACCOUNTABLE PLANS

If reimbursement is made under a nonaccountable plan, then it's reported in full on the employee's W-2 form. It becomes income to the employee. Then the employee can claim an offsetting deduction for business use of the car. However, such deduction is a miscellaneous itemized deduction subject to the 2 percent-of-AGI floor.

Expense Accounts for Travel and Entertainment

Most business owners travel to see clients and customers, wine and dine them, and incur other travel and entertainment costs related to their company. Fortunately, most travel and entertainment costs are deductible, although some limits apply.

From the employee perspective, *how* reimbursement of expenses is made determines the tax treatment on personal returns. If reimbursement is made under an accountable plan, explained earlier in this chapter in connection with company cars, then the employee has no income to report. If reimbursement is made under a nonaccountable plan that lets the employee retain any excess reimbursements or advances, then the company reports the full reimbursements as income to the employee. The employee can then deduct the portion of the reimbursement qualifying as a business expense as an itemized deduction subject to the 2-percent-of-AGI floor.

Travel Costs

Travel costs may involve local transportation in day-to-day activities. Or they may relate to out-of-town trips.

LOCAL TRANSPORTATION COSTS

The cost of local business travel is deductible. This includes business use of a car, or taxi, bus, or train fare incurred to see clients, customers, or suppliers, or otherwise conduct business. If the business pays the cost through an accountable plan, employees do not report any income and the company saves on FICA tax.

However, commuting costs to and from work generally are nondeductible personal expenses regardless of the length of the trip or whether you conduct business en route (e.g., talk on a cell phone to customers or display a company logo on the side of a car or van). The cost of travel between a business conducted at a home office and another business location is deductible, however, although most other types of commuting are not deductible.

TRAVEL COSTS

The cost of travel away from home (i.e., travel generally requiring an overnight stay) is deductible. Travel costs include not only transportation, such as airfare, but also lodging, meals, and incidental expenses (laundry, etc.).

Company owners frequently use business travel as an opportunity to combine business with pleasure. In doing so, though, only part of the costs may be deductible.

CAUTION

The cost of meals and entertainment is only 50 percent deductible, whether incurred in town or on business trips. However, there have been proposals to up the deductible limit for small business owners.

- If the trip is within the United States and primarily for business, then travel costs related to business are fully deductible. Whether the trip is primarily for business depends on the facts and circumstances. There is no set rule.

- If the trip is within the United States and primarily for personal purposes, then no part of the travel costs are deductible. But expenses related to business (for example, business dinners or local transportation costs to see customers) are deductible.

- If the trip is outside the United States and is "entirely" for business, then all transportation costs are fully deductible even if some time is spent on sightseeing or other personal purposes. "Entirely" has a special meaning in the tax law. It means (1) that the trip is only for a week or less (not counting the day of departure), (2) that less than 25 percent of the time outside the United States is spent on nonbusiness activities (regardless of the length of the trip), (3) that personal activities were not the major consideration in arranging the trip, or (4) the personal traveling does not have substantial control over arranging the trip (something virtually impossible for a small business owner to prove).

- If the trip is outside the United States and is "primarily" for business, then the allocable portion of transportation costs is deductible. For example, if a trip from the United States to Europe is 17 days (10 days on business, 5 days on sightseeing, and 2 days on travel), $12/17$ of the transportation costs is deductible.

- If the trip is outside the United States and is primarily for vacation, even though some business is conducted, then no portion of the transportation costs is deductible. But any costs related to the business, such as a business dinner, are deductible.

TRAVEL WITH ANOTHER PERSON

Travel costs of a spouse or other companion on a business trip generally are not deductible. There are, however, exceptions:

- *Spouse is an employee.* Travel costs are deductible if a spouse also works for the company and certain conditions are met. The spouse's presence on the trip must serve a bona fide business purpose and the costs would have been deductible had they been incurred for someone not accompanying the employee.

- *Costs would have been incurred anyway.* Only the additional cost of a spouse's travel is nondeductible. So, for example, the cost of a room for an employee is fully deductible if there's a flat

Example

The additional airfare on a business trip for bringing a spouse is $400. If this amount is treated as compensation to the employee, the employee is taxed at no more than $158.40 ($400 × 39.6%). If the employee had to pay for the expense out-of-pocket with after-tax dollars, he or she would have had to earn about $660 (assuming the top tax bracket).

room rate (whether or not a spouse is present). But even if only the cost of a single room is covered, then the cost of taking a double room to accommodate a spouse usually means that more than half the cost is deductible (a single room is typically about two-thirds, not half, the cost of a double).

Even if a spouse's travel costs are not otherwise deductible, the company can convert them into a deductible expense. The company can fully deduct the cost of spousal travel by treating the additional cost as compensation to the employee. This preserves the deduction for the company. And the cost of the additional compensation to the employee is probably less than the out-of-pocket cost of bringing the spouse along.

Entertainment Costs

Power breakfasts, business lunches, theater tickets, and other semi-social activities are routine ways in which business is conducted. The cost of entertainment directly related to business, such as conducting business talks at lunch, or associated with business, such as having lunch following business talks, generally is deductible.

However, there's a limitation on deductions for meals and entertainment: Only 50 percent of costs are deductible. Also, the costs cannot be lavish or extravagant. There's no dollar limit, so what's lavish and extravagant depends on the situation. But the fact that the business can only deduct 50 percent of costs has no effect on employees. They aren't taxed on the nondeductible portion. It's merely a cost of doing business that can't be written off.

There are certain exceptions to the 50 percent limit. The company can fully deduct the cost of meals for promotional activities, such as a free meal provided to prospective customers who listen to a sales presentation. Also, the cost of meals paid for social or recreational activities, such as a company picnic, is fully deductible. In a family business, a company picnic can virtually be a family outing as long as the event is open to all employees. Finally, the company can deduct the cost of an employee cafeteria on the premises.

Record Keeping for Travel and Entertainment Costs

In order for travel and entertainment costs to be deductible within the limits allowed, the law requires that certain records be kept for these expenses. One of the problems with family-owned businesses is the casual attitude that often blurs the lines between business and personal items. Unfortunately, this casual attitude can carry over into record keeping.

Record keeping for travel and entertainment expenses entails two aspects:

1. Recording in a diary, travel log, expense report, or other written record certain information about the travel or entertainment expense item. PalmPilots can be used for this purpose if a record of expenses is then given to the company.

2. Retaining receipts, canceled checks, charge slips, and other documentary evidence of the expense. The exception: No receipt is required for items (other than lodging) costing under $75.

Fringe Benefit Plans

The Internal Revenue Code contains a number of fringe benefit plans that can be provided to company workers on a tax-advantaged basis. A company is not required to offer these benefits, but if it chooses to do so, then benefits must be provided on a nondiscriminatory basis. They cannot be limited to owners or other key employees.

But, as explained next, even certain benefit plans may not be of significant help to owners in small companies. This is because nondiscriminatory rules require a certain percentage of benefits go to nonowners and highly compensated executives.

However, companies need to review benefit options on a plan-by-plan basis and offer those plans most needed or helpful in particular situations. In addition to medical coverage discussed earlier, here's a listing of other fringe benefit plans, also called statutory fringe benefits, that companies may offer to employees.

Adoption Assistance

Company-paid adoption assistance is tax free to employees up to $5,000 ($6,000 for a child with special needs) as long as the employee's adjusted gross income is below a threshold amount of $75,000, regardless of tax filing status. The exclusion phases out for income between $75,000 and $115,000, so that assistance becomes fully taxable for employees with adjusted gross income over $115,000. This exclusion is set to expire for amounts paid or incurred after December 31, 2001, unless Congress enacts an extension.

The company can deduct its costs. To provide adoption assistance in this tax-advantaged manner, the company must set up a separate written plan. The plan cannot provide more than 5 percent of total benefits to owner-employees ("5 percent test"). Thus, in very small companies, owner-employees may not want their companies to incur these costs where they personally cannot reap much benefit from them.

Dependent Care Assistance

Company-paid dependent care assistance up to $5,000 is tax free to employees. The company can deduct its payments in full (even amounts in excess of the $5,000 exclusion limit). The plan must be nondiscriminatory but need not meet the 5 percent test.

Educational Assistance

Company-paid educational assistance for undergraduate courses (whether work-related or not) up to $5,250 is tax free to employees. This exclusion does not apply to graduate-level courses. The exclusion is set to expire on December 31, 2001, unless Congress enacts an extension. Company-paid educational assistance for work-related courses may also be excludable as a working condition fringe benefit (explained later in this chapter). There's no dollar limit to the working condition fringe benefit. This fringe benefit can also cover laid-off workers for whom job training is provided.

The company can, of course, deduct its outlays. If the courses are job-related, they're treated as noncompensatory business expenses. If they're not job-related, then they're treated as wages. The difference: Wages, but not noncompensatory business expenses, are subject to FICA tax.

While educational assistance is a highly prized benefit among many workers, educational assistance plans may not make sense for

> **Tip**
>
> Educational assistance plans can be used to benefit an owner's child who attains the age of 21 and is no longer a dependent. As long as such child does not own any stock in the corporation, then he or she is not part of that owner group for whom no more than 5 percent of benefits can be provided. Whether this factor makes the use of an educational assistance plan worthwhile for your family business depends on which other employees are involved in the program.

small employers. As in the case of adoption assistance, the 5 percent rule applies to educational assistance so that no more than 5 percent of benefits provided under the plan can be used to benefit owners, their spouses, or their dependents.

Group-Term Life Insurance

The company can deduct premiums paid for group-term life insurance. Employees are not taxed on the first $50,000 of coverage. Coverage in excess of $50,000 is taxed according to a special IRS table that imputes income for this excess coverage based on the employee's age. This imputed income is far less than the actual cost of the coverage. (See Figure 6.4.)

If the group-term life insurance plan is considered discriminatory, favoring owners and key employees, then these individuals have imputed income from *all* coverage (not just excess coverage). What's more, imputed income in this case is the greater of actual cost or amounts figured under the IRS table.

Coverage can be continued for former employees. So, for example, when a founder retires, the company can continue to pay the premiums. Coverage can also be provided on a tax-free basis for a spouse and dependent of an employee up to $2,000.

> **Example**
>
> The company pays for $100,000 of group-term coverage for an employee age 53. The imputed income from the excess $50,000 of coverage is only $138 ($0.23 × 50 × 12 months).

FIGURE 6.4   Imputed Income for Excess Group-Term Life Insurance

Age as of December 31	Monthly Cost of Excess Coverage per $1,000
Under 25	$0.05
25–29	$0.06
30–34	$0.08
35–39	$0.09
40–44	$0.10
45–49	$0.15
50–54	$0.23
55–59	$0.43
60–64	$0.66
65–69	$1.27
70 and older	$2.06

Meals and Lodging

The cost of meals and lodging provided on company premises for the convenience of the employer (and in the case of lodging required as a condition of employment) is not taxed to employees. So, for example, motel owners and employees who live on the grounds aren't taxed on the value of their rooms.

Cafeteria Plans

Instead of providing the aforementioned benefits for all employees, it may be more cost-effective to offer employees a menu of benefits from which they can choose those most important to them. In this way, the company pays only for selected benefits (while meeting nondiscrimination tests).

A cafeteria plan is a written plan that allows employees to choose among two or more benefits consisting of cash and nontaxable benefits (such as group-term life insurance). The company deducts its cost of providing the benefits.

In small businesses, cafeteria plans make good economic sense. They limit company costs while having the ability to offer a wide range of benefits.

Nonstatutory Fringe Benefits

Nonstatutory fringe benefits are perks for which there's no separate section in the Internal Revenue Code. But they may also be tax-advantaged benefits for both the business and recipients. Employees are not taxed on these benefits. What's more, there are no employment taxes on the benefits, so the company saves on FICA and FUTA taxes.

- *No additional cost service.* Benefits provided in the ordinary course of the company's business aren't taxed to employees. For example, if your business runs a ferry service, employees who receive free ferry rides aren't taxed on the fares they save. The business doesn't get to deduct any additional amounts for offering this benefit (the business accounts for its expenses in other ways, for example, deducting the cost of fuel, depreciation on the ferry, etc.).

- *Qualified employee discounts.* Price reductions in goods offered to employees are not taxed if the discount is not in excess of gross profit (total sales price of the property less the cost of the property, divided by the total sales price of the property). In the case of company services, the discount must be limited to 20 percent of the price ordinarily charged to customers. The business accounts for the discounts in various ways. For example, in the case of goods, the discount is taken into account as part of the cost of goods sold.

- *Working condition fringe benefits.* Benefits provided to employees that would have been deductible by them if they'd paid for them are not taxable benefits. For example, job-related courses and use of a car for business fall within this category.

- De minimis *fringe benefits.* Items of small or nominal value aren't taxable to employees. This includes holiday turkeys, cab fare, and supper money. However, cash in any amount is always taxable as additional compensation.

- *Qualified transportation fringe benefits.* Company-provided free parking, transit passes, and commuter vans are tax-free fringe benefits within certain limits. The 2001 limit on free parking is $180 a month. This is determined by the value of the parking, so if parking is provided free to customers, it has no value for purposes of determining the value of the benefit for employees. However, partners and more-than-2-percent S corporation shareholders cannot receive this free benefit. They're taxed on the value of free parking regardless of the dollar amount. The 2001 limit on transit passes and commuter vans is $65 per month. If the dollar limits are exceeded, only the excess is taxable to employees. However, if partners receive monthly transit passes in excess of the dollar limit, then the entire benefit becomes taxable to them. If employees are given the choice between receiving cash of equal value or the fringe benefit, they're not taxed on the benefit (within the limits discussed earlier), but they're taxed if they choose the cash instead.

- *Moving expenses.* If the company pays the cost of moving an employee's household goods, either directly or as a reimbursement, the employee isn't taxed on this benefit if the employee would have been able to deduct the cost on his or her personal return. There's no dollar limit to this benefit. However, reimbursement or payment for what would have been nondeductible moving costs (such as financial help with selling a home) are treated as taxable compensation.

- *Athletic facilities.* Company on-site athletic facilities are a tax-free fringe benefit. This is so even if use is permitted to spouses and dependents of employees. However, membership dues paid to other health clubs or facilities are taxable compensation to employees but are not deductible by the business.

Miscellaneous Benefits

The company can tailor certain benefits for owners or other important personnel. It can provide such benefits to selected individuals when and to the extent desired.

Split-Dollar Life Insurance

The company can help owners or other key executives pay the cost of permanent insurance by using a split-dollar life insurance arrangement. Under this arrangement, the company takes out a whole-life policy on the employee and agrees to pay the portion of the premiums to the extent of the annual increases in the cash surrender value of the policy. The company retains an interest in the proceeds to the extent of premiums paid. Thus, eventually the business should recoup its out-of-pocket costs for providing this assistance. The employee names a beneficiary to receive the proceeds (in excess of the company's interest) and pays the difference between annual premium costs and what the company pays. The employee reports as income the one-year term cost of the coverage. The company deducts this amount as compensation (but cannot deduct its full out-of-pocket premium costs).

Club Dues

Company memberships in golf clubs, tennis clubs, or other recreational facilities are perks that some business owners want or expect to receive. From a tax standpoint, there's some flexibility in how to treat the costs. Generally, club dues are nondeductible. However, the business can elect to treat membership privileges provided to employees as additional compensation (deductible by the company and taxable to employees). This option applies only if the club is used exclusively for business purposes (100 percent for entertaining business clients). This election can be made on a per-employee basis. Thus, for example, the company can elect to treat club dues paid for nonfamily members as additional compensation while dues paid for an owner are not treated as compensation. When it is advisable to make this election must be determined according to the circumstances of your situation.

No-Cost Fringe Benefits

Certainly health coverage and company cars are highly valued by employees. But the company can also provide fringe benefits that will be appreciated by employees yet cost the company nothing. Here are some ideas to consider:

- *Flextime.* Allowing workers, both family and others, to arrange their work schedules according to personal preference is a highly appreciated benefit. A survey of recent college graduates rated flextime as a more highly prized benefit than bonuses and a company car! If the company adopts a flextime program, in order to avoid discord it should allow all workers the same options and not limit this benefit to family members only.

- *Job training and policy communication.* Companies often throw workers into positions without adequate training. What's more, workers may not be told the ropes—administrative procedures for getting things done. Workers greatly appreciate job training that will enable them to perform at their best and an explanation of how things work in the company.

- *Casual dress code.* According to one survey, this benefit was credited with keeping workers happy on the job.

CHAPTER 7

Retirement Plans

etirement plans are important to family businesses for several reasons. They provide a prefunded source of income for owners after they cease working for the company. They provide a means of attracting and keeping nonfamily workers with the company. And they offer tax advantages to the company, its owners, and other employees covered by the plans.

Despite these considerations, less than half of all small businesses (those with 100 or fewer employees) have yet to set up qualified retirement plans. It's believed that owners simply don't know their options or don't fully understand them (although Congress is considering substantial changes to retirement plan rules to make them more appealing to small businesses). They think employees would prefer a current salary amount to a future retirement benefit. And they don't understand the positive impact that this benefit can have on the company's workforce.

Small family-owned businesses have the same retirement plan choices as are available to nonfamily businesses. However, family businesses may employ different considerations than other businesses when choosing among plan options. In this chapter you'll learn about qualified retirement plans and what must be done to make them qualified. You'll find out about the types of tax-approved retirement plans open to small businesses. You'll also see what special arrangements can be made in family businesses and how to select the best plan for your company.

Overview of Qualified Retirement Plans

The tax law gives special treatment to qualified retirement plans. These include the following:

- Contributions to these plans are deductible by the business (within set limits).
- Earnings on contributions are not currently taxable.
- Distributions from the plan may qualify for special tax benefits in certain limited situations.

CAUTION

Your business isn't required by law to have a retirement plan for employees. But if you want benefits for yourself and family members working for the company and decide to provide them through a retirement plan, you must comply with law requirements. Failure to do so can result in steep penalties for the business.

To be "qualified," the plan must meet certain requirements. These requirements entail both tax law (supervised by the Internal Revenue Service of the Treasury Department) and labor law (supervised by the Pension and Welfare Benefits Administration of the Department of Labor).

Many of the requirements are very complicated. However, they are all intended to make things fair for workers. The requirements ensure that the plan cannot be used only to provide benefits for owners and other family members while excluding rank-and-file employees. They require employees to be notified of plan rules and performance. They keep company owners from using funds in the plan for the business or their own personal purposes. And they mandate certain investment responsibilities and other standards of conduct for those administering the plan.

Making a Plan Tax-Qualified

To be a qualified retirement plan, certain requirements must be satisfied. The following is a brief description of the key requirements that must be met to ensure that a plan is tax-qualified.

Tip

It's essential for a family business to work with a knowledgeable retirement plan expert to determine which plan is optimum under the circumstances and to ensure that the plan meets all law requirements. Consult with a pension benefits expert, or a CPA or attorney specializing in this area.

Coverage

A plan is "qualified" only if it allows employees who meet certain requirements to participate and receive benefits. There are three main coverage tests. A plan is qualified if it meets any one of these tests:

- The plan covers at least 70 percent of all "non-highly compensated employees" ("percentage test").
- The plan covers a percentage of non-highly compensated employees that is at least 70 percent of the percentage of highly compensated employees ("ratio test").
- The plan provides a minimum level of benefits to non-highly compensated employees ("average benefit percentage test" or ABP test).

Non-highly compensated employees are simply employees who don't fall within the classification of highly compensated employees. Highly compensated employees include owners with at least a 5 percent interest in the business (based on direct ownership and indirect ownership through a spouse, children, grandchildren, and parents, but *not* in-laws). Highly compensated employees also include certain highly paid workers. Highly paid workers are those receiving more than $80,000, adjusted annually for inflation, during the current year and a look-back year. For 2000, this means employees earning more than $85,000.

In family businesses, there may be only (or primarily) owners working for the company. This does not mean that their retirement plans automatically fail the coverage requirements. Plans covering only owners may still be treated as nondiscriminatory if there are no other workers so no rank-and-file employees are prevented from enjoying plan benefits. If there are some nonowner employees, then the plan may be treated as "top-heavy." This also doesn't make the plan discriminatory. It simply imposes certain additional requirements in operating the plan.

Participation

This is the right of employees to be covered by a plan after meeting service and age requirements. Generally, a plan must allow employees to participate after completing one year of employment (called service with the company). A year of service usually means working at least 1,000 hours during the year. This works out to just 20 hours a week for 50 weeks a year.

Caution

A plan cannot have a maximum age of participation. As long as an employee works for the company and meets other requirements, he or she must be included in the plan. This means that company founders and others can continue to amass retirement benefits beyond what's normally considered retirement age—65—as long as they still work for the business.

A plan can choose to prevent participation before age 21 if it wants to impose a three-year service requirement. Of course, if a family business wants a younger relative to participate, then the lower age limit must apply to nonfamily members as well. A two-year service requirement can be used only if there is immediate and full vesting of benefits (explained later in this chapter).

Under a safe harbor for 401(k) plans, coverage and participation tests are met if employers contribute at least 3 percent of compensation to the plan (whether or not employees contribute to the plan). Or they can match 100 percent of employee contributions made as elective deferrals under salary reduction agreements with the company (effectively up to 4 percent of compensation).

Vesting

Once plans permit employees to be covered does not mean such employees are then entitled to benefits. A plan can delay absolute ownership of benefits until participants become vested. Vesting is merely a matter of time, and a plan can delay vesting only so long. A qualified plan cannot defer vesting beyond certain limits. A plan must satisfy at least one of the following two vesting schedules:

- *Cliff vesting*—no vesting before five years in the plan, with full vesting thereafter.
- *Seven-year graded vesting*—gradual vesting of 20 percent after three years of service, plus 20 percent for each additional year of service (i.e., full vesting after seven years).

A plan can, of course, choose more rapid vesting. For instance, if an owner wants immediate vesting for himself and his relatives working for the company, such vesting is permissible.

Plans weighted more heavily to owners and highly compensated employees are considered top-heavy and *must* adopt more rapid vesting schedules. Top-heavy plans must satisfy either of the following two vesting schedules:

- *Cliff vesting*—no vesting before three years in the plan, with full vesting thereafter.
- *Six-year graded vesting*—gradual vesting of 20 percent after two years of service, plus 20 percent for each additional year of service (i.e., full vesting after six years).

Compensation

Generally, in figuring contributions and benefits under a qualified retirement plan, only a limited amount of compensation may be taken into account. For 2000, the limit is $170,000. This amount may be adjusted annually for inflation. Compensation is a broad term, including salary, bonuses, commissions, fringe benefits, expense allowances, and most other amounts paid for personal services.

For self-employed owners who do not receive compensation, contributions and benefits are based on net earnings from self-employment. This is the same net earnings used for determining self-employment income. Because limited partners aren't subject to self-employment tax on their distributive share of partnership income, they do not have net earnings from self-employment on which to base retirement plan benefits and contributions. Whether members of limited liability companies receive net earnings from self-employment remains to be seen.

Where both spouses work for the same company, each can receive contributions based on his or her own compensation up to the compensation limit. In the past, spouses working for the same company had been treated as one unit, and contributions had to be allocated between them according to their relative salaries.

Funding

Qualified plans must satisfy certain funding requirements. Failure to meet these requirements results in a 10 percent penalty (certain

Caution

If the company uses a deferred compensation agreement (discussed in Chapter 8) in addition to a qualified retirement plan, use care in agreeing to salary deferrals. Coordinate salary deferrals under the nonqualified deferred compensation agreement with potential contributions to the qualified retirement plan. The reason: Salary deferrals may adversely impact contributions to the qualified plan.

plans have a 5 percent penalty) applied to the amount of the funding deficiency. Funding requirements ensure that funds will be available to provide the promised benefits under the plans. These requirements apply only to certain types of plans, such as pension plans. The funding requirement generally means the plan must have sufficient assets to pay out benefits for the current year. (Pension plans with more than 100 participants and certain other plans may be subject to additional funding requirements.)

TIP

Employers suffering temporary substantial business hardships may ask the IRS for a waiver of the minimum funding standards. These requests usually are granted if there's a reasonable basis for the request. Then, employers must amortize the deficiency over five years using a special IRS interest rate.

A plan subject to the minimum funding requirement must use a device, called a funding standard account, to administer the funding requirements. Essentially, this special bookkeeping account is adjusted annually for plan contributions (a positive adjustment), an assumed rate of return (a positive adjustment), and the normal costs of benefits for the year (a negative adjustment). At the end of the year, if the account has a negative balance, the employer must make contributions to make up the deficit. If the account has a positive balance, this must be taken into account in figuring contributions for the year.

Contributions can no longer be made to a plan once its assets equal or exceed its liabilities. No deduction can be claimed once a plan is fully funded. A plan is fully funded if it meets its full funding limitation. Full funding means the excess of the applicable percentage from Figure 7.1 or the plan's accrued liabilities, whichever is less, over the value of plan assets.

Retirement Plan Options in General

Qualified retirement plans differ from each other in several respects:

- The amount of money that can be put into the plan.
- Participation and coverage requirements.

FIGURE 7.1   Full Funding Limitation Percentage

Plan Year Beginning In . . .	Percentage
2000	155%
2001 or 2002	160%
2003 or 2004	165%
2005 and later years	170%

- Limits on deductions for contributions.
- Costs of setting up and administering the plans.
- Reporting requirements.

There are two main categories of qualified retirement plans: defined contribution plans and defined benefit plans.

In defined contribution plans, retirement funds for employees depend on the investment performance of contributions, much like ordinary savings accounts. Contributions to these plans are fixed in relation to employee compensation. Generally, such contributions are a percentage of compensation within limits allowed by law. Examples of defined contribution plans: profit-sharing plans, money purchase plans, and 401(k) plans.

In defined benefit plans, retirement benefits are fixed according to compensation regardless of plan performance. Contributions to these plans are determined by an actuary to be sufficient to pay out those fixed benefits. Examples of defined benefit plans: pension plans and cash balance pension plans.

> **CAUTION**
>
> **Contributions to plans subject to funding requirements should be carefully monitored. You want to satisfy minimum funding requirements, but you don't want to exceed funding needs. Generally the company can't recoup excess amounts from overfunded plans without penalty.**

Retirement Plans for Small Businesses

Small business owners can use any type of plan available to large companies. But small companies have additional choices to consider. A survey of retirement plan options for small businesses follows.

Pension Plans

These are defined benefit plans that agree to provide a pension starting at a set age. Benefits payable under the plan cannot exceed $90,000 (adjusted annually for inflation). This dollar limit for 2000 is $135,000. The contribution is determined actuarily to ensure that the plan will have sufficient funds to pay out promised benefits. The older the employee (the closer to retirement) and the greater the salary, the larger the contribution necessary to fund the benefit.

Profit-Sharing Plans

These are defined contribution plans limiting employer contributions to 15 percent of compensation for a maximum contribution of

$30,000 in 2000. However, as a practical matter, since no more than $170,000 can be taken into account in figuring contributions in 2000, the practical limit is $25,500 (15 percent of $170,000).

While the name of these plans includes the word "profit," there's no requirement that a company actually show a profit in order to make a contribution. However, a company isn't penalized if it fails to make a contribution because it suffers losses in a particular year.

A company can use both a pension plan and a profit-sharing or other defined contribution plan at the same time. Before 2000, however, a special formula imposed a limit on the maximum benefits and contributions permitted. This limitation no longer applies.

Money Purchase Plans

These are defined contribution plans limiting employer contributions to 25 percent of compensation for a maximum contribution of $30,000 in 2000. Contributions to these plans are mandatory (i.e., they must be made even if the business has losses). The $30,000 limit may be adjusted annually for inflation.

401(k) Plans

These are a type of profit-sharing plan in which employees make contributions on a pretax basis. Instead of receiving a full salary, they agree to use a portion as a contribution to the plan. That contribution, called a salary reduction, isn't taxable for income tax purposes but is still subject to FICA tax.

Employers may also make contributions to the plan on behalf of employees. Employer contributions can be used to encourage participation so that the plan will meet participation requirements. Alternatively, employers may make contributions under the safe harbor provision to ensure nondiscrimination.

> ## Note
>
> Profit-sharing, money purchase, or defined benefit pension plans used by self-employed business owners used to be designated as Keogh plans (named after the U.S. senator who sponsored self-employed retirement plans) but the term is no longer used. These plans effectively treat owners as if they were employees. Contributions on behalf of owners under this plan are geared to net earnings from self-employment since self-employed individuals do not receive compensation like employees. However, certain restrictions apply to self-employed owners under the plan that do not apply to shareholders who work for their corporations.

Simplified Employee Pensions (SEP Plans)

These are IRAs set up to receive employer contributions on behalf of employees. As the name implies, these plans are easy to set up and administer and don't entail any annual government reporting associated with other types of qualified plans.

While there is no technical requirement limiting SEPs to small businesses, as a practical matter they are used only by such companies. The reason: SEPs have more modest contribution limits (no more than the lesser of 15 percent of compensation or, in 2000, $25,500) and more generous participation requirements than other plans. SEPs can, however, be combined with other qualified plans to provide greater benefits. If the SEP is combined with a 401(k) plan, then the maximum contribution to that plan of 15 percent of compensation must be reduced by the percentage contributed to the SEP. If the SEP is combined with a money purchase plan, the maximum contribution to that plan of 25 percent must be reduced by the percentage contributed to the SEP.

> **CAUTION**
>
> In small companies, employers should expect to make contributions—either matching contributions serving as incentives or safe harbor contributions. The reason: This is the only way that owners will be able to enjoy maximum salary reduction contributions themselves.

Businesses that use SEPs must observe special participation rules. The plans must allow an employee to participate if he or she is at least age 21, earns at least $450 in 2000 (adjusted for inflation), and has completed at least three years of service (which means performing services in these three prior years). SEPs cannot exclude part-timers. Employees older than $70\frac{1}{2}$ can continue to participate in SEPs even though the plans are really IRA plans from which required minimum distributions must be taken. In effect, these older employees will receive contributions and take distributions at the same time. But, depending on the rate of return on investments, such employees may see their retirement benefits continue to grow. Once an employee participates, all contributions are fully vested.

> **Note**
>
> In the past, SEPs could be combined with salary reduction arrangements allowing employees to make contributions on a pretax basis. Such SARSEPs established before 1997 can continue to accept employee contributions. However, no new SARSEPs can be established. Total contributions to a SARSEP cannot exceed the lesser of 15 percent of compensation or $30,000.

The annual limit on contributions to a SEP is 15 percent of compensation up to $30,000 in 2000. However, as a practical matter, since no more than $170,000 can be taken into account in figuring contributions in 2000, the practical limit is $25,500 (15 percent of $170,000).

A SEP must adopt a contribution formula. The formula is a percentage of compensation. While 15 percent is the maximum percentage, the company can adopt a lesser percentage. It can change percentages from year to year.

Savings Incentive Match Plan for Employees (SIMPLE Plans)

These are defined contribution plans limited to small employers who do not maintain any other qualified retirement plan. They can be set up as either SIMPLE-IRAs or SIMPLE-401(k) plans. While SIMPLE plans can provide a solid retirement benefit for employees at a modest cost for employers, one-third of small employers with no existing qualified retirement plan haven't even heard of them.

Businesses that use SIMPLE plans must allow all employees to participate regardless of age, earnings, or years of service. In 2000, an employee can opt to contribute up to $6,000 of compensation via a salary reduction agreement (i.e., on a pretax basis). All employer contributions are fully vested.

SIMPLE plans meet nondiscrimination requirements as long as employers make certain contributions. There's a choice of contribution formulas:

- Matching dollar-for-dollar the contributions made by employees up to 3 percent of employee contribution (or, for a SIMPLE-IRA only, a lower percentage under certain circumstances). For example, if an employee earning $40,000 contributes $6,000 to a SIMPLE plan, the company must contribute $1,200 (3 percent of $40,000). The maximum matching contribution to a SIMPLE-401(k) plan in 2000 is $5,100 (3 percent of $170,000, the maximum compensation that can be taken into account). But there's

---

Note

A "small employer": for purposes of SIMPLE plans is one with 100 or fewer employees who received at least $5,000 in compensation in the preceding year. For purposes of this limit, all employees employed at any time during the year are taken into account. A company remains a small employer for two years after its payroll exceeds 100 employees (a two-year grace period).

no limit to compensation taken into account for SIMPLE-IRAs, so there's no limit to the matching contribution in this case.

- Nonelective contributions of 2 percent of compensation (regardless of whether an employee participates). For example, if an employee earns $40,000, the company must contribute $800 to the SIMPLE plan, whether or not the employee makes a contribution. The maximum contribution by the company is $3,400 (2 percent of $170,000).

Self-employed individuals can contribute to a SIMPLE plan as if they were employees. Their contributions are based on net earnings from self-employment (the same basis used for other types of retirement plans). They can also make an employer contribution on their own behalf, again based on their net earnings from self-employment.

While SIMPLE plans appear to provide for modest contributions, in family-owned businesses they can be effective for providing substantial benefits for owners. For example, a husband and wife who own a local pizzeria are able to put away $18,000 each year in a SIMPLE-IRA. They each take a salary of $100,000 from the business and each contributes the maximum ($6,000 through salary reduction, plus a 3 percent matching contribution, or $3,000). Their five employees, whose salaries total $120,000, cost the company a maximum contribution of $3,600 (assuming these employees make contributions that can then be matched). And since this employer contribution is deductible, the after-tax cost to the company is even less.

Choosing the Right Plan for Your Family Business

The choice of plan for your business depends on several factors: Cost to the company (and the ability to pay it), the administrative burden, the nature of the business, the age and income of the owners, and the objectives of the owners. The following factors should be considered when evaluating your plan alternatives.

Cost of Contributions

Owners are naturally concerned with the cost to their company of starting and maintaining a qualified retirement plan. If you want to have a retirement plan but keep costs down, you can shift part of the burden to employees through salary reduction alternatives such as 401(k) plans and SIMPLE plans. While employer contributions may be required to make the plan nondiscriminatory, the cost to the company for these plans may be less than that under other plan alternatives.

> **Note**
>
> Think that sponsoring a retirement plan will have a negative impact on your company's bottom line? Think again. According to a recent survey of small employers, companies sponsoring plans had higher gross revenues than those that did not. Only 2 percent of small employers without retirement plans had annual gross revenue of $5 million or more. This compares with 22 percent of small employers already sponsoring qualified retirement plans.

If you want to minimize company contribution costs, consider limiting the contribution formulas to provide only modest contributions. For example, while you may contribute up to 15 percent of compensation to a profit-sharing plan, you are permitted to adopt a lesser percentage. Of course, weigh the cost savings to the company against the loss of potential benefits for yourself and other family members working for the company.

Or consider using a SIMPLE plan where the company can estimate its maximum contribution exposure based on payroll. And, depending on the contribution formula selected, this estimation may prove greater than actual contributions the company must make if employees don't make projected contributions or employees' compensation is lower than expected because of terminations.

Finally, if your company isn't yet well established, then select a plan that lets you decide from year to year whether to make contributions. While pension plans and money purchase plans commit the company to ongoing contributions, even in lean times, profit-sharing plans, SEPs, and SIMPLE plans afford flexibility in this regard.

Timing of Contributions

Generally, the company can make contributions up to the due date of its return for the year (including filing extensions). For example, a C corporation on a calendar year basis that obtains an automatic six-month filing extension for its 2000 return until September 17, 2001 (September 15 is a Saturday), has until this date to make contributions that are deductible for 2000.

However, certain plans subject to funding requirements must make contributions in quarterly installments much like estimated taxes after their first year. More specifically, pension plans with a current funding liability percentage of less than 100 percent must make quarterly payments of 25 percent of required annual payments of the lesser of: 90 percent of the required current contribution, or

Example

Corporation X has a defined benefit plan. For 2000, it is required to contribute $60,000. Its required contribution for 1999 was $40,000. X can avoid any penalties for 2000 by contributing $10,000 in quarterly payments (25 percent of 100 percent of the prior year contribution).

100 percent of the amount of the required contribution for the preceding year.

A company that has difficulty managing cash flow may prefer the long time horizon for making contributions for certain plans. Another company in a similar financial position may prefer the discipline of making quarterly contributions. It depends on you.

Other Costs

In addition to the cost of contributions, consider other costs associated with qualified plans when selecting plan options. Additional costs include the following:

- *Setup costs.* You may have to pay professionals to set up your plan. Depending on the type of plan, these costs can run high. For example, if you have a tailor-made plan, you'll need to request a determination letter from the IRS that your plan is a qualified plan. The law doesn't require you to do this, but if you don't get approval and later discover errors in the plan documents, you could be in for penalties and cause benefits to become immediately taxable. If you use a prototype plan provided by a bank, brokerage firm, insurance company, or mutual fund

Caution

Contributions are timely under the minimum funding requirements only if made within $8^1/_2$ months of the close of the tax year. So even though contributions are deductible if made up to the extended due date of the return, they will not relate back to the prior year for purposes of the minimum funding rules to be deductible unless they are actually made within $8^1/_2$ months of the close of the tax year. In a calendar-year C corporation, this means contributions must be made no later than August 15 to satisfy minimum funding requirements for the prior tax year.

company, the financial institution will have obtained qualified status (and will pass its costs of doing so on to you). You don't need professionals to set up SEPs and SIMPLE plans. To set up these plans, you only need to complete a simple IRS form. But even for other plans, you may be able to use standard plans provided by brokerage firms, mutual funds, banks, and insurance companies.

- *Bonding requirements.* To make sure you don't abscond with the pension funds leaving participants without benefits, you must post a bond if you have any control over the plan or its assets. For example, if you can transfer funds or make disbursements from the plan, then you have control and must post a bond. The bond must be at least 10 percent of the amount over which you have control. The minimum bond is at least $1,000, but the bond need not exceed $500,000. You don't need a bond if the plan covers you as the only owner, whether you're self-employed or a sole shareholder, or only partners and their spouses. To avoid bonding requirements, use SEPs or SIMPLE plans where participants have their own individual accounts.

- *Updating plans.* As tax laws change, you must amend the plan accordingly. This may require you to pay professional fees for updating plan documents. If you have a prototype plan, you'll probably pay financial institutions disguised fees for updating through their fee structure.

- *Actuarial costs.* If you have a defined benefit plan, you need the services of an actuary each year to figure the amount of your contributions. There are no actuarial costs for a defined contribution plan of any type.

- *Premiums to the Pension Benefit Guaranty Corporation (PBGC).* If you have a defined benefit plan, you're required to pay annual premiums to the PBGC, a quasi-federal agency charged with protecting employee pension plans in the event the employer goes out of business. There are two types of premiums: $19 per participant, and a variable-rate premium for underfunded plans (those that have not contributed sufficiently to pay all of their anticipated pension liabilities). There are no premium requirements for a defined contribution plan of any type.

- *Accounting costs.* Plans may be required to file annual information returns with the Department of Labor, and you may want or need an accountant to complete these forms. Generally, no accounting costs are incurred for SEPs or SIMPLE plans.

Administrative Burden

You're running a business. Your time and ability to run a retirement plan as well are certainly limited. To minimize your administrative burden (or the cost to you of shifting this burden to professionals), consider the following:

- SIMPLE plans do not require any annual reporting to the government. What's more, you can even let employees choose their own financial institutions through which they make their own investment choices with the contributions made by them and the company. For this purpose, adopt a SIMPLE plan using IRS Form 5304-SIMPLE. If you want to select the financial institution for your employees, then use IRS Form 5305-SIMPLE.

> **TIP**
> Shift investment decisions to plan participants. Let them decide how aggressive or conservative they want to be with their contributions. Use plans that accomplish this goal: 401(k) plans, SIMPLE plans, and SEPs.

- SEPs do not require any annual reporting to the government. All that's required to set up the plan is to complete IRS Form 5305-SEP.

Nature of the Business

Certain plans require an ongoing commitment from the business to make contributions regardless of available cash to do so. For a company just starting out or for those that have revenues that fluctuate annually, defined benefit plans are generally not advisable. It locks the company into making contributions (even if it has to borrow to do so). Instead, opt for a profit-sharing plan that allows for flexibility in deciding on the level of contributions from year to year. Other choices providing flexibility: SEPs and SIMPLE plans.

Providing Benefits to Owners

Many owners hope to get the biggest bang for their bucks by garnering the lion's portion of retirement benefits from the plan. Despite tax law requirements that plans be fair and not discriminate against rank-and-file employees, there is still room for some planning to meet owner objectives in this regard. Strategies for doing so are discussed later in this chapter.

Where owners are older and perhaps nearing retirement age, a defined benefit plan would provide the greatest opportunity for savings on their behalf. In contrast to a defined contribution plan that generally fixes contributions regardless of age solely on the basis of compensation, defined benefit plans allow for greater contributions on behalf of older employees.

Maximizing Benefits to Owners and Their Families While Minimizing Company Costs

Some small business owners recognize both the tangible and intangible benefits of having qualified retirement plans. The company can write off the costs associated with administering the plan and making contributions to it. And the provision of benefits to employees is a means of attracting and keeping good workers.

But some small business owners want to have retirement plans for their own benefit and would prefer not to provide benefits for employees. It can't be done through qualified retirement plans. So, these owners need to find ways to maximize benefits on their own behalf and keep overall costs down.

Maximizing Benefits for Owners

Obviously, owners who work for their companies are probably the best paid and, therefore, will outpace other employees in terms of benefits from or contributions under the plan. But an even greater share can go to owners if they adopt certain types of plans.

- *Age-based profit-sharing plan.* This is a profit-sharing plan that bases contributions on both compensation and age. Employer contributions are allocated to participants on the basis of the present value of a single life annuity starting at an age specified in the plan (such as 65). Where owners are older than other company personnel, they'll receive a greater allocation of contributions, not only because of their higher compensation but also because of their age.
- *Unit benefit plan.* This is a defined benefit (pension) plan that provides the greatest pensions for those with the longest employment. Since owners and other family members will have been with the company longer than nonfamily employees, it's probable that they'll enjoy the greatest pensions under this type of plan.
- *Target benefit plan.* This is a combination of a pension plan and money purchase plan. Annual contributions are based on anticipated pension benefits to participants. But those contributions are then allocated to individual participant accounts. Where ac-

counts perform better than expected, the added funds are used to increase benefits to participants (rather than to adjust future contributions).

Pensions for Low-Paid Family Members

The tax law allows a pension plan to make annual minimum distributions of $10,000 to family members who participate in the plan even though they've never earned that much in salary a year. The company simply figures on making these minimum distributions and funds the plan accordingly.

The $10,000 minimum pension distribution must be reduced by 10 percent for each year your relative has worked for less than 10 years. Thus, for example, if your spouse has worked only eight years, the $10,000 is reduced to $8,000 ($10,000 less 20 percent).

Permitted Disparity

As an employer you are already providing retirement benefits for employees through Social Security. You can keep down the cost of company contributions by taking this fact into account. This is called "permitted disparity" (it used to be called "integration"). Taking into account the benefits that participants will receive through Social Security isn't considered to be discriminatory as long as it meets integration level requirements. The rules on permitted disparity are highly complex. But application can result in substantial savings to the company without diminishing benefits for owners.

CAUTION

Family members must still work at least 1,000 hours to be credited with a year of service. This amounts to 20 hours a week for 50 weeks a year. But if a spouse or child works this minimum amount, the relative would receive the minimum pension distribution if he or she earned less than $10 an hour.

CAUTION

Top-heavy plans cannot use permitted disparity to meet the minimum annual retirement benefit for a defined benefit plan or the minimum annual contribution for a defined contribution plan.

Tip

Owners who do not want to provide retirement benefits for rank-and-file employees can obtain personal benefits through plans based solely on directors' fees. Since directors' fees are treated as self-employment income, owners serving on their company boards can fund their own retirement savings based on this income alone.

Plans for Directors

Family members who receive directors' fees for serving on the company's board can set up their own retirement plans based on these fees. These plans are in addition to any plans set up by the company. It is a very favorable strategy since it allows individuals to shelter directors' fees in retirement plans.

However, certain restrictions apply to inside directors—individuals who are both employees and directors of the same corporation. In family businesses, this dual role is common. Unless certain requirements are satisfied, both the director's individual plan and the company's plan can be disqualified.

For more information about retirement plans for small businesses, see IRS Publication 560, which is available from the IRS Web site at www.irs.gov.

CHAPTER 8

Nonqualified Retirement Plans

Family businesses may not want or be able to provide qualified retirement plans for employees. Or if they do have qualified plans, benefits can only go so far. Instead family businesses may rely more heavily on nonqualified plans to ensure retirement income for family members. Nonqualified plans can be tailored to meet individual circumstances. They provide great flexibility in benefit planning for family members and other key employees.

In this chapter you'll see how nonqualified retirement plans differ from qualified plans. You'll find out about how to structure plans for optimum tax results. You'll learn how plans can be set up as nonqualified plans to provide a measure of protection for you, your family members, and other employees covered by the plans. And you'll see what other strategies can be used to provide retirement benefits to owners and other family members.

Overview of Nonqualified Retirement Plans

Nonqualified retirement plans are plans that provide retirement benefits to owners and others. There are two main categories of nonqualified retirement plans: plans based on deferral of current compensation, and other types of plans that provide benefits without regard to current

NOTE

How important are deferred compensation plans and SERPs to your retirement income? According to some figures, as much as 65 percent of your retirement income may be derived from these sources.

compensation. Nonqualified retirement plans have a variety of names, from deferred compensation plans to SERPs (supplemental executive retirement plans, explained later in this chapter). Regardless of the title given to the plan, all nonqualified retirement plans have a number of things in common.

While both qualified retirement plans (discussed in Chapter 7) and nonqualified plans provide retirement income, these plans differ in several key ways. Unlike qualified retirement plans that must meet strict nondiscrimination rules to provide fairness to rank-and-file employees, nonqualified retirement plans can be structured to benefit a select few. Thus, nonqualified plans typically are used to benefit just family members and perhaps some other key employees. Nonqualified plans can even be designed to cover just one owner-employee.

TIP

Nonqualified retirement plans can be used at the same time as qualified retirement plans to augment benefits as desired. Companies don't have to choose between qualified and nonqualified plans.

Nonqualified retirement plans are also free from restrictions on contributions and benefits payable under the plan. There are no dollar limits on benefits or earnings under the plan. Nonqualified retirement plans can be as generous as companies can afford. If your company is doing well, you can transform its earnings into a source of retirement income.

Nonqualified plans do not have any formal annual reporting requirements. In contrast, qualified retirement plans generally must report annually to the government on the status of the plans. Since nonqualified plans don't have to meet qualified plan requirements or file annual reports with the government, plan administration and its attendant costs and time are reduced.

Tax Consequences of Nonqualified Retirement Plans

Nonqualified retirement plans also differ from qualified plans in terms of tax consequences to both the company and the plan participants. Nonqualified retirement plans do not provide the same tax benefits for the company as qualified plans. In qualified plans, the employer claims a tax deduction in the year contributions are made to the plan. In contrast, a deduction for payments under a nonqualified plan can be taken only when such payments are made to you. This deduction rule applies to both cash-basis and accrual-basis companies.

> ### Example
>
> Company A has a deferred compensation plan, a type of nonqualified retirement plan. Under the plan, Henry, the company's president, can set aside 10 percent of his annual compensation. Assume Henry's annual compensation is fixed at $100,000, so he agrees to receive $90,000 currently and to defer $10,000 under the deferred compensation plan. Company A can deduct compensation of $90,000 this year. It can deduct the additional $10,000 when it is paid to Henry at some future time.

This deduction rule also applies to both compensation deferred under the plan as well as interest credited on deferred amounts. While labeled "interest," such earnings are viewed as additional compensation and are subject to the same deduction rule. For example, should Company A in the example agree to pay 10 percent annually on compensation deferred under its plan, then the company could deduct this interest only when it's paid out from the plan in the form of additional benefits.

From the employees' perspective, nonqualified plans can provide the same tax deferral opportunity possible under qualified retirement plans. Contributions on their behalf are not currently taxable to them as long as they are not in constructive receipt of the funds or receive any economic benefit from them. Similarly, earnings on contributions are not currently taxable to them. It is anticipated that benefits will be received in retirement when the former employee's tax bracket may be lower so that more of the money earned can be retained after tax.

Constructive receipt means the money is set aside or credited to your account and is currently available for your use. For example, if you tell the company to hold your check, you're in constructive receipt and taxable on the money at that time even if you actually receive the check later on. *Economic benefit* means the right to financial enjoyment of the money, such as the ability to use the money as collateral for a loan.

Participants are not taxed on deferred amounts as long as there is a risk of forfeiture of benefits. This risk exists where benefits can be lost for violating the terms of an employment contract or leaving employment prior to the retirement age under the deferred compensation plan.

But even if there is no risk of forfeiture (participants are fully vested in benefits), they may still not be currently taxable. Whether participants are currently taxable under nonqualified plans depends on whether the plan is viewed as funded or unfunded. In unfunded plans employer contributions remain assets of the company subject to the claims of general creditors. The contributions may be separate entries on the company books or even placed into a trust. However, if the company becomes insolvent or goes under, creditors could have a claim against them. Funded plans are plans that have assets segregated from the company's assets and can't be touched by the company's general creditors. To summarize:

- *Funded plans*—employees are currently taxable on benefits, even if the benefits are not received until some future time.

- *Unfunded plans*—employees are not taxed until benefits are actually or constructively received.

As an employee of your company, understand that there's risk involved with unfunded plans. They're totally dependent on the promise of the company to make good on deferred compensation arrangements. Should the company suffer severe losses, you could find yourself without promised benefits.

On the other hand, while funded plans provide protection to you and other covered employees that benefits will be paid, this assurance comes at the price of current income taxation. In family-owned businesses where the life of the company is key to all involved, as an owner-employee you may be willing to risk future compensation on the promise of the company you own. After all, you are the company, so effectively you're giving your word to yourself.

Nonqualified plans of family-owned businesses must be careful to determine whether they're subject to minimum funding and coverage requirements imposed by law. Check to see whether they qualify for a "top hat" exemption from these requirements for plans covering a select group of owners and highly compensated employees. According to the Department of Labor, plans covering less than 5 percent of the company's workforce are automatically presumed to qualify for the top hat exemption. Plans covering between 5 percent and 20 percent may or may not be eligible for this exemption. Plans covering more than 20 percent of the workforce probably are not exempt.

CAUTION

Even though they are not qualified retirement plans, top hat plans are subject to special reporting and disclosure rules.

Employment Taxes

When compensation is deferred, employment taxes are due when the compensation is earned, not when it's paid. This rule applies even though the company cannot deduct the compensation until it's

Example

In 2001, your salary is $125,000, and you agree to defer $25,000 to retirement. Since your salary (without regard to the deferred amount) is already above the ceiling of $80,400, there are no additional Social Security taxes imposed on the deferred amount. (The Medicare portion of FICA tax is imposed on the full $125,000 since there is no ceiling for this tax.) Say you retire in 2010 and receive the $25,000. Since it was already subject to FICA tax (even though there was no Social Security tax on it), there is no further employment tax obligation.

paid. For example, if you agree to defer $25,000 of your compensation until retirement, FICA and FUTA taxes are figured in the year of deferral, not the year of retirement. This can produce tax savings for you and the corporation.

Employment tax rules are discussed in IRS Publication 15, Circular E, "Employer's Tax Guide," available through the IRS Web site at www.irs.gov.

Figure 8.1 provides a comparison of the tax consequences and other aspects of qualified and nonqualified plans.

Nonqualified Plans and Unincorporated Businesses

Partnerships and limited liability companies can use nonqualified retirement plans in much the same way as corporations can. The plan merely defines the owners or others to be covered under the plan and the amount of benefits each can earn from the plan.

Partnership plans must be carefully structured to protect benefits from self-employment tax. Generally, periodic payments from a nonqualified plan that continue until a former partner's death are not subject to self-employment tax. This exclusion from self-employment tax

Tip

Where a retired partner provides postretirement services to the partnership, the arrangement should be carefully structured as an independent contractor relationship. Put this agreement in writing. Make sure that the partnership agreement does *not* require a former partner to pay any postretirement income to the partnership.

FIGURE 8.1   Comparison of Qualified Plans to Nonqualified Plans

Aspect	Qualified Retirement Plans	Nonqualified Retirement Plans
Nondiscrimination requirements	Yes	No
Limit on benefits and contributions	Yes	No
Deductibility of contributions	Currently deductible	Deductible when benefits are paid
Employees taxed on benefits	When paid	When paid if plans are unfunded When contributions are made if plans are funded
Asset protection	Yes	No (if plans are unfunded)
Annual reporting	Yes	No
Employment taxes	Benefits are exempt	Subject to employment taxes in year deferred compensation is earned

applies as long as the partner does not render any services to the partnership when receiving benefits and the partner has no interest in the partnership (other than the right to receive benefits under its non-qualified retirement plan).

Sole proprietors cannot use nonqualified plans for their own benefit. Since they are currently taxed on all net profits from their business, they can't set any amount aside for the future. Sole proprietors are restricted to using qualified retirement plans for purposes of their own retirement savings. Of course, sole proprietorships can use nonqualified plans for their rank-and-file employees. Sole proprietors who employ family members may want to consider nonqualified retirement plans to provide retirement income to these family members.

Setting Up Nonqualified Plans

Nonqualified plans are written plans designed to defer income for you and other plan participants to some future date. These plans usually need to be set up with the assistance of a benefits expert, accountant, or attorney versed in nonqualified retirement plans. This involves an initial fee for advice and plan creation. However, once the plan is set up, future professional fees should be minimal (for example, only on an as-needed basis when plan changes are desired).

Nonqualified retirement plans should be adopted by the board of directors and reflected in the corporate minutes. Shareholder approval may also be required under state law or the corporation's bylaws or articles of incorporation. However, shareholder approval usually is required only when company stock is used to provide benefits, something never done in family-owned businesses. The company may be required to notify the Secretary of Labor of the plan's adoption within 120 days of this action.

Providing Flexibility

Setting up a plan today does not lock the company or you and other plan participants into the arrangement indefinitely. The plan can give the company or participants the option to stop future deferrals for any reason. This lets the company stop agreeing to deferrals if liabilities under the plan may become excessive. It also lets you stop agreeing to deferrals if you become concerned about the company's future solvency or you become certain that your future tax bracket will be the same as your current tax bracket (thereby eliminating a key reason for deferral in the first place).

> **TIP**
>
> The plan may permit a change of deferral by a participant in the case of a financial hardship. It's advisable to have a change reviewed by a committee to avoid constructive receipt problems for the participant.

Deferred Amounts

Nonqualified deferred compensation plans can be designed in several different ways. Generally, they give covered employees the opportunity either to defer compensation or to gain additional benefits on top of current compensation. For example, in the deferred compensation type of plan, you can agree to defer a percentage of your current compensation. Or deferral can relate solely to your annual bonuses. In the additional benefits type of plan, the company adds a percentage of your current compensation to the plan.

A deferred compensation plan must be set up *before* compensation is earned. Attempts to defer compensation after it's earned can result in current taxation to you or other covered employees. You may be considered in constructive receipt of the deferred amounts even though now you can't take distributions from the plan until retirement or some other future date.

Payout Events

The plan must describe the terms and conditions under which payments will be made. Generally, benefits are paid upon any of the following events:

- Retirement
- Disability
- Termination of employment
- Death

Plans may want to limit the payout to retirement only. If the company promises to make payments upon death or disability, this promise can be viewed as an economic benefit. You may become immediately taxable on the value of these promised benefits (for example, the value of a comparable benefit provided through life insurance).

Payout Options

Plans can tailor payout options as desired. They can permit lump-sum payments of accrued benefits. They can provide for monthly payments. They can provide payments through a commercial annuity. Or they can give participants the choice of payout method.

AVOIDING CONSTRUCTIVE RECEIPT ON PAYOUT OPTIONS

To ensure that you aren't immediately taxed on benefits by virtue of your payout option, follow these alternatives. Select the type of payout:

- When commencing participation in the plan.
- Well before benefits are set to commence (for example, two or three years prior to retirement age).
- Within 60 days of being able to select a lump-sum payout, irrevocably opt for an annuity.

LIMITING COMPANY EXPOSURE

A nonqualified plan that has several participants presents a potential financial threat to the company. Under a worst-case scenario, if all participants retire at the same time and want their benefits paid in full, the company can be faced with a severe liability. Thus, it's advisable to set limits on annual amounts that can be paid from the plan. This will

---

Caution

Where participants have a choice of payout options and can exercise that choice at the time when benefits commence, participants are treated as in constructive receipt of all benefits at that time. This is so even if monthly payments are selected. However, it may be possible to avoid this constructive receipt treatment if certain steps are taken.

limit the company's exposure to payments. For example, the plan can cap annual payments from the plan at $50,000 per participant. In this way, the company is assured that its maximum cash requirement in any year is this dollar amount times the number of participants.

Strategies for Providing Benefit Security

Family businesses that use deferred compensation arrangements for owners and other key employees may want to build in some measure of protection for these people. Perhaps security isn't necessary for you and other family members. But nonfamily employees covered by the plan may not have your same level of comfort. Providing a measure of protection means walking a careful line; too much protection can trigger immediate taxation to plan participants.

There are several strategies that can be used to give participants of a deferred compensation plan some security:

- Rabbi trusts
- Secular trusts
- Annuities
- Insurance

Rabbi Trusts

The company can set up a special type of trust for the purpose of providing deferred compensation. If properly structured, the trust provides protection from changes in management without triggering current tax to owners participating in the deferred compensation plan. The IRS has sanctioned this special type of trust and has even provided model trusts. Using model trusts assures the company and employees participating in the company's deferred compensation plan that intended tax treatment will be obtained.

A *rabbi trust* is an irrevocable trust established by a company to provide future benefits to officers, directors, and other key employees. Its name derives from the first such trust set up by a congregation for its rabbi.

While the trust is irrevocable, the funds within the trust remain subject to the claims of the company's general creditors. The assets within the trust are reported as part of the company's financial statement. The benefit of a rabbi trust over an ordinary deferred compensation arrangement merely entered on the company books is protection for participants against changes in management and management views. For example, if there's a company takeover, beneficiaries of the rabbi trust are protected. More importantly, employees participating in this type of deferred compensation plan are protected from the claims of the participants' creditors. A participant's interest in the trust is not subject to attachment and cannot be encumbered by the participant (e.g., pledged as security for a loan).

In setting up a rabbi trust, consider certain modifications to a basic trust agreement. These modifications can provide additional protection for you and other participants.

- *Modifications only by supermajority.* Have the trust require that amendments to the trust or replacement of a trustee take place only upon the consent of a supermajority of the plan participants (beneficiaries of the trust). For example, require that 75 percent or 80 percent of participants agree to any changes.

- *Automatic plan termination.* Have the trust terminate automatically upon the occurrence of certain events that could jeopardize the financial security of the company. For example, the trust may be terminated if the company faces certain regulatory action or fails to meet certain financial benchmarks (for example, net worth, net income, or share price). Termination will, of course, mean that benefits under the plan become immediately taxable to you and other participants. But at least you will avoid risk of loss should the company become insolvent as a result of the regulatory action or the failure to meet the financial benchmarks.

- *Haircut.* This is a provision allowing a participant to take an immediate payout of benefits, less an amount forfeited. A typical forfeiture under a haircut provision is 10 percent of the deferred amount. However, the IRS has not yet ruled on the impact of the haircut provision or the amount of forfeiture that is appropriate.

- *Investment restrictions.* Have the trust limit the types of permissible investments. Conservative investments by the trust can help to ensure funds to pay out benefits to plan participants.

Taxwise, a rabbi trust produces the following tax consequences:

- The company cannot deduct contributions to the trust.
- The company is taxed on earnings on contributions to the trust.
- You as a participant (beneficiary) are taxed on distributions from the trust.
- The company can deduct distributions from the trust that are made to participants.

WHO SHOULD ACT AS TRUSTEE OF THE TRUST?

The trustee has the job of administering the trust. This means making investment decisions, paying out benefits, and otherwise observing state law fiduciary requirements for the benefit of participants. The company may want to consider using an outside trustee for this purpose. There are two reasons:

1. As an owner, if you are a beneficiary of the trust, then you can't act alone as trustee. In effect, there's a conflict of interest in being both a beneficiary and the trustee. The same holds true for any other owner who is a plan participant.

2. As owner or company officer you may better spend your time and efforts on company business. You may not have investment expertise needed to manage the trust.

Secular Trusts and Other Trusts

In addition to rabbi trusts, other trusts may be used to provide deferred compensation. Each alternative has pros and cons to consider.

SECULAR TRUSTS

Secular trusts are irrevocable trusts designed to allow funding for deferred compensation plans while providing added protection for participants in the event of the company's insolvency or bankruptcy. Funds contributed to these trusts are beyond the reach of the company's creditors, thereby protecting participants. The downside to secular trusts includes the following:

- Participants are viewed in constructive receipt of the contributions and are immediately taxable on these amounts.

- The trust is taxed on earnings. These earnings are again taxed when distributed to participants.

The upside to participants and the company includes the following:

- All future payouts of principal to participants are tax free (participants have already paid tax on these amounts).

- While funds remain in the trust they are protected from any claims of participants' creditors.

- The company can claim an immediate income tax deduction for its contributions to the trust.

Are secular trusts worth the bother in a family-owned business? Probably not. Usually, the company must "gross up" a participant's income to provide cash for taxes on currently taxable deferred compensation.

SPRINGING TRUSTS

These are irrevocable trusts set up currently to provide a measure of protection for deferred compensation arrangements. The trusts are unfunded and remain so indefinitely. However, if there's a change in the ownership or control of the business, then the trust "springs" into action, requiring the company to set up a rabbi trust at that time. The rabbi trust would then hold the funds for participants. The funds remain subject to the claims of the company's creditors.

Annuities

Commercial annuities can be used to provide security for the company's promise to pay benefits. The company purchases an annuity in the name of the participant and pays the premiums for the contract. The amount of the contract is correlated to the projected benefits that will be payable to the participant.

You are not taxed on the annuity as long as the company owns it, and you don't have any rights in it (for example, you are subject to a risk of forfeiture). When the company transfers title of the policy to you upon retirement or some other triggering event and the annuity commences, you then become taxable on the annuity payments.

Alternatively, you may own the contract. In this case, you are taxed at the time the company pays the premiums. When you annuitize (meaning you commence receipt of payments, usually upon your retirement), a portion of each payment representing your return of investment (amounts previously taxed) is tax free. More specifically, the taxable portion of each annuity payment is the ratio of previously taxed premiums to the total annuity payments expected to be made. This expectation depends on the provisions of the annuity. For example, payments may be fixed for a term certain or payable for life or even the joint lives of you and your spouse.

The downside to using commercial annuities is added cost. Instead of simply paying the funds to you, the company in effect is paying those funds plus fees and charges to the annuity company. Also, as long as the company owns the annuity, it remains subject to the claims of its creditors.

Insurance

It may be possible to use insurance to protect promised benefits from deferred compensation plans.

SPLIT-DOLLAR LIFE INSURANCE

This arrangement is similar to the use of commercial annuities. It provides the same financial protection to you and other participants.

> **Caution**
>
> There is some question about whether the buildup of the cash surrender value results in current taxation to you. In one instance the IRS charged that annual increases in the cash surrender value over the premiums paid was taxable income. However, this IRS position has been criticized, and it's not certain whether it will be followed.

In split-dollar life insurance, the company and you have an ongoing relationship. You are the owner of the policy; the company pays the premiums. When you die, the company recoups its premium outlay.

The aim of the split-dollar life insurance arrangement in the deferred compensation context is to build up cash surrender value. As cash surrender value grows, so too does security for benefits promised under the deferred compensation plan.

> **CAUTION**
>
> If you use insurance to protect your interests under a deferred compensation plan, be sure to review coverage every few years. As benefits grow, so too will the needed coverage.

SURETY BOND OR INDEMNITY INSURANCE

You can purchase insurance protection against the company's promise to pay you benefits. Buying such coverage usually will not trigger immediate taxation of the benefits under the deferred compensation plan. The benefit of coverage obviously is the assurance that you'll receive benefits one way or the other. The drawback to coverage is the cost involved.

Other Nonqualified Retirement Plan Strategies

Instead of a deferred mechanism for current compensation, nonqualified plans can be structured to provide retirement income without diminishing current salary.

SERPs (Supplemental Executive Retirement Plans)

These are nonqualified plans set up much like defined benefit pension plans (discussed in Chapter 7). These plans provide a pension starting at retirement based on your final average pay of the last three years of employment. Typically, the retirement benefit under this plan results in retirement income of between 60 percent and 80 percent of what you had been earning on average during the last three years of employment. Enhanced benefits may be provided through a tie-in to company performance.

A SERP is a particularly attractive method of retaining nonfamily executives. Since such individuals will probably never achieve ownership of any significance in a family business, they can be rewarded for longevity with additional retirement income. This income is based on compensation paid to them in their final years when earnings typically rise, so the longer they stay, the larger their retirement incomes.

The plan is nonqualified because it benefits only a limited class of individuals. That class may include officers, directors, and other highly compensated individuals.

Benefits under a SERP are not vested until retirement. Usually they are paid from the company's general assets when the individual retires. However, a rabbi trust can be used to provide some measure of protection for promised benefits under a SERP.

Golden Handcuffs

These are a type of nonqualified retirement plan designed to encourage individuals to remain with the company for the long haul. Golden handcuffs provide retirement benefits that supplement any qualified benefits or deferred compensation arrangements that may also be available. Suppose a company has middle-aged children of its founder working for the business who are unhappy about their limited roles in middle management and the continued presence of their parent, the founder. To ensure that the second generation remains with the company despite their limited roles, the company may create a golden handcuffs agreement with them. The agreement describes a promise to pay certain benefits upon retirement. Since the agreement is a mere promise to provide a benefit in the future, there is no immediate cost to the business. Also, there are no immediate tax consequences to either of the parties.

Other Arrangements

Phantom stock plans are another means of providing additional income to individuals on a deferred basis. These plans are discussed in Chapter 5.

CHAPTER 9

Home-Based Businesses

It used to be that a man's home was his castle. For many it was also a place of business—the family farm or an apartment above the store. Today a home is also a place for many different kinds of businesses. The advent of technology has enabled people to work as productively from home as from any office, store, or other location in the world. And so homes are being used as the base for family businesses.

Working at home at the family business presents both opportunities to take advantage of and problems to resolve. This chapter provides a picture of who's working from home today—and why. It discusses some legal and financial concerns about conducting business in your home. And it also explains the tax write-offs you may be entitled to.

Families Working at Home

Home isn't only the place to *bake* your bread. It's also the place to *make* your bread for a growing number of people. Statistics vary greatly, but according to the U.S. Department of Labor, as of 1998 about 6 percent of all U.S. households had home-based businesses. Half of all sole proprietors work from home. Home-based businesses are the fastest growing segment of our economy, with annual growth of 10 percent.

How many of these businesses are family businesses? No one has accurate statistics. However, it appears that many of these businesses probably fall into this category. Many husbands are running contracting, electrical, and plumbing businesses from home, with their wives keeping the books and preparing payroll for their employees each week. Other couples are working together in multilevel marketing (also called MLM or network marketing) of vitamins, cosmetics, cleaning materials, plastic containers, lingerie, or other things, and operate these activities from their homes. Parents are operating businesses from home, employing their teenagers, and creating family businesses.

Working from home is an ideal work arrangement for some individuals. Here are some benefits to consider:

- The cost and time of commuting is eliminated. From a cost perspective, this can run to thousands of dollars annually per couple. From a time perspective, this can be 10 hours or more per week for each commuter.

- Parents can be on-site for child-care responsibilities. Working at home enables parents to raise their children instead of leaving it up to child-care workers. In addition to the personal considerations, there's a significant cost savings here, too. Child care can cost as much as several hundred dollars per child each week.

- Adult children can be on-site for the care of their elderly parents. An increasing number of adults are shouldering the responsibility of caring for their elderly parents or other relatives. Working from home provides the flexibility for managing this task.

Legal and Financial Concerns about Working at Home

Running your family business at home is a little like putting all your eggs in one basket. You're combining what may be your two biggest

Caution

Couples who work together outside the home certainly need to address personal issues of togetherness. But those working together in the home have an even greater need to decide how much togetherness they can stand. To survive this business arrangement, some couples may want to develop outside interests, create separate work spaces, or figure out other ways to maintain their individuality.

assets: your business and your home. Make sure you're legally entitled to operate your business from home. Make certain to comply with all local, state, and federal laws applicable to your business. And be sure to have adequate insurance protection for the use of your home. Resolve the zoning and insurance issues before you start.

Zoning Issues

While families have worked from home for centuries, zoning laws in the past 100 years have tried to limit this work arrangement. In an effort to preserve the residential character of a neighborhood, local zoning laws may limit the types of business activities that can be conducted at home. Violation of these laws can result in stiff penalties or fines. A husband-and-wife team operating a nationwide medical referral service from their finished basement found this out the hard way when a disgruntled employee alerted the town to the fact that there were more than half a dozen unrelated employees on the premises in violation of local zoning law. Penalties for them ran into thousands of dollars, and they were forced out of their home office.

What kind of business are you running from home? Do you have employees? Generally the answers to these two questions govern whether you can legally operate a business from home.

Zoning laws generally recognize traditional home-based businesses. These include such businesses as professional suites for doctors, dentists, accountants, architects, and other professionals; music teachers; and seamstresses. However, in many locations, zoning laws haven't kept pace with the changing work environment. Today, an Internet-based business can sell worldwide from a single spare bedroom in the family home. Whether this business or others can be conducted from a home varies from locality to locality.

Most towns and cities have no trouble with freelance writers, consultants, and other solo endeavors. They may also permit other types of businesses where there are no nonresident employees. This means that if the business uses only the labor of family members living on the premises, it would not violate zoning law. However, if the business hires someone who does not live in the home, even if that person is a relative, it might violate zoning law.

Bottom line: You must check with your city or town zoning board (or other government office) to find out about your local restrictions. Zoning laws may affect how many employees you can have (in addition to those living in your home), what parking you're required to provide, and the size of a sign, if any, you can display. If the type of business you run does not comply with the zoning rules, you're not necessarily out of luck. You may be able to obtain a variance from your city or town.

This is special permission for your business to operate from your home. For example, one mother-daughter day-care operation was found to be in violation of local zoning law after a neighbor complained about the noise. They were given a variance to continue their operation but were required to limit outside playtime to certain hours.

Also check on whether there are any fees required to run a business from home. Some localities have used zoning laws as a means of raising additional local revenue.

Other Legal Issues

Running a family business from home does not exempt the company from other government regulations. You are still subject to the same federal and state laws applicable to businesses that are not run from home. For example, you are still subject to the federal Fair Labor Standards Act governing child labor, the minimum wage, and equal pay requirements, even though you operate from home and employ your own children.

Of course, as a small business, you may be exempt from certain federal and/or state laws imposed on larger companies. For example, you need not comply with the federal Family and Medical Leave Act (FMLA), requiring a business to provide up to 12 weeks of unpaid leave time for certain family and medical situations, if your business does not employ at least 50 workers within a 75-mile area. But just because you operate from home as a small business doesn't exempt you automatically. You need to meet all the exemption requirements for the particular regulation.

Note

Employing your children? Even though you operate from home, the following provisions of the Fair Labor Standards Act apply:

- Children ages 14 and 15 can perform any nonhazardous work within the following hour limitations: no more than 3 hours on a school day (up to 18 hours in a school week) or 8 hours on a nonschool day (up to 40 hours in a nonschool week). Work can't start before 7:00 A.M. or run past 7:00 P.M. (except from June 1 through Labor Day, when hours can extend to 9:00 P.M.).

- Children ages 16 and 17 can perform any nonhazardous work for unlimited hours.

- Children 18 and older aren't subject to limitations on the type of work or hours they can work.

Insurance Issues

What happens if a fire destroys your home office? What happens if a thief walks off with your computer? What happens if a customer falls on the floor of your home office? You need to determine what insurance protection you have for each of these situations and whether you need to make adjustments to coverage. Insurance protection with respect to a business you run from home has two key components:

1. *Property coverage (also called casualty insurance)*—covers damage, destruction, or theft of property.

2. *Liability coverage*—provides compensation to third parties who are injured on your premises. This would include clients, customers, suppliers, and people who make deliveries.

There's another concern you may want to consider. What happens if your computer data is lost due to a storm or other event? Insurance can cover the cost of data reconstruction.

Your homeowner's policy may or may not cover your business needs. A homeowner's policy may have dollar limits on business equipment (for example, $5,000), which may be insufficient for your purposes. Or it may not cover *any* business equipment. Similarly, it may not cover liability arising from business visitors to your home.

You may be able to adjust your homeowner's policy to cover your business needs. An inexpensive rider to your policy may, for example, extend liability coverage for occasional business visitors if you don't regularly have customers in your home. Or you may have a special endorsement to cover your computer and other business equipment.

> **TIP**
> You can obviate the need for insuring your computer data if you regularly back up your data and store it in a safe place. Consider storing it off premises such as in a bank safe-deposit box or at home in a fireproof safe. There are also online storage sites available for this purpose.

In the event that it would be too expensive to adjust coverage under a homeowner's policy, or the policy won't allow for adjustments, you can obtain a separate policy to cover your home office. This separate policy typically covers property damage, liability coverage, and data reconstruction. Generally the cost of coverage for a separate policy runs only a few hundred dollars a year (depending, of course, on the extent of coverage you require). For example, one financial planner who operates a home business from a converted garage, employing his two teenagers for computer work, pays just under $300 a year for property coverage of his contents up to

$15,000, liability coverage of $500,000 per occurrence, and data reconstruction of $10,000.

Companies offering home-office insurance packages are listed in Figure 9.1.

Writing Off Home Office Expenses and Related Items

A spare bedroom, a converted garage, an attic, or a basement family room may be an ideal location for your family business. Running the family business from home lets you better handle personal issues, such as time management (you don't have to commute) and child (or parent) care responsibilities. What's more, whether your family business is full-time or part-time, operating from home enables you to save money, thereby keeping more of what you earn.

- You save on overhead costs. You're already paying for overhead—your home—so by operating the business from there you save on overhead expenses you'd otherwise have to pay if the business were in an outside office, in a storefront, or somewhere else.

- You can deduct what are essentially personal expenses you are already paying for. The tax law lets you claim a home office deduction against your business income. This deduction operates as an umbrella for all the expenses associated with operating from home, such as maintenance, insurance, real estate taxes, mortgage interest, a depreciation allowance if you own the home (or rent if you lease it), and utility costs. The term "home office" isn't limited to conventional office space or use. It can include any part of a home. For example, a basement workshop of a cabinetmaker or a backyard greenhouse of an orchid grower can be considered a home office.

FIGURE 9.1 Insurance for Home Offices

Insurance Company	Telephone	Web Site
Fireman's Fund	415-899-2000	www.the-fund.com
The Hartford	860-547-5000	www.thehartford.com
Travelers Property Casualty	800-238-6225	www.travelers.com
Zurich Small Business	800-648-9789	www.zurichsmallbusiness.com

Example

If you run a contracting business from home, you earn your money at job sites. But if you use your home office to estimate jobs, order supplies, and keep your books and records, then your home is treated as your principal place of business.

Qualifying for a Home Office Deduction

To claim a home office deduction, you must meet two tests:

1. Your home office generally must be your principal place of business.

2. You use your home office regularly and exclusively for business.

TEST 1

Your home office generally must be your principal place of business. Generally this is the place where you earn your money. For example, if you run a travel agency or public relations (PR) company from your home, you earn your money there. But even if you don't generate income out of a home office, it's still considered your principal place of business if you use it for substantial management or administrative activities and you have no other fixed location for such activities.

Substantial administrative or management activities include:

- Billing customers, clients, and patients
- Estimating jobs
- Forwarding orders
- Keeping books and records
- Ordering supplies
- Reading trade or professional journals
- Scheduling appointments or jobs
- Writing reports or papers

Your home office is still your principal place of business even if you use your cell phone in your car to conduct business. It's not a fixed location. The same is true for business conducted in a motel room while you're on the road.

You may still be entitled to a home office deduction even if it's not your principal place of business. A deduction is allowed if you use your home as a place to meet or deal with clients, customers, or patients in the normal course of business. A deduction is also allowed if you use a separate structure not attached to the residence in connection with your business (for example, a freestanding greenhouse used in a plant sale business).

TEST 2

You must use your home office regularly and exclusively for business. This generally means you must use the space *only* for business. For example, under this test if you use a family room as an office during the day, your family can't use it for recreation at night. This doesn't mean you must set aside a full room for business. You qualify for a home office deduction even if you use only part of a room as long as that use is exclusive. No physical partition is required.

There are two exceptions to the exclusive use requirement:

1. Day-care activities within the home. The law recognizes that you can't coop up children in a single room for extended periods of time, but instead you must give them the run of the house. Special rules (not discussed here but explained in the instructions to IRS Form 8829) apply to figuring the portion of your home used for business.
2. Storage of inventory or samples for a retail or wholesale business you run from home.

Also, you must use the home office more than occasionally. Thus, meeting with customers at your home once in a while probably isn't sufficient by itself to support a home office deduction.

What's Deductible?

Expenses related to your home office fall into two categories: direct expenses and indirect expenses. Direct expenses are those that relate solely to your home office. Direct expenses are fully deductible. Indirect expenses are expenses that relate to your entire home. Only the portion of indirect expenses relating to your home office is deductible.

Generally, indirect expenses are apportioned on a square footage basis. So, for example, if your home is 3,000 square feet and you

---

Example

If you paint your home office, it's a direct expense. But if you paint the outside of your home, it's an indirect expense.

use a room as your office that's 300 square feet, then 10 percent of every indirect expense becomes deductible. The law allows apportionment on a per-room basis if the rooms are about equal in size. So, for example, if you have a four-room apartment and use one room as a home office, then 25 percent of your indirect expenses are deductible.

The following are examples of expenses to consider:

- Casualty and theft losses
- Cleaning
- Depreciation (if you own your home)
- Insurance
- Interest on a home mortgage (if you own your home)
- Property taxes (if you own your home)
- Rent (if you lease your home)
- Repairs
- Security systems
- Snow removal
- Utilities

CAUTION

Some expenses may be direct or indirect, depending on the circumstances. For example, if a flood damages your entire home, this casualty loss is an indirect expense. But if a tree falls through your office ceiling, this casualty loss is a direct expense.

Some expenses are not deductible. You cannot deduct any part of the cost of landscaping or lawn care for your home. Similarly, you cannot deduct the basic monthly cost of the first telephone line to your home. You can deduct the cost of long-distance calls made for business, as well as business services (call waiting, call forwarding, and call answering). And you can separately deduct a second (or third) phone line used for business.

Most expenses comprising the home office deduction are self-explanatory. Many of these expenses are listed on the IRS form used to figure the home office deduction (Figure 9.2—Form 8829, Expenses for Business Use of Your Home, for self-employed individuals, and a worksheet that's virtually identical to Form 8829, for employees and partners using a home office).

While most expenses on Form 8829 are clear, depreciation on your home office requires more explanation.

Depreciation is a noncash deduction that allows you to write off the cost of property over a number of years (fixed by law). A depreciation allowance may be claimed even though the value of the property actually appreciates.

Form **8829**

Department of the Treasury
Internal Revenue Service (99)

Expenses for Business Use of Your Home

▶ File only with Schedule C (Form 1040). Use a separate Form 8829 for each home you used for business during the year.

▶ See separate instructions.

OMB No. 1545-1266

2000

Attachment
Sequence No. **66**

Name(s) of proprietor(s)

Your social security number

Part I   Part of Your Home Used for Business

1	Area used regularly and exclusively for business, regularly for day care, or for storage of inventory or product samples. See instructions	**1**	
2	Total area of home	**2**	
3	Divide line 1 by line 2. Enter the result as a percentage.	**3**	%

- For day-care facilities not used exclusively for business, also complete lines 4–6.
- All others, skip lines 4–6 and enter the amount from line 3 on line 7.

4	Multiply days used for day care during year by hours used per day.	**4**	hr.
5	Total hours available for use during the year (366 days × 24 hours). See instructions	**5**	8,784 hr.
6	Divide line 4 by line 5. Enter the result as a decimal amount . . .	**6**	.
7	Business percentage. For day-care facilities not used exclusively for business, multiply line 6 by line 3 (enter the result as a percentage). All others, enter the amount from line 3 . . . . . ▶	**7**	%

Part II   Figure Your Allowable Deduction

8	Enter the amount from Schedule C, line 29, **plus** any net gain or (loss) derived from the business use of your home and shown on Schedule D or Form 4797. If more than one place of business, see instructions	**8**	

See instructions for columns (a) and (b) before completing lines 9–20.

		(a) Direct expenses	(b) Indirect expenses	
9	Casualty losses. See instructions	**9**		
10	Deductible mortgage interest. See instructions .	**10**		
11	Real estate taxes. See instructions	**11**		
12	Add lines 9, 10, and 11.	**12**		
13	Multiply line 12, column (b) by line 7 . . .	**13**		
14	Add line 12, column (a) and line 13. . . .		**14**	
15	Subtract line 14 from line 8. If zero or less, enter -0- .		**15**	
16	Excess mortgage interest. See instructions . .	**16**		
17	Insurance	**17**		
18	Repairs and maintenance	**18**		
19	Utilities	**19**		
20	Other expenses. See instructions	**20**		
21	Add lines 16 through 20	**21**		
22	Multiply line 21, column (b) by line 7	**22**		
23	Carryover of operating expenses from 1999 Form 8829, line 41 . .	**23**		
24	Add line 21 in column (a), line 22, and line 23		**24**	
25	Allowable operating expenses. Enter the **smaller** of line 15 or line 24		**25**	
26	Limit on excess casualty losses and depreciation. Subtract line 25 from line 15		**26**	
27	Excess casualty losses. See instructions	**27**		
28	Depreciation of your home from Part III below	**28**		
29	Carryover of excess casualty losses and depreciation from 1999 Form 8829, line 42	**29**		
30	Add lines 27 through 29		**30**	
31	Allowable excess casualty losses and depreciation. Enter the **smaller** of line 26 or line 30 . .		**31**	
32	Add lines 14, 25, and 31		**32**	
33	Casualty loss portion, if any, from lines 14 and 31. Carry amount to **Form 4684,** Section B .		**33**	
34	Allowable expenses for business use of your home. Subtract line 33 from line 32. Enter here and on Schedule C, line 30. If your home was used for more than one business, see instructions ▶		**34**	

Part III   Depreciation of Your Home

35	Enter the **smaller** of your home's adjusted basis or its fair market value. See instructions . .	**35**	
36	Value of land included on line 35	**36**	
37	Basis of building. Subtract line 36 from line 35.	**37**	
38	Business basis of building. Multiply line 37 by line 7.	**38**	
39	Depreciation percentage. See instructions	**39**	%
40	Depreciation allowable. Multiply line 38 by line 39. Enter here and on line 28 above. See instructions	**40**	

Part IV   Carryover of Unallowed Expenses to 2001

41	Operating expenses. Subtract line 25 from line 24. If less than zero, enter -0-	**41**	
42	Excess casualty losses and depreciation. Subtract line 31 from line 30. If less than zero, enter -0-	**42**	

For Paperwork Reduction Act Notice, see page 4 of separate instructions.

Cat. No. 13232M

Form **8829** (2000)

FIGURE 9.2   IRS Form 8829

FIGURE 9.3   Depreciation Percentages for Home Offices

Year	January	February	March	April	May
1	2.461%	2.247%	2.033%	1.819%	1.605%
2–39	2.564%	2.564%	2.564%	2.564%	2.564%
40	0.107%	0.321%	0.535%	0.749%	0.963%

Year	June	July	August	September
1	1.391%	1.177%	0.963%	0.749%
2–39	2.564%	2.564%	2.564%	2.564%
40	1.177%	0.391%	1.605%	1.819%

Year	October	November	December
1	0.535%	0.321%	0.107%
2–39	2.564%	2.564%	2.564%
40	2.033%	2.247%	2.461%

Depreciation is figured on the basis used for the business portion of your home. If you convert your residence to business use, then your basis for depreciation is the lower of the fair market value of the home office at the time of conversion or its basis (what you paid for it). In making this determination, don't include the value of the land on which the home sits; use only the home itself.

Once you have the basis of your home office, you then apply the percentage allowed by law. This percentage depends on the month in which you start using your home office for business and the current year of claiming depreciation. (See Figure 9.3.)

If you remodel your home to create a home office, you can't simply deduct your construction costs. You must depreciate the cost of converting a garage, attic, or basement or adding on a room in your home for business use.

Gross Income Limit

The home office deduction is limited to gross income from your home-based business. If this business is your main business, this gross income limit probably isn't a problem. But if it's a sideline business, the gross income limit may determine what you can write off this year. Unused home office deductions can be carried

> ### Example
>
> You and your spouse start up a home-based business in May and begin using your home office at that time. Your home office is 10 percent of your home's square footage. You paid $225,000 for your home several years ago ($25,000 of which was the land). Today it's worth $350,000. Your basis is 10 percent of the lower of the home's cost (exclusive of land)—$200,000—or the fair market value—$350,000. Your basis for depreciation is thus $20,000. Since you started using your home in May, your depreciation write-off for the first year is $321 ($20,000 × 1.605%). Your annual depreciation for years 2 through 39 is $512.80 ($20,000 × 2.564%). If you still own your home 40 years from now and continue to use it for business, your final depreciation deduction will be $192.60 ($20,000 × 0.963%).

CAUTION

Depreciation isn't easy to figure and has negative consequences upon a later home sale. But you can't choose *not* to take it if you're entitled to it. So if the home office is your principal place of business and you use the home office regularly and exclusively for business, you must figure this write-off.

forward and used when and to the extent there is gross income from the same home office activity. There's no limit on the carryforward.

Corporate Businesses

What happens if your business is incorporated? Under the tax law, if you lease your home office to the corporation, you can't claim a home office deduction. Your only write-offs with respect to your home are those allowed to all homeowners, which include mortgage interest, real estate taxes, and casualty losses. Your corporation can deduct any rent it pays to you. However, you must report this rent as income against which no deductions are allowed. So, it's generally not advisable for your corporation to lease space in your home.

If you don't lease your home office to the corporation, you may still be entitled to claim a home office deduction. As an employee of your corporation, you can take this deduction if you personally meet the two home office deduction tests and you use your home office for the convenience of your employer (the corporation). Generally this means that the corporation requires you to work from home because it doesn't provide the space you need to perform your job. For example, if your corporation occupies an office that closes up each night but your duties as company owner require you to work after hours, you may need to use a home office in this instance. In such a case, you could deduct home office expenses as unreimbursed employee business expenses on your personal income tax return. Such expenses, however, are deductible only to the extent your miscellaneous itemized deductions exceed 2 percent of your adjusted gross income. So if your income is high, you may not get any benefit from your write-off.

Ancillary Write-Offs

Running a family business from home allows you to take other write-offs. Travel from your home to any business location and back again is a deductible business expense. In effect, there's no such thing as commuting if you work from a home office whose expenses are deductible. How important is this write-off to you? It depends on how often you leave your home office on business. But if you're constantly in the field, then your car or truck expenses become deductible.

More than two-thirds of home businesses use computers. If yours is one of them, you can write off the cost of your computer using first-year expensing or accelerating depreciation. Generally, these write-offs are allowed only if "listed property", which includes a computer, is used more than 50 percent of the time for business. But listed property used in a tax-deductible home office is assumed to meet this test. You don't have to keep records of business use of your computer in order to qualify for these deductions.

If you must make structural changes to your home to accommodate the elderly or disabled, you may be entitled to special business write-offs. This is so even if you're not required to do so under the Americans with Disabilities Act or other government rules. The write-offs are also permitted even if the only person to benefit from the structural change is you or a family member as long as the changes are made for business reasons (for example, you work at home and need to make your workspace more accessible). Write-offs for these structural changes are more favorable than ordinary depreciation. There are two special write-offs available:

1. You can deduct up to $15,000 spent in widening doorways, installing a ramp, or making other accommodations for the elderly or disabled.

2. You can claim a tax credit of 50 percent of your costs of at least $250, but not more than $10,250, for a maximum credit of $5,000 (50 percent of $10,000). The disabled access credit

is limited to small businesses—those with no more than 30 full-time employees and annual gross receipts of no more than $1 million.

If expenditures qualify for either write-off, you must choose one or the other (you can't double dip). Generally the credit provides the greater benefit, but you must run the numbers to be sure in your situation. Except for local building permits, you generally don't need government approval to make your changes. However, you must retain records of your construction project, such as blueprints, contracts, and building permits, for possible examination by the IRS.

Home office deduction rules are explained in IRS Publication 587, "Business Use of Your Home," which you can download from the IRS Web site at www.irs.gov.

Impact of Your Home Office on a Future Sale of Your Residence

If you have a home office, you can enjoy current tax deductions for its use. But when you sell your home in the future, there's a price to pay for this tax benefit. Ordinarily, gain on the sale of a home is tax-free up to $250,000 (or $500,000 on a joint return) if you own and use your home as your principal residence for at least two out of five years preceding the date of sale. But if you've used a home office, you may have to report gain on the sale. And you'll have to make special computations to figure that gain. The tax implications of having a home office depend on how long you've used a portion of your home for business.

- *You use your home office for three or more years prior to sale.* In this case you don't qualify for the home sale exclusion on the home office portion of your home (you fail the two-out-of-five-year personal use requirement). You must allocate the sales proceeds to the business portion of the home and figure your gain accordingly. In figuring gain, you must reduce your basis by all depreciation taken for the home office. Gain up to this amount of depreciation is taxed at the rate of 25 percent, with the remainder of gain on the business portion of the home taxed at up to 20 percent.

- *You use your home office for less than three years prior to sale.* This means you used that portion of your home more than two years as a principal residence (and not as a home office). As such you're entitled to apply the home sale exclusion to your entire gain. You don't need to allocate the sales proceeds. However, you must still pay tax, at the rate of 25 percent, on the gain equal to the depreciation claimed with respect to your home office after May 6, 1997 (an arbitrary date fixed by statute). This taxable amount is called "unrecaptured gain" on Schedule D of Form 1040.

CHAPTER 10

Protecting Your Business Interests in Divorce

Divorce usually is a difficult personal experience for all parties—spouses, children, grandparents, siblings, and other relatives. But when those parties are in business together, complications abound. Should or must one spouse leave the business if the couple splits up? When a couple divorces, must an in-law leave the family business? If both spouses own the company and one wants out, how does the other arrange a buyout? What financial and tax consequences do the parties need to consider? And what steps can business owners take to avoid problems in case their marriage (or their children's marriage) ends in divorce?

There are no easy answers to these questions. Each couple's situation is different. Each needs a special solution. However, understanding the financial and tax consequences of a marital dissolution to both the business and the parties is important. This chapter explains what a divorce can mean to the company and to the family. It discusses how to use prenuptial and postnuptial agreements and other strategies as preemptive steps to protect business interests. It also explains the tax implications of property settlements so spouses can plan effectively for a division of the business interests upon a separation or divorce.

Impact of Divorce on the Business and the Family

Divorce generally is unpleasant all around. It not only brings emotional changes to the parties and their families, but also can be extremely time-consuming and costly. All these things—emotions, time, and money—usually detract from a person's ability to work productively. Now layer onto these negatives the fact that a couple may be co-owners or coworkers in a family enterprise. This certainly means added complexities for the situation.

Here are some of the issues for divorce in the context of a family business:

- If both spouses work for the company, will one or both of them leave this work arrangement after a separation or divorce? If one is forced to go, must it always be the spouse who married into the family?

- If spouses jointly own the business, how will ownership of the business be parsed? Will one buy out the other? Will both sell the business and divide the proceeds?

- If one spouse owns the business, does the other spouse have an interest in it? And if so, how will the nonowner spouse be compensated for this interest?

- What input do other family members in the business have on the divorcing couple's resolution of working and owning the company?

There are no cookie-cutter answers to these questions. Each situation is unique. Sometimes divorce does not disrupt the business. One couple that co-owned a transportation company divorced after more than 20 years of marriage. Emotionally they had simply grown apart. Despite this breakup, they continued to co-own the business and work together each day. In their situation, divorce was not the result of a breakdown in trust or loss of respect for each other, so they could

Note

According to the United States Census Bureau and the National Center for Health Statistics, there's about a 50 percent chance of a first marriage ending in divorce. These odds increase to 60 percent for remarriages. The average cost of divorce is $15,000, but it can run to $200,000 or more when there is company stock to divvy up. And it can take a year or more to come to terms on property issues.

continue to work together as co-owners. In fact, they claim to get along better now that they're divorced, and the marital dissolution had no effect (other than perhaps a positive one) on their business.

Similar results arose in another family-owned business that managed commercial real estate. Here, the son-in-law worked for his father-in-law, the founder of the company. After the son-in-law and the founder's daughter divorced, he continued to work for the company and his relationship with the founder remained sound.

But these stories are unique. Certainly, in many divorce situations, the breakup is acrimonious and families are torn apart. In one family, the husband, who co-owned the business with his wife, had to give her the house and just about every other asset he had in order to buy out her interest in the company. When the divorce settlement was over, he owned the company but not much else. And in another family business that operates teen tours, the son-in-law, who had worked in the business for more than 10 years, was forced out by his wife and her siblings when the couple split up.

There are two distinct issues that must be resolved when a couple divorces:

1. The working relationship
2. The ownership interests

Working on the Working Relationship

Usually the parties need to work out this issue between them. In deciding whether one or both spouses need to go, consider the skills they bring to the job (and what it would cost the company to replace the person) as well as the working relationships among the spouses and other company employees.

From the business perspective, the continued participation of both spouses following divorce may be desirable. This is so where each person brings unique talents and abilities to the company.

But where personal animosity would disrupt the business operations, poisoning the workplace and jeopardizing the continued success of the company, then one spouse should withdraw. Whichever type of property law applies, it's generally best to work out a gradual withdrawal. This will give time for employees, customers, suppliers, and others to acclimate to the new dynamics.

If a spouse must go, then work out arrangements that will not be detrimental to the business. You don't want to create a void that can undermine the continued success of the company. For example, in one ice cream and sandwich shop, a sister and her husband worked for the owners, her brother, and his wife. When the sister left her husband, it was agreed that she leave the shop as well and find other employment. The brother-in-law was the shop's manager and indispensable to the business. He got on well with the owners and could continue to work well with other employees.

Working Out the Ownership Interests

Parties can certainly make any property settlements they can agree to at the time of divorce. But if they fail to reach an agreement, it's up to a court to divide up the couple's property, which may include ownership interests in a family business. A judge may determine that each spouse is entitled to a share of the business (or assets equivalent to the value of that share). Generally, the size of that share depends on the length of the marriage, the state in which the couple resides, and the contributions of the spouses to the business. State laws on property distributions fall into three main categories:

- *Equitable distribution.* Unless the parties agree to their own property settlement, a judge will decide how much of the couple's property each is entitled to. This may be an equal share or some other portion of assets. Usually, the longer the marriage, the greater the share of a nonworking spouse in the assets created by the other spouse during the marriage.

- *Equal division.* Again, unless the parties agree to their own property settlement, a judge will order that the couple's property be divided equally between them. This doesn't necessarily mean that if a business is involved, the interest in the business must be split between the parties. But it does mean that each would be entitled to property of equal value. So if one spouse kept the business interest, the other would receive different but equally valued property.

- *Community property.* Under community property law, property acquired during the marriage generally is viewed as community

---

Caution

Property owned before the marriage usually remains separate property and does not become community property. However, in some states, any appreciation of separate property during the marriage is treated as community property. Business owners who lived or currently live in a community property state should consult with an attorney familiar with the laws of the applicable state to determine their potential exposure under community property rules.

property. In effect, each owns half of the community property, regardless of who holds title to such property. So, for example, if one spouse starts a business during the marriage, the other spouse has a community property interest in the business even though title is held by only the owner-spouse. The following states have community property laws: Arizona, California, Idaho, Louisiana, Nevada, New Mexico, Texas, Washington, and Wisconsin.

Structuring Property Settlements Involving Family Business

Where one or both spouses have an ownership interest in a family business, a property settlement must be devised to resolve this ownership. The property settlement depends on their ownership interests.

Where One Spouse Has a Business Interest

If the nonowner spouse is entitled to a share in the business but doesn't want to give up any ownership interest, then the nonowner spouse becomes entitled to property of equal value. Unless the owner-spouse has other assets of equal value, then a structured settlement must be worked out to pay off a set amount over time. Generally the amount required is keyed to the length of the marriage (the longer the marriage, the greater the share payable to the nonowner spouse). In structuring a settlement, keep these points in mind:

- Property settlements generally are not currently taxable. But certain aspects can produce income to one spouse or the other. The tax treatment of property settlements is explained later in the chapter.

- An interest rate payable on outstanding amounts should be set. In New York, for example, there is a statutory rate of 9 percent.

- Property settlements, unlike alimony and maintenance awards, are dischargeable in bankruptcy. To protect against this possibility, which would wipe out the property settlement, the attorney for the nonowner spouse may insist that language be included in the agreement suggesting that the property settlement was relied upon to supplement alimony or child support. Such language may be effective in preventing a discharge.

Where Both Spouses Own a Business Together

The property settlement in this instance depends on what the parties want to accomplish. Each may simply retain his or her share of the business and go on as before the divorce. This was the case with the co-owners of the transportation company mentioned earlier in this chapter.

Or the couple may decide to go their separate ways. In this case one spouse may choose to buy out the interest of the other. If the business is incorporated, there are alternative ways of buying out the interest of a departing spouse. But care must be taken to avoid adverse tax results. Arranging a redemption of corporate stock is discussed later in this chapter.

Tax Treatment of Property Settlements

In deciding how to split up ownership interests in a family business, the tax rules for property settlements must be kept in mind. Generally, property settlements are not taxable events. Couples can divide up their assets without causing immediate taxation. However, the spouse receiving property takes the other spouse's basis for tax purposes. This means that when such property is eventually sold, the recipient-spouse will report gain or loss as determined by the other spouse's basis.

This means it's essential to factor in the tax cost to the recipient-spouse. In the example, Suzie does not really receive property worth $60X because she simultaneously receives a tax liability of $10X ($50X gain times 20 percent tax on capital gain). In effect, she receives only $50X worth of property ($60X value less $10X potential tax liability).

While the property settlement itself is not taxable, certain aspects of the settlement may be taxable. For example, if one spouse pays the other a property settlement in installments with interest, the interest is currently taxable to the recipient-spouse (even though the underlying installments are not).

If the settlement involves items that have not yet been taxed, then the recipient-spouse will be taxed on those items. For example, if one spouse is given a share of the other spouse's IRA, the recipient-spouse will owe income tax on funds in the IRA when they are distributed to him/her.

Example

Suzie and Sam split up after eight years of marriage. Sam owned 100 percent of a contracting business for which Suzie worked as estimator/bookkeeper. He also owned a stock portfolio of equal value to the business. Assume that Sam wants to retain ownership of his business, so Suzie gets the portfolio in a property settlement. Sam paid $10X for that portfolio. At the time of the divorce, it's worth $60X. If Suzie sells the portfolio at that time, she has a $50X capital gain ($60X minus $10X basis).

> **Caution**
>
> If a couple are co-owners of an S corporation and have suspended losses because their basis is insufficient to allow a current deduction for those losses, a divorce can wipe those losses out. For example, if one spouse transfers shares to the other, the transferor-spouse cannot take the suspended losses because of insufficient basis. And the transferee-spouse cannot take those losses because the losses belong only to the original shareholder. The losses are forfeited on a transfer even though made incidental to divorce.

Legal Fees

A spouse who incurs legal fees to protect a business interest in a divorce generally cannot deduct those fees. They are considered nondeductible personal expenses even though they relate to a business interest. The only portion of legal fees that may be deductible is the portion that relates to the receipt of tax advice.

If the business pays legal fees to resist one spouse's attempt to take it over during the course of a divorce, the business can deduct its expenses. For example, where one spouse tied up the assets of the business while the other spouse lay in a hospital bed, the legal fees that the business paid to extricate its assets during the couple's divorce proceedings were deductible by the company.

Arranging Redemptions of Corporate Stock

What happens when both spouses own shares in a family business? Often the corporation may have the funds (or the borrowing ability to raise the funds) to acquire a spouse's interest. In contrast, the other spouse may lack such economic ability. If spouses are 50/50 owners of a corporation, and if the corporation redeems the shares of one spouse, then the other becomes the sole shareholder. In divorce, redemptions may be considered as a way of buying out the interest of one spouse. But if a redemption is used to acquire one spouse's shares in the corporation, care must be used to avoid adverse tax consequences. Potential adverse consequences include:

- Taxable income to the spouse whose shares are redeemed. Instead of the usual tax-free treatment that results in a property settlement incidental to divorce, the spouse may be subject to capital gains on the shares redeemed.
- Dividend treatment to the spouse who remains as the sole shareholder of the corporation.

Tax Treatment of the Spouse Whose Shares Are Redeemed

The tax treatment isn't clear. Courts are currently split on whether the spouse is taxable on the redemption of his or her shares by the corporation. Some view the transaction as made on behalf of the remaining shareholder. This makes the transaction nontaxable to the spouse whose shares are redeemed. For example, when coshareholders of a motor parts company divorced, the wife was ordered to sell all her stock to her husband or at his election to the corporation. He then elected to have the corporation purchase the wife's stock, which it did for a cash payment plus a promissory note for the balance. The wife did not report any income from the transaction. The Tax Court decided that the wife had no income from the transaction because the sale to the company was made on behalf of her husband (i.e., to benefit him).

In a similar case involving a pottery business that had been owned 51 percent by the husband, 47 percent by the wife and 2 percent by their child, the redemption of the wife's stock following the couple's divorce was also treated as a nontaxable event. Under the terms of their divorce, the corporation was obligated to redeem her shares, and the husband unconditionally guaranteed the corporation's installment payments to the wife because doing so was a "direct interest, benefit, and advantage" to him. This court even allowed the imputed interest on the installment payments (the portion of the installment payments that would otherwise be treated as interest rather than capital gains) to receive nontaxable treatment as well.

However, the IRS and some courts view the redemption as a taxable transaction even though it is done pursuant to a divorce decree. For example, in one family business, a husband gave his wife stock in a property settlement. She was permitted to negotiate with the corporation to have her shares redeemed (if she needed to raise cash), which she chose to do. The husband was not a party to this negotiation. As a result, the redemption is not viewed as made on the husband's behalf, and so the wife is taxable on the redemption.

> **CAUTION**
>
> It is essential to discuss potential stock sales with a knowledgeable attorney. State law and tax rules may govern the tax results in your situation.

Tax Treatment of the Remaining Shareholder

If the divorce decree requires the spouse to purchase the other spouse's shares and the corporation helps out by redeeming them, then the remaining shareholder is treated as having received a constructive dividend (and is taxable on it). Why? Because the corporation satisfied the spouse's obligation, which put that spouse into the sole ownership position. The spouse whose shares are redeemed is viewed as any other creditor. So a payoff to the other spouse's creditor by the corporation is a taxable dividend.

It would seem that the key to tax treatment for the remaining spouse is whether there is a primary and unconditional obligation to acquire the other spouse's shares. If such obligation exists and the corporation satisfies it, then the spouse is taxable as a result.

Arranging Payouts from Company Retirement Plans and IRAs

After the couple's interest in the business and their home, assets in company retirement plans and IRAs may be their most significant assets. Care must be taken in giving a spouse an interest in these assets. If it's done incorrectly, then it may be considered a taxable distribution. It would then be immediately taxable and possibly subject to penalties.

Qualified Retirement Plans

If the family business maintains a qualified retirement plan, then a spouse may have amassed considerable assets in that plan. Under the terms of a property settlement, the other spouse may be entitled to a portion of those assets. In giving a spouse an interest in a company retirement plan, the settlement must be considered payable under a qualified domestic relations order (QDRO). If so, then the spouse isn't taxed on shifting benefits to the other spouse. And the other spouse isn't taxed until benefits are distributed from the plan. So the recipient-spouse can roll over newly acquired benefits to an IRA and defer income until benefits are withdrawn from the IRA.

For benefits to be treated as payable under a QDRO (and not immediately taxable to the participant-spouse), all of the following conditions must be satisfied:

- Payments must be made under a judgment, decree, or court order (including approval of a property settlement agreement).

Caution

The qualified status of the company's retirement plan can be called into question if distributions are made to a nonparticipant-spouse *other* than pursuant to a QDRO. If you are acting as plan administrator, it's your duty to make sure that the QDRO complies with the law so that you protect the qualified status of the plan.

- The amount of qualified benefits to be paid must be specified. This can be a dollar amount or a percentage of benefits.

- The number of payments or the period to which the order applies must be stated.

- The name and address of the recipient of benefits, referred to as the alternate payee, must be stated, as well as the address of the participant-spouse.

- Written notice must be given to the plan administrator.

Once the QDRO is in place, then benefits can be paid to the spouse designated as the alternate payee. Depending on the terms of the plan, these benefits may be payable immediately or delayed until a specified time, such as after the participant-spouse reaches age 50, or leaves the company, or reaches the early retirement age under the plan. If benefits can be payable immediately, the alternate payee can take a distribution and pay tax on the benefits or postpone tax by rolling the benefits over to an IRA.

Preemptive Steps for Protecting Business Interests

No one marries with the anticipation that the union will break up later on. But if people go in with their eyes wide open, they can take steps that will minimize wrangling over business interests and other property if there is a divorce. Obviously, the best time to make plans is before the marriage takes place. But even if that has already happened, strategies are available to protect business interests in case of divorce.

Divorce can cripple a family business and wipe out a lifetime of work. But there are three main ways to plan ahead for the disposition of business interests in case of divorce:

1. Prenuptial agreements.
2. Postnuptial agreements.
3. Buy-sell agreements.

Which type of agreement to use depends on the ownership interests of the parties and the stage of their relationship.

In some situations, none of these agreements may provide a satisfactory solution. The parties may be unwilling to sign prenuptial or postnuptial agreements. Or the terms of the agreements just never seem to be worked out, so nothing gets signed. In this case, other strategies, such as restrictions on stock transfers or the use of trusts to hold ownership interests, can be used to protect family business interests in case of divorce.

Prenuptial Agreements

Prenuptial agreements (also called antenuptial agreements) are contracts entered into before the marriage takes place. These agreements specify what happens in the event that the marriage doesn't work out. (It may also say what happens upon the death of one spouse.) The terms of these agreements supersede state laws on community property, equal division, or equitable distribution of property that otherwise govern property settlements following divorce. (The terms of these agreements also supersede state laws on intestacy—who inherits what if there is no will.) While the terms of the agreement aim to limit the interests of a divorcing spouse, having the agreement doesn't prevent the parties from agreeing to more generous terms if they actually divorce.

NOTE

There are no statistics available on the percentage of couples who opt for prenuptial agreements. They are more commonly used in second marriages than first marriages. However, they are gaining in popularity even in first marriages, especially where the parties each have interests in dot-coms or other high-tech companies.

There is no set format for prenuptial agreements. Instead, they can be tailored to individual needs. For people who have an interest in a family business, use of prenuptial agreements is important to ensure the continued ownership by family members only.

In order for the agreements to stand up in the event of divorce (or death), certain requirements must be met:

- Each party must be represented by a separate and independent attorney. This requirement ensures that each party understands the terms of the agreement, including any rights he or she may be giving up. It also avoids any claims of fraud, duress, coercion, or overreaching in having one party agree to the terms.

- The terms of the agreement must be fair, both at the time the agreement is made as well as when it becomes effective (on divorce, separation, etc.). For example, a court will not enforce a prenuptial agreement that would create the possibility that one party might need public assistance.

- The terms of the agreement cannot promote divorce. In other words, one party cannot be given such an attractive payout on divorce that it would be financially better to divorce than to stay married.

- There must be full and complete financial disclosure by both parties to the agreement. This means that each person must list all sources of income, assets (and value), liabilities, and any other information that can affect a person's financial situation. This full disclosure requirement ensures that each party is making an informed decision.

> **TIP**
>
> If one party currently has a business interest, that interest must be properly valued in the prenuptial agreement. In order to do this, it is necessary to get an appraisal of the business. Finding a qualified appraiser is explained in Chapter 12.

Negotiations for the prenuptial agreement may require delicacy and tact. Where the family of one party pushes for an agreement in order to protect the family business, the other party may view the relationship as one of distrust. Generally, the terms of a prenuptial agreement should be worked out well before the marriage. Having one party sign on the dotted line moments before marching down the aisle may be viewed as coercion or overreaching. This action can effectively void the terms of the agreement.

TERMS OF THE PRENUPTIAL AGREEMENT

Where one party has (or expects to have) an interest in a family business, the agreement usually provides that the other party has no claim against that interest. Care must be taken to prevent the nonowner spouse from being viewed as having acquired an interest in the business during the marriage. A prenuptial agreement will provide full protection only if the agreement states that the business remains separate property even if the nonowner spouse provides help to the business or the other spouse. This help may be in the form of direct help to the business, such as working for the company, or it can be indirect help, such as providing homemaker services to enable the owner-spouse to run the company.

> **TIP**
>
> Where the main reason for a prenuptial agreement is protection of the family business, the parties may want to limit the agreement to cover only this issue. The limited prenuptial agreement may satisfy family members while creating a more general partnership between the couple with respect to their other assets.

WHO SHOULD HAVE PRENUPTIAL AGREEMENTS?

In the past, only the Rockefellers and Vanderbilts used these agreements to protect vast family fortunes from potential fortune hunters. Today, they are increasingly popular among even those of modest means. In order to protect business interests, it's a good idea to have a prenuptial agreement if:

- You own a business (or an interest in one). In this way, your ownership interest is protected. The agreement must specify that this interest remains separate property even if the nonowner spouse provides direct or indirect help with the business.

- You plan to start a business. A business can create great wealth, even overnight in some cases. Struggling newlyweds may find this hard to grasp, but newly rich dot-com owners may find out too late the importance of protecting their business ownership interest.

- You are the child of a business owner. You may not own an interest in the business now, but you may become an owner someday. If you (or your parent) want this yet-to-be-acquired interest protected, you need to think ahead and obtain protection through a prenuptial agreement.

AMENDING PRENUPTIAL AGREEMENTS

Generally, the terms of an agreement can be changed after the marriage only if the same requirements for fairness and disclosure are met. This means each spouse is represented by counsel and there is a new financial disclosure.

Postnuptial Agreements

A spouse who did not sign a prenuptial agreement may decide later on to have a postnuptial agreement. As the name implies, a postnuptial agreement is a contract made after a couple has married. Like a prenuptial agreement, a postnuptial agreement spells out what happens to a couple's property in the event of divorce (and/or death). The reason for wanting such an agreement may be that one spouse has now started a business that may prove or has already proved to be successful and wants to protect that interest in case of divorce. For example, two computer nerds married right out of college and didn't have a dime between them. But they had a great idea for an Internet business that is now poised to go public. This couple may become multimillionaires in no time. But what happens if they should someday divorce? Do they both stay with the company? Do they continue their ownership interests? This couple may want to spell out what happens to them and their company in case of divorce.

Since postnuptial agreements are relatively new and certainly not common, only a few states have laws on how to treat them. Each state's requirements for postnuptial agreements and their views on them may be different.

- Florida and New York enforce postnuptial agreements if they meet the same requirements as prenuptial agreements (i.e., the parties are represented by separate counsel, the terms of the agreement are basically fair, and there is full disclosure of financial information).
- Louisiana and North Carolina require court approval of postnuptial agreements for them to be enforceable.
- Hawaii and New Jersey also require court approval of postnuptial agreements. Under the law in these states, the agreements must be fair *both* at the time they are written *and* at the time of divorce.

Buy-Sell Agreements

Buy-sell agreements are contracts between owners or between owners and their company to spell out what happens with ownership interests under certain circumstances. These events usually include death, retirement, disability, and bankruptcy. However, where spouses co-own a business, divorce may be treated as an event covered by the agreement.

For example, a buy-sell agreement involving spouses may stipulate that in case of divorce, one spouse is required to sell his or her interest in the business to the other. A buy-sell agreement, combined with restriction on stock, can also be used where only one spouse is an owner in the business. If a divorce settlement awards the nonowner spouse shares in the company, the other may have the right to acquire the shares under the terms of a buy-sell agreement.

The buy-sell agreement should provide a means for arriving at the value of that interest. For example, the agreement can require an independent appraisal of the business at the time of divorce and base the buyout on that value. Or the agreement may include a formula for determining value, such as a multiple of book value or business net earnings.

Finally, the buy-sell agreement should detail how the buyout will work. For example, it may provide that the buyout be made in installments over a set number of years. Or the buyout may have to be made in a lump sum, requiring the acquiring spouse

CAUTION

Where spouses also have a prenuptial agreement, be sure to coordinate the terms of the buy-sell agreement. If the terms of the two agreements conflict, the result may be uncertainty for the spouses and the business. They'll also incur added time and legal fees to resolve the conflict.

to take a loan or otherwise come up with the necessary cash to meet the terms of the buyout.

Buy-sell agreements are discussed in greater detail in Chapter 12.

Other Strategies

If you own shares in a corporation, that ownership interest can be protected without relying on separate agreements. Here are some alternative ways of protecting interests in a family business from passing to outsiders.

RESTRICTIONS ON TRANSFERABILITY

Restrictions on transferability can be placed on the stock to keep it from being transferred to a spouse during a divorce. Of course, the spouse may be entitled to property of equal value. But the value of stock subject to restrictions is less than such stock without restrictions.

TRUSTS

One spouse's interest in a family business can be protected if that interest is owned by a trust. For example, one father who owned a magazine publishing company wanted to bring his sons into the business. But he feared that in the event of divorce his daughters-in-law would receive a portion of his sons' interests, something he did not want to happen. Since his sons didn't have prenuptial agreements (and didn't want to ask their wives to sign postnuptial agreements), the father put the sons' interests into a trust. The trust contained a "spendthrift provision" barring the transfer of any trust assets to satisfy the claims by creditors of the trust beneficiaries (the sons). In this context, the daughters-in-law were potential creditors.

> **CAUTION**
>
> One spouse cannot create a trust to shield his or her assets from the other spouse. This self-serving trust is still fair game in case of divorce.

For this strategy to be successful, the beneficiaries cannot be given any control over the trust. For example, they cannot be given the power to make distributions from the trust.

Of course, in using a trust approach, there is a trade-off to be considered. The family business is protected from outside parties, but the beneficiaries do not have direct ownership of the company.

If a parent wants to use this strategy, it is advisable to discuss the situation with children before taking any action.

PART 3

Selling or Transferring a Family Business

CHAPTER 11

Getting Out Gracefully

Like a good guest who knows not to overstay his or her welcome, an owner in a family business should also know when it's time to leave. And the owner should exit in such a way as not to disrupt the business or sow the seeds of potential future conflict within the family. Unfortunately, most family businesses aren't prepared for a change in leadership. No plans have been made. No person has been selected to fill the shoes of a departing owner.

This chapter focuses on one aspect of succession planning—the change in leadership. You'll see what this change in leadership can mean to the family and to the business. This chapter discusses the events that can trigger a departure of a family member from the business and what steps to take if death of an owner occurs when no succession plans have been made. It discusses what retirement means to the business from a management perspective as well as retirement income planning for a departing owner. And it explains planning ideas for the disability of an owner.

The other aspect of succession planning—a change in ownership—is covered in the balance of this book.

Overview of Succession Planning

Kings and queens have succession plans in place. By custom or law, the oldest son or child becomes the ruler when the parent abdicates or dies. There isn't much else to plan for other than to have children and hope that the oldest one is capable of handling the position to which he or she is born.

In the past, even family businesses, by custom, had automatic succession plans in place. Under the custom of primogeniture, the oldest son succeeded to everything that the father owned. So when the father died, the son took over the business. This was so without regard to this child's abilities to handle the company's helm or the wants or abilities of the other children.

But in family businesses today, things are more complicated. The old custom of primogeniture is no longer routinely followed. Today, there may be several children involved in a family business. Daughters as well as sons may be active participants. Each child may have different aptitudes, training, experience, and goals.

NOTE

Within the next five years it's been estimated that 43 percent of family businesses will have a change in leadership. Yet one-third of these businesses with CEOs over the age of 60 are still without any succession plans.

Succession planning involves a twofold approach: planning for a change in the leadership of the company and planning for a change in ownership. These are two separate and distinct considerations. There can be a change in leadership without a change in ownership. And there may even be a change in ownership without a change in leadership. The changes in leadership and ownership may or may not occur at the same time. Of course, it's important to coordinate these two changes. (Planning for a change in ownership is discussed in Chapters 12 through 15.)

Some owners don't plan ever to leave the business. They'll die with their boots on and then let their children wrangle over leadership after they die.

Every family business that has been around for some time has its own story about departing founders. In one company, mom and dad, founders of a highly successful stationery company in New England, decided to retire to Florida and pass on the mantle of leadership to their two sons. In this story the older generation voluntarily left the business. Their children didn't have to force them out.

But in a Midwestern mining equipment company, there was a different story. Here the elderly father who founded the company just wouldn't go. He not only stopped contributing to daily operations, choosing instead merely to put in an appearance at the office, but he also disrupted things with his increasingly surly demeanor. His daughter, who was waiting in the wings to take the helm, had to nudge him out the door so she could direct the day-to-day operations of the company. She did this by bumping him upstairs to become chairman of the board that had just been created.

Unlike succession plans of royalty that are triggered solely by abdication or death, succession plans for a family business need to address a wide range of possibilities. Departure may be voluntary or involuntary. The older generation may depart because of retirement— voluntary or forced retirement. Or there may be a change because of other events, such as disability or death. Or there may even be a change because of divorce (discussed in Chapter 10).

If you're the senior family member, you generally can't be forced out because of age. Under a federal law called the Age Discrimination in Employment Act (ADEA), private companies engaged in commerce that have 20 or more employees cannot discriminate against workers age 40 and older (and state law may prohibit discrimination at any age). This means that if you're in this age category, you can't be fired or demoted on the basis of age.

However, the ADEA permits a company to adopt a mandatory retirement policy for an executive or high policy maker under certain conditions. A mandatory retirement policy for an executive or high policy maker does not violate the law if the person has held this position for two years before mandatory retirement at age 65 and is entitled to receive a nonforfeitable annual retirement benefit of at least $44,000. This benefit may be paid through a pension plan, profit-sharing plan, savings plan, deferred compensation plan, or any combination of plans. The $44,000 retirement benefit amount is a fixed dollar limit that is *not* adjusted annually for inflation.

Whether or not permissible, it's highly unusual for family businesses to fix any mandatory retirement. Indeed, with increased longevity, an increasing number of founders well into their 90s may continue to work and even head up their companies if they choose to do so.

Making Plans for a Change in Leadership

If you fail to make plans for a change in leadership, you're sowing the seeds of disaster that can wreck both the family and the business. Hurt feelings, distrust, and misunderstandings can tear the family apart. Lack of certainty as to who will be the head of the company and lack of adequate training for this person can undermine the business. Lack of adequate succession planning is the leading cause of failure of family businesses to endure. Remember that only about one-third survive past the first generation, and only between 5 percent or 10 percent to the third generation. Bottom line: You need to take steps to create a plan for succession.

Note

In an examination of a number of failures among family businesses, statistics show that nearly 48 percent failed after the founder's death because of inadequate succession planning. This compared with only a 16.4 percent failure rate where there had been a planned transition to a son or daughter after the founder's death and just 6.1 percent where the transition occurred upon the founder's retirement.

TIP

Some experts suggest that succession planning commence at least 10 years before the anticipated change in leadership. In practical terms, this would mean that planning should start when an owner is about 55 years old. But it can also start when children join the business. The owner may be younger or older than 55 at this time.

Who should initiate succession planning? There is no right answer. Certainly the current leader would be wise to start the planning process and is in the best position to act. But the impetus to commence planning can come from potential successors. The important thing to remember is to start planning and start early.

In a family business, even more than in other enterprises, the needs of all parties must be considered to avoid bad feelings among relatives and prevent disruptions in business operations. Do older members wish to stay or leave? Do younger members want control now? The sooner that family members address a change in leadership, the better off all parties will be.

Strategies for Developing Your Succession Plan

FIX A FRAMEWORK FOR THE PLAN

The older family member needs to make concrete plans for his or her departure. To do this, it's helpful to set both a time frame and an exit strategy. Leaving it to some vague time in the future ("when I feel like it," "when the time is right," or "not until I drop dead") can create frustration for younger members. And it can create chaos if there's a sudden death and no plans are in place. Departure plans include not only *when* to leave but also *who* will succeed to the leadership position. Generally there's a single child or other relative who assumes this role. But the duties of a company head can be split among children.

Departure by a senior member doesn't mean the end of his or her relationship with the business. An older member can adopt a spectrum of changes, the consequences of which are explained later in this chapter. Possible exit strategies include:

- *Full retirement.* Here the senior member stops working for the company altogether.
- *Semiretirement.* Here the senior member shifts the leadership role to someone else but continues to work for the company on a reduced schedule.
- *Full retirement with a consulting agreement.* Here the senior member no longer is an employee of the company. Instead, he or she provides assistance when needed.

NOTE

According to one survey, about 10 percent of family businesses are already using co-CEOs. Another 42 percent have coleadership under consideration for the next generation.

Each of these alternatives requires different planning for both the management of the business and the compensation to the departing senior. For example, if a senior member opts for full retirement, it can be problematic if he or she reappears regularly at the offices to offer unsolicited advice. Thus, the departure strategy should be clearly understood by all parties.

NAME A SUCCESSOR

Departing the company without picking a successor and providing adequate training for the person assuming the new role can create a management void. But how can a parent pick a successor from among his or her children? It's not an easy task and may require the wisdom of a Solomon. In some families there may be a natural heir—a child with the greatest leadership qualities. But in other families, there may be no obvious choice. More than one child may want the top spot and children may be in competition for it.

The parent should try to be objective in making a choice. Make a list of potential successors and then rank them according to their ability to do the job. This ranking should not be affected by gender of children or their order of birth, but should be based solely on their ability. Ability includes certain tangible qualities, such as training or education, experience in a leadership position, and intellectual capacity. But ability to be the head of a company also includes an important intangible quality: the ability to work well with the other relatives.

Discuss the choice of successor with all affected relatives. In some families, those who are not selected to head up the company may harbor bad feelings for both the parent who makes the selection and the new leader. The sooner these

TIP

In making plans, it may become apparent that no child is capable—now or ever—of assuming the leadership position. A departing leader may have to turn to someone outside the family in order to assure the continued life of the company. Nonfamily CEOs are discussed in Chapter 3.

feelings can be aired, the easier it will be to resolve potential conflicts. For example, a disappointed office seeker may decide to leave the company, and the company will need to fill the vacancy.

GO SLOW

In most cases, there's no need to make swift changes. Taking things slowly lets all the parties have input into the process. It also lets all involved acclimate to the changes. And going slowly prevents disruptions within the operations of the company.

COMMUNICATE

The succession plan should not be a highly guarded secret by the departing leader. Instead, it should be a plan developed through input from all affected members. Make sure the intended successor wants the responsibility of leadership. Not everyone feels up to the task emotionally even though the person's skills would enable him or her to handle the job. Whether a child wants the top spot sometimes depends on the age of the heir apparent. If the proposed successor is too young (under the age of about 30) or too old (over the age of about 60), he or she just might not want to assume the leadership position. In such a case, a parent may have to rely on a second choice.

BE FLEXIBLE

The terms of the plan must be structured to withstand change. For example, the plan may name a certain child as successor. But in the interim, that child may suffer a disability or may choose to go off on his or her own to start up a dot-com company. The plan should allow for an alternate successor.

Similarly, the plan may have certain financial provisions for the departing owner. If the company suffers financial reverses, it may be impossible to fulfill these terms. Again, the plan should be designed to adapt to changing circumstances of the business.

BALANCE THE INTERESTS OF THE OWNER WITH THE NEEDS OF THE COMPANY

The plan should not be only a financial device to fill the pockets of the departing owner. It must consider the impact of any financial aspects on the business itself. If a payout is too burdensome to the company, it can cripple its chances for continued success.

GET PROFESSIONAL HELP

Some families can create and implement a succession plan with no problems. But other families may require the intervention of an outside person who is objective and can guide all of the relatives to a resolution. There are consultants who specialize in family succession planning. Check with the Service Corps of Retired Executives (SCORE) at 800-634-0245 or click on www.score.org. SCORE is an arm of the Small Business Administration that offers free advice on succession planning.

Or use the services of a private management firm specializing in succession planning. The cost of such assistance varies widely, so check on fees or charges up front.

A listing of university-based family business institutes providing help in succession planning may be found in Appendix A. Services offered through these institutes may include counseling, programs, and information.

And six states, including New York, currently offer subsidized succession planning. Check with your state's economic development department to find out if such services are available.

Owner's Death in the Absence of a Succession Plan

Death can come at any age. In one multimillion-dollar paper distribution company, the 39-year-old CEO drowned in a boating accident. Since he was so young, the company had not yet made plans for a successor. When death occurs and there's no succession plan in place, what happens to the management of the company? It all depends on how the company is run *before* the event of death.

Where other family members participate in day-to-day operations, there may be someone ready and able to fill the void created by an owner's death. One child, for example, may be a vice president who assumed the helm when the parent took extended vacations and can easily move up when the parent dies.

In selecting someone to head up the company under these circumstances, the same considerations as for normal succession planning apply. The person must be qualified in terms of experience, ability, training, and temperament.

Where an owner who dies suddenly without creating a succession plan had run the company with an iron hand, things can get dicey. Siblings may compete bitterly for the leadership position. A surviving spouse with no prior experience in the company who inherits an interest in the company may be thrust into a leadership position solely because of the new ownership interest. Such a leader may need to enroll the help of others—nonrelatives within the company or outside professionals—to keep things afloat.

The major difference between a normal succession plan and one necessitated by a sudden death is the need for speed. While a normal succession plan generally is developed slowly over time, the emergency succession plan must be implemented quickly. The company needs leadership immediately. Family members may need to put personal feelings on hold to ensure the survival of the company.

Planning for Full Retirement

When an older family member leaves the company, his or her presence within the company may be missed. In some family businesses, a founder may be the alter ego of the business, imprinting upon it a personality that has become identified with the company. A succession plan to replace the founder and fill the leadership position must be implemented at the time of the founder's retirement (if it has not already been implemented).

From the perspective of the departing owner, retirement can mean a time of great personal and financial changes. Where a founder was used to putting in 15-hour days, the person now needs to fill up the hours with other activities. Where a founder was calling the shots that affected the lives of many people, now the person needs to find other meaningful things to do.

CAUTION

In developing a retirement income plan for a departing owner, heed the words of many experts: "Never make parents dependent on their children." A departing owner should have sufficient retirement income to remain independent for the rest of his or her life.

Financially, a retiree may or may not require the same income to maintain the same lifestyle. While some experts suggest that retirement may necessitate an income of only about 80 percent of that in preretirement, individual experiences may differ. It all depends on what a person does in retirement. Activities such as travel and philanthropy may mean the same or even a greater income need.

In developing a succession plan, the retiree needs to consider his or her retirement income needs. Generally retirement income comes from four main sources:

- Social Security benefits.
- Retirement benefits from qualified retirement plans and IRAs.
- Personal investments and the income they produce.
- Deferred compensation.

A business owner may have yet another source of income: payouts from the sale of his or her interest in the business. This very important source of income is discussed in Chapters 12 and 14.

SOCIAL SECURITY BENEFITS

Social Security benefits generally will not provide a meaningful source of income. Benefits are limited even though a retiree has earned high salaries through a working career. This is because only a limited amount of salary or net earnings from self-employment is used annually to figure Social Security taxes. For example, in 2001, the taxable earnings limit is $80,400, regardless of actual earnings.

Social Security benefits are a lot like the old Woody Allen joke about the cuisine at a borscht belt resort: It tastes terrible—and such small portions! So not only are benefits not substantial, but they're subject to income tax if your income exceeds a certain amount. More specifically, benefits are included in income according to the following rules that depend on modified adjusted gross income (MAGI). This is essentially adjusted gross income plus interest from municipal bonds.

- When MAGI exceeds $32,000 on a joint return or $25,000 if single, then up to 50 percent of benefits are included in income.
- When MAGI exceeds $44,000 on a joint return, $34,000 if single, and zero if married filing separately, then up to 85 percent of benefits are included in income.

From a planning perspective, an owner will have some idea of the benefits to expect because the Social Security Administration (SSA) automatically provides this information. The SSA sends a benefits estimate statement three months before each birthday detailing an earnings record and providing an estimate of benefits at the earliest retirement age (age 62), the normal retirement age (currently 65 but increasing in stages to 67), and delayed retirement at age 70. Starting benefits at age 62 means you'll collect only a percentage of the benefits payable starting at the normal retirement age. If you delay collection until 70, you'll receive enhanced benefits. If you do not receive your benefits estimate statement, contact the SSA at 800-772-1213 or click on www.ssa.gov.

BENEFITS FROM QUALIFIED RETIREMENT PLANS AND IRAS

These plans are intended to provide a source of income during retirement years. How much income depends, of course, on the plans in-

Example

You're married and have MAGI on a joint return of $120,000. Your Social Security benefits for the year are $15,000. Of this amount $12,750 (85 percent of $15,700) are included in your income. If you're in the 31 percent bracket, this means that you'll have only $11,047 in spendable benefits ($15,000 less taxes of $3,953).

volved. Some owners have sizable benefits from company-sponsored qualified plans. Others may have little or nothing from such plans.

If the plan permits it, you can take all or some of your benefits, according to your needs, when you leave employment. Some plans, however, dictate payout provisions. These plans may pay out only a monthly amount and prohibit greater distributions.

Distributions generally are taxed as ordinary income. Only those who were born before 1936 and receive a lump-sum distribution can use 10-year averaging to figure the tax on the distribution.

There's no 10 percent early distribution penalty for distributions from qualified plans and IRAs after age $59\frac{1}{2}$. In fact, there's no early distribution penalty for distributions from a qualified retirement plan after age 55 if you "separate from service" (which means you no longer work for the company). And there's no such penalty if you take distributions at any age on account of disability.

> **TIP**
>
> If you have a Roth IRA, there are no required lifetime distributions. You need not take withdrawals from a Roth IRA at age $70\frac{1}{2}$ unless you want to or need to. Since earnings from a Roth IRA can be withdrawn tax free if certain conditions are met, it's advisable to leave money in this account to accumulate on a tax-free basis as long as possible.

From a tax perspective, it's generally advisable to take as little as possible from these plans, relying instead on income from other sources. This is because investments in these plans can continue to grow on a tax-deferred basis. But be sure to observe required minimum distribution rules in order to avoid a 50 percent penalty on underwithdrawals. Generally, minimum distributions must commence by April 1 of the year following the year in which you turn age $70\frac{1}{2}$. However, if you continue to work for your company past this age, you can postpone taking benefits from a qualified plan (but not from an IRA) until you actually retire. You can, of course, take more than the required minimum distribution at this time.

Planning for required minimum distributions is a highly complex undertaking. You need to balance your income needs now against your desire to provide benefits to a spouse, children, or others in the future. It's generally advisable to discuss distribution planning with a tax professional.

INCOME FROM PERSONAL INVESTMENTS

While you worked, your investments may have been geared toward appreciation. When you retire, you may need to reposition your portfolio to provide you with income. For example, if all your savings before retirement are in growth mutual funds, you may want to shift some money to bond funds for retirement income. Alternatively, you can continue to hold your growth mutual funds, selling a portion of your holdings in them to provide you with an income at a tax-favored rate. Gain on shares in stock mutual funds held long-term are taxed at no more than 20 percent compared with a tax of 39.6 percent on ordinary income such as interest from Treasury notes or dividends from preferred stock.

Like planning for distributions from retirement plans, income planning from personal investments is a complicated undertaking. It depends not only on market conditions, inflation, and changes in tax laws, but also on such intangibles as your tolerance for risk. Again, working with an investment planner or other professional may prove helpful in this matter.

DEFERRED COMPENSATION

If the company has a deferred compensation arrangement, a retiree may have an important source of retirement income. A deferred compensation plan allows a worker to defer receipt of current income to the future, typically at retirement. How income in a deferred compensation plan is tapped—in monthly payments or a lump sum—usually depends on the terms of the company's plan.

From a tax perspective, payments from a deferred compensation plan are fully taxable as ordinary income. This is because contributions to the plan are not taxed when made (i.e., tax was deferred), assuming the funds within the plan have remained subject to the claims of the company's general creditors. But for purposes of Social Security and Medicare taxes, distributions from deferred compensation plans are not taxable when they are paid out (they were already taxed when earned). Deferred compensation plans are discussed in greater detail in Chapter 8.

Planning for Semiretirement

For some individuals, slowing down may not mean moving on. These individuals may opt for semiretirement. Instead of stopping work completely, the person cuts back in the number of hours or days worked at the company. This cutback necessitates a change in leadership. A part timer usually can't be in control of daily operations.

The benefit of semiretirement from the business perspective is continuity of management. Customers, suppliers, and even employees can take comfort in the continued presence of a semiretired owner. Company history and experience are preserved.

Semiretirement also gives the younger generation a cushion when assuming leadership of the business. There's someone to fall back on if necessary. Hopefully there's guidance when needed (without meddling or interference). Certainly you want to avoid the problem created in one PR firm when the founder "retired" but never really relinquished control to his son. The frustration of the son in trying to run the company while warring with his father was so great that he thought he would have a nervous breakdown if things didn't change. Fortunately, the father eventually saw the stress created by his continued presence and reluctantly stopped putting his two cents' worth in on his days at the office.

For management purposes it's advisable to clearly delineate the function of the semiretiree. This will keep the person from trying to influence too many aspects of the business. For example, where a founder skilled in marketing opts for semiretirement, he or she may wish to limit responsibilities to this phase of the business. Or the founder may simply move upstairs to the boardroom as discussed earlier in this chapter. Fiscally, compensation to the semiretiree should reflect the reduced role in the company. The company may not be able to justify the same salary to a semiretiree that had been paid before the reduction in hours as being "reasonable." And if such salary isn't reasonable, it isn't deductible by the company.

From an income perspective, a semiretiree has the benefits of both a continued paycheck and other sources of retirement income. The only limitation may be that distributions from the company's qualified plan may be restricted before a full retirement. This depends on the terms of the qualified plan.

> **TIP**
>
> Working past age 65 won't reduce Social Security benefits. The earnings limit for those age 65 and older has been repealed. However, if you retire before age 65 and start to collect benefits, you'll lose $1 of benefits for each $2 over the earnings limit, which adjusts annually for inflation ($10,680 for 2001).

Planning for a Consulting Arrangement

In some businesses, both the company and the departing owner want to preserve a relationship. The company may need the counsel and advice of a seasoned owner. And the owner may be unable emotionally to sever all ties and instead wants to keep his or her hand in the pot. Where there is a mutual agreement for a continued association, an independent contractor relationship may fit the bill.

Generally, a departing owner may continue the relationship with the company through a consulting agreement. This agreement may call for regular consulting services or services on an as-needed basis.

In drafting a consulting agreement, the company can use the same type of agreements used in the past with outside consultants. Make sure that both the consultant and the new company leader fully understand the terms of the agreement. Be sure to address the following terms in a consulting agreement:

- *Work responsibility.* What areas will the retired owner-turned-consultant be operating in? Depending on the company, this may be a general responsibility or confined to a specific department or aspect of the business (for example, marketing or product development). The scope of authority should also be clearly delineated. While a retired owner may have wielded unfettered authority before the change in roles, he or she may now be limited to making suggestions rather than commanding actions.

- *Time commitment.* This depends on the scope of the agreement. It may require regular participation, such as 10 hours a week, or it may be limited to participation in certain projects. In this case, the consultant may put in long hours but only for a limited time.

- *Compensation.* This too depends on the situation. Payment for a consulting agreement can be structured on an annual retainer basis or pay-for-work (at a fixed hourly rate). Just make sure the pay is reasonable for the work performed in order to preserve a full deduction for payments made by the company.

Caution

Beware of excessive payments. Some parents who arrange for consulting agreements insist on enormous payments, viewing the money as compensation for past contributions to the business rather than for current performance. This view is flawed for two reasons. First, it often creates resentment from the children and other current owners who must work to meet these high obligations. Second, the payments may simply be unreasonable in light of what the company receives in exchange, and deductions for such payments may be partially disallowed.

- *Term of the agreement.* While some agreements may be open-ended and go on forever, most have set limits. It's customary to limit the agreement to one to three years. Then provide renewal options to extend the agreement if mutually desirable. It's also a good idea to give the consultant the option of terminating the agreement so he or she can bow out gracefully if no longer able to perform the terms of the agreement.

Planning for Disability

What would happen to your business if you should become disabled? Disability may be temporary—for example, where an injury caused by an accident or some minor illness lasts for just a while. Or disability can be permanent, such as disability resulting from a chronic illness or condition (for example, Alzheimer's or Parkinson's disease). Who would fill your shoes as head of the company? How will you receive an ongoing income if you need one?

You need to plan ahead for this possibility. If you fail to make plans and then become disabled, your family will have to go to court to obtain authority to manage your business and your other financial assets. This judicial process entails both time and money. If you make plans now for disability, you can ensure that your business will operate without substantial disruption and your finances will be managed according to your wishes.

There are two main devices to use for the management of your business and your finances in case of disability:

- Durable power of attorney
- Trust

Using a Durable Power of Attorney

You can use a durable power of attorney to name someone, called an attorney-in-fact, to act on your behalf. A durable power of attorney is a written document delegating certain powers to your attorney-in-fact. It's called a *durable* power of attorney because it remains effective even though you, the principal, become disabled.

Attorney-in-fact is a person named in a power of attorney to act as agent on behalf of the principal, the person signing the document. The agent does not have to be an attorney.

The durable power of attorney can be effective immediately upon signing. It's simply not used until the need arises. Or, in a number of states, you can use a springing durable power of attorney. As the name

implies, the power springs into effect upon the occurrence of an event such as disability. The document or state law defines the terms and conditions
for the springing durable power of attorney to take
effect.

NAMING A POWER OF ATTORNEY

Just about anyone over the age of 18 can act as
your agent. (The rules may differ slightly from
state to state.) However, since you want this person to handle your business affairs, you need to
name someone capable of handling this responsibility. It may be a spouse or an offspring who
works in your company. In keeping with a succession plan, it may be advisable to name your successor to act as your agent if you're disabled.

You can name two people to act as your agents.
In doing so, you can mandate that all actions require unanimity by your agents (sometimes re-
ferred to as joint and several action). Or you can give them the
authority to act alone. For example, one agent can vote your shares
of stock at company board meetings while your other agent makes investment decisions for your holdings.

Generally, the person you name as agent isn't compensated for his
or her actions. But where the agent's job includes management of
the company, you can and should provide for compensation.

Durable powers of attorney are available in preprinted form from
most stationery stores. However, since you want to give authority over
the management of your business, it's a better idea to have an attorney
draft a power of attorney tailored to your needs. The cost for preparing
a durable power of attorney is minimal. The attorney can make sure
that the form complies with state law. And if you maintain homes in
more than one state—for example, you work and have a main home in
New Jersey and a winter vacation home in Florida—it's advisable to
have powers drawn up in both states to avoid any problems with asset
management in both localities.

> **CAUTION**
>
> There are no checks or balances on the actions of your agent named in a power of attorney. The actions of the agent aren't reviewed by a court, and the agent isn't required to account for spending or other activities. Therefore, it's essential that you name someone who is not only capable of handling your business and financial matters but who is also completely trustworthy.

Using Trusts for Asset Management

Instead of, or in addition to, a durable power of attorney, you can
use a trust for asset management in case of disability. The trust can
be funded (by placing assets in it) or unfunded. If the trust is unfunded, you need a durable power of attorney to give an agent the
authority to shift assets into the trust in the event of disability.

The trust can be revocable, allowing you to cancel the trust and recoup the property you placed in it. Or the trust can be irrevocable so that once you transfer your ownership interest to the trust you no longer have control over it. A revocable trust becomes irrevocable upon incapacity. Incapacity is different from disability. You are incapacitated if you lack the legal ability to understand what's going on and to make decisions. Disability, such as blindness, may merely prevent you from going to and from work each day. In such a case you may need assistance with handling your finances but you're still legally competent to control the trust.

The person who governs the trust is called a trustee. Again, you may have one trustee or multiple trustees. If you have more than one trustee you can empower them to act alone or require concerted action. A trustee can be an individual, such as a spouse or adult child. Or it can be a trust department in a bank experienced in acting in this capacity. Or you can use a combination of a relative and a trust department. It's generally assumed that a relative may be more sensitive to your needs, while a trust department may be more competent to handle money. By using both parties as trustees, you get the best of both worlds.

A trustee may or may not receive compensation (obviously a trust department won't accept the position without adequate compensation). State law provides for a fee structure for a trustee. However, a trustee may accept appointment under the terms of a trust that conditions appointment on the waiver of such fees.

> **TIP**
>
> **Work with a knowledgeable attorney to structure the trust arrangement to meet your needs. The attorney you use for this purpose may not be the same one you use for company business. Attorney's fees for the creation of a trust typically average a few thousand dollars.**

Income Planning for Disability

If you become disabled and can't work for your business, what happens to your income? In some companies, your salary can continue for some time, but may not be paid indefinitely. If you don't have the resources to meet your financial needs if your paycheck stops, then consider your options.

COMPANY PLAN FOR DISABILITY PENSIONS

Your company can set up a plan to pay benefits in case of severe permanent physical injuries. Benefits payable under such a plan are tax free to you. The plan must be nondiscriminatory, which means the plan must cover rank-and-file employees as well as family members and other owners who work for the company. The plan can be part of a profit-sharing plan as long as it clearly provides that benefits are payable because of injury and not because of longevity with the company. The plan should include a schedule of payments geared to different types of injuries or conditions.

If the company has a disability plan that is discriminatory or provides payments for other than severe disability, then benefits are taxable to you. If you're under the minimum retirement age set by the plan, you report the benefits as salary. If you've reached that minimum retirement age, you report the benefits as pension income. Whether benefits are reported as income or as a pension, taxwise things come out the same.

RETIREMENT BENEFITS

If you have a qualified retirement plan and/or IRAs, you may tap into these resources to provide you with an income. You may take distributions penalty-free on account of disability even if you're under age 59 ½. This exception to the 10 percent early distribution penalty applies for someone who is essentially totally and permanently disabled. The definition of disability follows the strict Social Security definition explained later.

DISABILITY INSURANCE

Consider carrying private disability insurance to provide a monthly income in case of disability. Disability policies are sold by many major insurance carriers directly to you or the company. Disability policies are also available through various trade associations and professional groups.

Your business may offer disability coverage as a benefit to its employees. Or it can increase your pay to allow you to buy your coverage personally. In deciding whether to pay for coverage yourself or have such coverage paid by the company, consider the following tax treatment of benefits:

- If you pay the premiums, then benefits paid under the disability policy are tax free.
- If the company pays the premiums and this fringe benefit is tax free, you are taxable on benefits paid under the disability policy.

Regardless of who pays the premiums, in selecting a policy be sure to evaluate the terms of coverage. The key thing to check for is the definition of disability provided under the policy. The best (but most expensive) policies will pay benefits if you are unable to perform your current job. Some policies will pay benefits only if you are totally and permanently disabled, which means you can't perform any substantial gainful activity.

TIP

Buy the best policy you can afford. To help you make this policy affordable, you can cut your premiums by opting for a longer exclusion period (the time before which benefits are paid). For example, instead of a 30-day exclusion period, consider a 90-day or 180-day exclusion period.

Also consider how long the policy should pay benefits. For example, it may pay benefits for up to five years. Or it may continue to pay benefits until the normal age of retirement for Social Security (currently age 65, but increasing in stages to age 67). Obviously, the longer the potential coverage, the higher the premiums.

Generally, private insurance policies coordinate their benefits with Social Security benefits paid on account of disability. For example, benefits under a policy may be reduced to the extent of Social Security disability benefits received.

SOCIAL SECURITY DISABILITY BENEFITS

If you become disabled before the normal retirement age for Social Security, you may qualify for benefits. Assuming you've worked long enough, you qualify if you meet a strict standard of disability. This is defined as the inability to engage in any substantial gainful activity by reason of any medically determinable physical or mental impairment that can be expected to result in death or which has lasted or can be expected to last for a continuous period of not less than 12 months. "Substantial gainful activity" means earnings of $500 a month (or $1,000 if legally blind). So even if a medical condition prevents you from being CEO, you may not qualify for Social Security disability benefits if you can still earn a living (even part-time). Essentially you must be totally and permanently disabled to qualify for Social Security disability benefits.

TIP

If you qualify for Social Security disability benefits, you are entitled to Medicare health insurance after two years of disability benefits. While the Social Security benefits may not be significant, it pays to apply if you're eligible for them to lock in your right to Medicare before age 65.

If you do meet the strict definition of disability, you can receive Social Security disability benefits that are figured in much the same way as retirement benefits. (They're taxable in the same way as Social Security retirement benefits.) However, no Social Security disability benefits are paid for the first five months of disability. Once you satisfy this five-month waiting period, then you can recoup benefits for up to 12 months before the month you filed your claim ("back payments"). And your spouse may be entitled to benefits because of your disability. Even so, these benefits are hardly likely to replace all the income you earned as head of your company.

CHAPTER 12

Buy-Sell Agreements for Lifetime and Death Transfers

Succession planning has two main components: planning for a change in leadership and planning for a change in ownership. One way to ensure an orderly change in ownership is with a device called a buy-sell agreement. The use of this device is especially important in a family business to keep control within the family by preventing outsiders from acquiring an interest in the company and to avoid internal disputes among owners and their families. Don't assume that in a family business the interests of a departing owner will automatically stay within the family. Action must be taken to ensure that the interests won't pass to outsiders.

This chapter explains what buy-sell agreements are all about and how they operate. It suggests ways in which to fix the value of a business interest under a buy-sell agreement. It also suggests ways to provide the funds required under the terms of a buy-sell agreement to acquire the departing owner's interest. Finally, this chapter explains the tax ramifications to the parties in a buy-sell agreement.

Overview of Buy-Sell Agreements

A buy-sell agreement is a written contract for the purchase of an owner's interest in a business upon the occurrence of an event. The

TIP

Instead of using a buy-sell agreement to restrict transfers to outsiders, other types of agreements among owners may be used. These other agreements include a partnership agreement or a shareholder agreement.

death of an owner would always be a triggering event. But the triggering event may also be an owner's retirement, disability, or even personal bankruptcy.

There are several reasons for using a buy-sell agreement in a family business:

- *Continuing the business.* The failure to provide continuity for ownership of the business following death or other departure of an owner can leave the business high and dry, forcing it to fold.

- *Providing a ready market for a departing owner's interest.* Having a ready market puts cash into the hands of the departing owner or his or her family upon the owner's death.

- *Restricting transfers of interests to nonfamily members.* This prevents outsiders from gaining an ownership foothold. A family business won't remain as such if interests pass to outsiders, something that won't happen under the terms of a buy-sell agreement.

- *Fixing the value of interests in a family business.* This provides certainty for the buyout amount as well as potentially fixing the value of a deceased owner's interest for estate tax purposes.

- *Providing funding to meet purchase requirements.* This ensures that the agreement won't be merely a hollow promise but will, in fact, allow the purchase to proceed according to plan.

Continuation of the Business

When an owner dies, the business may crumble. Or it may pass into the hands of outsiders. A buy-sell agreement ensures that the business will continue and who will own it.

> **Example**
>
> Assume a contracting business is owned equally by three brothers and there's no buy-sell agreement in place. When one of the brothers dies, his interest in the company passes to his wife under the terms of his will. Now the two brothers are in business with an in-law who may know little or nothing about the business. She may or may not even get along with her brothers-in-law. But she needs the income from the business that ownership entitles her to. And she may even want to sell her newly acquired interest to an outside third party.

Ready Market

Unless the company is a public corporation whose shares are traded on a national exchange, then there's no ready market for the departing owner's interest. This status leaves both the family and the business in a vulnerable position when an owner dies or otherwise leaves the company.

If the brothers in the example had been parties to a buy-sell agreement, then on the death of one of the brothers the other two could have acquired his interest. This would have fixed the value of the business interest, prevented a sale of the interest to an outsider, and given the brother's widow money for the interest in the company that she inherited. Usually the buy-sell agreement is tied to a funding mechanism (discussed later in this chapter) to ensure that there's sufficient cash to execute the terms of the agreement.

Restriction on Transfers to Outsiders

A buy-sell agreement prevents the sale of business interests to nonfamily members. In other words, a buy-sell agreement not only obligates certain parties to buy (creating the ready market), but it also requires the departing owner to sell *only* according to the terms of the buy-sell agreement.

Fixing Value

Obviously, a buyout under a buy-sell agreement is based on the value of the business at the time of sale. A buy-sell agreement provides a formula or other means for determining value. A buy-sell agreement can also be used to fix the value of the business for estate tax purposes when an owner dies. The value determined under the agreement for purposes of a sale of a deceased owner's interest will control for tax purposes only if such value is based on an independent appraisal at the time of the owner's death.

In an ideal world, a buy-sell agreement should be made when the business first starts out. Death and other unexpected events can happen at any time and at any age. However, if you do not yet have a buy-sell agreement, it's not too late for owners to make one.

TIP

If the business is an S corporation, a restriction on transfers to outsiders will protect the S election by preventing noneligible persons from becoming shareholders.

TIP

A buy-sell agreement isn't a do-it-yourself form that can simply be copied or downloaded from a resource. To accomplish the goals you intend, you must make sure that the agreement contains the terms and conditions best suited for your situation. Consult with a knowledgeable attorney for this purpose.

Funding Mechanism

This is discussed later in this chapter.

Types of Buy-Sell Agreements

Buy-sell agreements may be long or short, simple or complicated. But there are two basic types of buy-sell agreements:

1. Cross-purchase agreements
2. Redemption-type agreements

Cross-Purchase Agreements

The remaining owners have a right to buy the departing owner's interest before it's offered for sale to outsiders. The remaining owners' basis in their newly acquired interests is their cost basis. Cost basis is what they pay for their interests, which is the value on the date the interests are acquired. In effect, the basis of the interest they acquire is stepped up to the value at the time of their acquisition.

The main drawback to a cross-purchase agreement is the potentially unfair burden placed on younger owners who will have to pay higher insurance premiums on the lives of older owners. And if older owners have larger ownership interests, the cost of the insurance burden on younger owners is even greater. However, compensation to younger owners can be increased to provide them with additional cash for premium costs (assuming total compensation to them remains reasonable).

There are some other important drawbacks to a cross-purchase agreement:

- Owners who pay for insurance on the lives of co-owners can't deduct their premium payments.
- If owners personally experience financial difficulty, their creditors can reach the insurance they carry.

Example

Amy, Beth, and Carol are three sisters who are equal owners of the X Corporation. When Amy dies, Beth and Carol each acquire one-half of Amy's one-third interest in X. Thus, after the purchase, Beth and Carol are still equal co-owners of X, now with each owning 50 percent of the outstanding shares in the corporation.

- The agreement may need to be updated following the death or other departure of an owner.

Redemption-Type Agreements (Also Called Entity Agreements)

In this type of buy-sell agreement the business buys back the departing owner's interest before it's offered for sale to the remaining owners or to outsiders. Where the business is incorporated, the corporation redeems the departing owner's shares. Where the business is a partnership or limited liability company, the business simply buys back the departing owner's interest. The interests of the remaining owners are proportionately increased by virtue of the company's action. (It's not the number of shares owned but the proportion of those shares to total shares outstanding that matters.) In a redemption-type agreement, since the owners don't acquire the interest directly, they don't receive any step-up in basis for their interests in the business.

Besides not receiving a stepped-up basis if a redemption-type agreement is used, there are other tax drawbacks to consider:

- The corporation can't deduct its premium payments.
- There is a potential alternative minimum tax (AMT) problem where the agreement is funded by life insurance. This tax can result when the corporation receives life insurance proceeds. The buildup in the policy in excess of what the corporation paid in premiums is factored into the "adjusted current earnings" (ACE) calculation used to figure corporate AMT. However, there is no AMT concern if the corporation is an S corporation, because the S corporation isn't subject to AMT. And there's no AMT concern if the corporation is a "small" C corporation, because they are exempt from AMT. A small C corporation is one with average annual gross receipts of no more than $5 million for three years.
- If the company experiences financial difficulties, any permanent insurance owned by the business can be acquired by the com-

Example

The situation is the same as in the previous example, but instead of Beth and Carol buying out Amy's interest, X Corporation redeems Amy's shares. After the redemption, Beth and Carol are still equal co-owners, with each owning 50 percent of the outstanding shares in the corporation. But their basis in their shares remains unchanged.

TIP

A cross-purchase agreement is the favored alternative because of the tax and financial advantages it offers. However, when the number of owners who are parties to the agreement exceeds four, it's just too impractical to use this alternative, and the redemption-type agreement is usually used.

pany's creditors. If so, it would not be available to fund the buy-sell agreement when needed.

Owners may want to retain flexibility by allowing the purchaser to be *either* the remaining owners *or* the business, depending on circumstances at the time the interests need to be acquired. In a C corporation, there is a danger in adopting this approach unless the buy-sell agreement is carefully drafted. If the terms of the buy-sell agreement require the owners to buy out the departing owner's shares but the corporation redeems the departing owner's shares, this may be viewed as a constructive dividend to the remaining shareholders (taxable to them as ordinary income).

A better approach is to give the shareholders only a right of first refusal to acquire the shares of a departing owner rather than an obligation to buy the shares. Then make the corporation obligated to redeem if the remaining owners don't exercise their right of first refusal. In this way, dividend treatment can be avoided, since the owners aren't obligated to acquire the departing owner's shares, but flexibility is preserved.

The parties can structure a buy-sell agreement to include both a cross-purchase and redemption-type feature. This is sometimes called a hybrid agreement. In this instance, the owners acquire some of the departing owner's interest, while the company acquires the balance. The division of the obligation between the owners and the company can be made in any percentage desired. This hybrid approach spreads the cost of acquisition among more participants.

Valuation of a Business Interest

In a family business that's not a public corporation, it may be difficult to determine the true value of the business. Owners may not have the

Example

Alvin and Betty are each 50 percent shareholders in Y Inc. When Betty dies, Alvin is required under the terms of their buy-sell agreement to buy Betty's interest, valued at $5 million. But Alvin instead lets Y redeem Betty's shares. Since he is relieved of the liability to acquire her shares, he's treated as receiving a constructive dividend of $5 million. This can result in an income tax bill to Alvin of nearly $2 million.

vaguest idea of their company's worth. Ask two owners of the same company and you'd probably receive two different answers. Even owners familiar with the company books may inflate the value because of some perceived goodwill or other intangible affecting value.

However, it's necessary to fix some value so that the departing owner's interest can be priced and acquired. There are several alternatives for fixing value in a buy-sell agreement: appraisal, annual agreed-upon value, and formula clauses.

Appraisal

Perhaps the most accurate method for fixing value is to have an expert appraiser provide a value. The valuation is based on IRS guidelines on valuing closely held businesses. These guidelines, familiar to tax professionals and appraisers, take into account the book value and financial condition of the business, its earnings capacity and dividend-paying ability, goodwill and other intangibles, any recent sales of stock or interests in the business, and comparisons of market price to other similar companies. However, this method can be costly (depending on the business involved), usually running $5,000 and up. For example, an appraiser may charge up to $1,000 a day and estimate that the job will take 10 to 15 business days. It's advisable to negotiate a fee up front and limit the maximum fee for the job ($5,000, $10,000, or other appropriate amount).

One way to find an appraiser is to contact an appraisers' trade association (see Figure 12.1). Other sources of appraisers for a business are certified public accountants who may know of expert appraisers or perform such appraisals themselves. However, do not use the company's CPA for an appraisal under a buy-sell agreement (this relationship may not be considered independent).

Annual Agreed-Upon Value

Owners can set a value in the agreement and then agree to reset value each year. The benefit of this method is to avoid the expense of an appraisal. But the problem with this method is that owners often

FIGURE 12.1 Appraisers' Trade Associations

Trade Association	Phone Number	Web Site
American Society of Appraisers	800-272-8258	www.appraisers.org
Institute of Business Appraisers	561-732-3202	www.instbusapp.org
National Association of Certified Valuation Analysis	801-486-0600	www.nacva.com

forget to renegotiate value. In view of this shortcoming, a buy-sell agreement that uses an agreed-upon value method should also include a formula clause (discussed next). This formula clause would kick in as a default valuation method if the owners failed to adjust the value of the business.

Formula Clauses

Instead of relying on an appraisal, which is costly, or an agreement among owners, which may not be obtained as needed, you can use a formula clause to fix value. Using a formula clause eliminates the need to update value annually or pay for high appraisal fees. Typically these formula clauses are based on book value (or book value with certain adjustments) or a multiple of net earnings over some period of time (or weighted earnings), or some combination of book value and an earnings multiple. The type of formula depends in part on the industry in which the business operates. But be aware that using book value alone usually results in a valuation that is too low and using a multiple of net earnings of 8 to 10 times usually results in a valuation that is too high. If you choose to rely on a formula, then use one that produces a more accurate valuation.

NOTE

According to one source, only about 40 percent of business owners have buy-sell agreements or other continuation plans in place. And of these, only approximately 28 percent have funded plans.

Funding for Buy-Sell Agreement

Creating a mechanism to buy out a departing owner's interest is certainly important. But it's only half the battle. It's essential to provide a means of paying for that interest. Depending on the value of the business and the personal wealth of the owners, it's doubtful that there is sufficient cash to pay for that interest outright. So a funding mechanism is required to meet the buy-out obligation.

Caution

Where the valuation of a buy-sell agreement is used to fix the value of a deceased owner's interest for federal estate tax purposes, beware of IRS scrutiny. The IRS looks closely at valuations involving a family business. To protect the valuation, it is essential to use the services of an independent appraiser and not to rely on mechanical formula clauses that may distort the real value of the business.

Funding for a Buyout at Death

Typically, life insurance is used to meet buyback obligations by the company or the other owners where the triggering event is death. The proceeds of the policy are received by the policy owner tax free and then used to buy the departing owner's interest. *Who* owns the policy depends on the type of buy-sell agreement used:

- *Cross-purchase agreement.* An owner takes out a life insurance policy on each other owner. For example, if Company A has three owners, six life insurance policies are required. Each of the three owners must take out a policy on the lives of the other two (three owners times two policies).

- *Redemption-type agreement.* The company carries insurance on the life of each owner. So in the preceding example, Company A would carry three policies, one on the life of each owner (one company times three policies).

> **TIP**
>
> A cross-purchase agreement can be funded with a single policy on each owner. The policy in this case is held in trust or in escrow. This limits the number of required policies to the same as that under a redemption-type agreement.

TAX CONSEQUENCES OF OWNERSHIP

The payment of premiums, either by the owners under a cross-purchase agreement or by the business in a redemption-type agreement, isn't deductible. By the same token, the receipt of the proceeds isn't subject to income tax. However, in the case of a C corporation that isn't a small corporation exempt from the alternative minimum tax (AMT), receipt of the proceeds may factor in to the AMT and result in some tax cost to the business.

Where insurance proceeds are payable to the business, they increase the value of the company. This in turn can boost the owner's estate taxes because a higher value is placed on the deceased owner's interest in the business.

TYPE OF INSURANCE

Which type of insurance to use for this purchase depends on circumstances. Where it is reasonably expected that an owner will retire within a few years and sell his or her interest at that time (i.e., the owner won't die and the life insurance policy won't pay off), it may be financially better to use a term policy. The premiums are lower than on permanent insurance. But where owners are young and have a long time horizon, whole-life or other permanent insurance should be used. The cash value that builds up in permanent insurance can be used either to fund the buyback or to pay the premiums on the policy.

Another variable to consider is split-dollar life insurance. This type of insurance arrangement can allow for the greatest flexibility of the parties. The agreement does not have to commit the owners or the company to buy the departing owner's interest but instead leaves that decision until the actual time of death. But the funding is based on the assumption that the owners, rather than the company, will do the buyout. (Remember that if the business is incorporated, give the shareholders only a right of first refusal rather than an obligation to buy so that if the corporation winds up redeeming the shares it won't create a constructive dividend.) When an owner dies, the other owners collect the proceeds. If the company ultimately executes the buyback, the owners can lend the proceeds to the company. The loan should carry an appropriate rate of interest.

IMPACT OF CHANGES IN BUY-SELL AGREEMENTS

Since the business isn't static, it's advisable to update the buy-sell agreement as needed. It may require a new valuation. Or, if owners come and go, it may require a complete revision in the type of buyback method used. For example, the owners of a business may have made a simple cross-purchase agreement when there were only three of them. But as children entered the business, there are now six owners, making the cross-purchase agreement too cumbersome to manage. At this juncture, a redemption-type agreement is probably preferable. By the same token, a company that had numerous owners and a redemption-type agreement may wish to streamline the agreement to a cross-purchase agreement as the number of owners diminishes. Or the business may have experienced a change of organization. Two partners of a catering business had a cross-purchase agreement in place. When the business prospered and they incorporated, they needed to revise the agreement to reflect the change in the business's form of organization.

Obviously a change in the type of agreement necessitates a change in the ownership of life insurance policies. Be careful in changing the ownership of existing life insurance policies when the type of agreement is changed. Certain transfers of life insurance are considered "transfer for value" so that proceeds received under such policy are *not* tax free. Transfers to the following are not subject to the transfer-for-value rule and won't prevent tax-free treatment for proceeds:

- An insured
- A partner of the insured
- A partnership in which the insured is a partner
- A corporation in which the insured is a shareholder

Caution

There must be a business reason for forming the partnership or LLC other than to avoid the transfer-for-value rule. If this is the only reason, then the IRS will view the transaction as tax avoidance and disregard it. But the partnership or LLC may be created to own assets that are used by the corporation, such as an office building or factory. If a partnership or LLC is used to avoid the transfer-for-value rule, the entity should be set up well before the policy is transferred to avoid the suggestion of tax avoidance.

However, a transfer by a corporation to its shareholder is subject to the transfer-for-value rule and should be avoided. The rule applies equally to S and C corporations.

But there's a strategy that can be used to avoid the transfer-for-value rule when making a transfer by the corporation. Instead of having the corporation transfer the policy to its shareholders, use an interim owner. For example, the shareholders can form a partnership or a limited liability company. The corporation would then transfer the policy to the partnership or LLC, and the partnership or LLC, in turn, would transfer the policy to its partners/members (the shareholders). In this way, the shareholders end up owning the policy without triggering the transfer-for-value rule.

Funding for Buybacks Triggered by an Event Other Than Death

Life insurance generally isn't used for a buyback other than death. However, some carriers now sell disability buyback insurance that will pay proceeds in a lump sum upon the disability of an owner. Coverage runs to age 65. Typically the payout is delayed for one to two years following the onset of a disability to require proof of complete disability to perform the activities of your own occupation.

Example

Based on policy illustrations from one insurance company, a policy to fund a disability buyback obligation of $1 million (after 24 months of disability) for a healthy male owner who is currently 45 years old would cost about $4,000 annually until the owner turns age 50, when premiums for the duration of the policy would escalate to $8,800.

> ### Note
>
> Disability buyback insurance is more difficult to obtain and more costly than life insurance. It requires a more thorough health examination than for life insurance, and generally it costs two to three times as much as term life coverage of equal value (depending on your industry and the carrier providing the coverage). It will be written only after you prove the valuation of the business. Disability buyback insurance is currently offered by many major carriers, such as Guardian Life Insurance Company (www.glic.com), MassMutual Financial Group (www.massmutual.com), and UnumProvident Corporation (www.unum.com).

There is no type of insurance you can buy to fund a buyback necessitated by the retirement of an owner. In this case, the owners or the company (depending on the type of agreement in place) must come up with the cash to meet the buyback obligation. Some methods for ensuring sufficient cash are discussed later.

Of course, a buyback for any reason—death, disability, or retirement—can be structured as installment payments. This will provide the retired owner with an annual income without imposing an extraordinary strain on the buyers. Installment sale rules are explained in Chapter 14.

Another funding mechanism to consider is the creation of a sinking fund. Typically, the company accumulates its earnings for this purpose rather than distributing the earnings. If the business is incorporated, accumulating earnings for this purpose will avoid an accumulated earnings penalty.

> ### TIP
>
> A cross-purchase agreement should be structured to limit an owner's liability under the agreement. For example, consider limiting liability to the extent of life insurance acquired for the purpose of executing the terms of the agreement.

Yet another funding mechanism for corporations to consider is to let their qualified retirement plans (other than pension plans) be the purchaser of the stock of a departing owner. Such plans are permitted to own employer securities if the terms of the plans allow it. Pension plans, however, are subject to a 10 percent limit on the ownership of employer securities.

Owners who are parties to a cross-purchase agreement need to appreciate their liability exposure, especially under unfunded agreements. By contractually agreeing to purchase a departing owner's interest, they become personally liable to the extent of this obligation.

Tax Treatment of the Parties to a Buy-Sell Agreement

Signing buy-sell agreements has no immediate tax cost to the parties. But when the terms of the agreement are triggered—for example, an owner dies and his or her interest is acquired—there's a tax cost to consider. How the buy-sell agreement is structured can affect the tax ramifications for the parties.

Departing Owner

The income tax treatment to the departing owner depends on the terms of the agreement. Selling an interest in a business generally results in capital gain to the departing owner. As such, up to 20 percent of the proceeds are lost to federal income taxes.

The redemption of shares in the company can also qualify for capital gain treatment. However, such treatment isn't automatic. In a family-owned business, special care is required. A complete redemption of an owner's interest produces capital gain treatment, which is taxed up to 20 percent, rather than dividend treatment, which is taxed as ordinary income at rates up to 39.6 percent. But, under "attribution rules" that view an owner's holdings as including not only shares owned personally but also shares owned by certain family members (indirect ownership), a redemption of the owner's shares doesn't eliminate his or her indirect ownership interest. The IRS and Tax Court both hold the view that family attribution rules apply even if the redemption is necessitated by family hostility and the parties don't speak to each other.

But an owner can waive family attribution and obtain capital gain treatment if he or she does not act as an officer, director, or employee of the corporation for at least 10 years following the redemption. Being a creditor is no problem, so if the owner continues to have loans outstanding, this will not prevent capital gain treatment upon a redemption of shares.

Where an owner dies and stock included in his or her estate is redeemed to pay estate taxes, a portion of the redemption is treated as capital gains. This portion is limited to death taxes (federal and state) and administration expenses. To qualify for this tax treatment, the value of the stock must be more than 35 percent of the decedent's adjusted gross estate (the gross estate less administration expenses and losses). And the redemption must take place no later than 90 days after the end of the limitation period on assessment of estate tax (generally three years after the filing of the estate tax return, which is due nine months after the decedent's death). The rules on redemption to pay estate taxes is discussed more fully in Chapter 15.

> ### Tip
>
> The redemption of stock included in an owner's estate can qualify for capital gain treatment even if the proceeds aren't actually used to pay estate tax. In other words, the estate may use life insurance proceeds to pay estate tax and use the cash raised on a redemption to pay a bequest to the surviving spouse. All that is necessary for capital gain treatment is that the estate had death taxes and expenses and the other requirements for redemption are satisfied.

Where the buyback is made in installments, interest payable on the installments is ordinary income, subject to federal income tax at rates up to 39.6 percent.

Where the buyback is tied to a noncompete agreement that prevents the departing owner from starting or working for a competing business, a portion of the buyback may be viewed as ordinary income. There's no fixed allocation that must be made between the capital gain for the sale of the business interest and the ordinary income for the noncompete agreement.

Owners

Owners cannot deduct their payments to acquire the interest of a departing member. However, the basis in their ownership interest increases accordingly. For example, if each remaining owner pays $1 million to acquire a departing partner's interest, then that owner's basis in his or her partnership basis increases by $1 million. When that owner ultimately sells his or her interest, the added basis will minimize gain on that sale.

Corporation

A redemption by the corporation is a nondeductible expense of the business. And the corporation may be taxed on life insurance proceeds if it owns the policy. While such proceeds are free from income tax, they may be subject to the corporate alternative minimum tax (AMT). A C corporation that isn't classified as a small corporation (discussed earlier in this chapter) is potentially subjecting up to 75 percent of the proceeds to the AMT. Since the tax rate for the corporate AMT is 20 percent, this results in an effective tax rate of 15 percent (20 percent of 75 percent of the proceeds). A corporation may be a small corporation now, but it may not be a small corporation when it receives the proceeds in the future. There's no way to be certain.

Making a Buy-Sell Agreement Work

If the agreement is to produce its intended results—keeping control within existing owners while providing cash to the departing owner (or his/her estate)—the owner and the company need to coordinate their actions. Here are some strategies that can be used to ensure success:

- *Reflect the agreement in the minutes of your board meetings.* While the agreement is an independent contract, it is still advisable to acknowledge its terms in the minutes of your company board meetings. This will prevent misunderstandings from arising down the road.

- *Operate consistently with the terms of the agreement.* If one owner retires but isn't bought out according to the terms of the agreement, this can create a dangerous precedent. While the parties may be happy to let this owner continue his or her interest, the same may not be true with a departure by another owner. He or she may feel no obligation to honor the terms of the agreement and sell if the agreement had not previously been followed.

- *Make a notation on stock certificates.* It's a good idea to note on corporate stock certificates that the shares are subject to a restriction (for example, "The sale or transfer of this certificate is subject to a buy-sell agreement dated _____"). This legend on the stock certificate will prevent a sale of such stock to an outsider who is otherwise unaware of the existence of the buy-sell agreement.

- *Secure deferred payments.* If the agreement calls for a payout in installments (an arrangement most likely to be used upon retirement of an owner where insurance isn't available to pay for the buyout), be sure to secure the deferred payments by the interest that's being purchased. If the remaining owners or the company fail to make required payments, the departed owner can reacquire an interest.

- *Review the agreement periodically.* The agreement you currently operate under might have addressed your needs when drafted. But things change. And your agreement may need to be modified accordingly. Make it a regular practice to review your agreement (for example, at the last board meeting of each year). Also review the agreement following the departure of an owner.

CHAPTER 13

Giving the Business to Your Children and Grandchildren

If you own the business, there are compelling personal, financial, and tax reasons for giving your children and grandchildren an interest in it. You may simply want them to have a stake in the business, especially if they're working in it. You may want to give them an income without having to write a check to them. And looking ahead, you may want to take steps now that can save your estate substantial tax dollars down the road.

This chapter explains why you may want to transfer ownership interests to your children. It also explains the basic tax rules for making gifts to your children. It tells you how to make gifts of different types of business interests. And it provides some more sophisticated strategies for gifting, including the use of family limited partnerships and reorganizing corporations to facilitate gifting.

Reasons for Gifting Interests in Your Business

Gifts aren't limited to birthdays, anniversaries, or other special occasions. They can be made at any time and for a variety of reasons. You may have one reason or many for giving your children an interest in the business.

Bringing Involved Children into the Workings of the Company

If your children work in the business, you may want to reward them for their performance. You may want to let them gradually experience what it means to be an owner—attending board meetings, making decisions, looking over the books, and feeling the effects in their pocketbooks when the business grows or slows. By letting them test-drive the company from an owner's perspective while you're still in the car, you may get a better feel for which child should ultimately be in the driver's seat.

Deciding which child to give an interest to and how much of an interest to give can be a difficult decision. Some parents opt for making gifts of equal amounts to children who work for the business. But this decision may be no fairer than giving equal pay to children even though they perform at different levels for the company. You need to devise a gift program that best suits your particular situation.

The key to making any gift program work within a family business context is good communication. Discuss the reasons for your immediate steps and what your long-term gifting plans include.

In one appliance company, two talented children in their mid-30s wanted to take over the business from their father, the founder. He wasn't quite ready to step aside but recognized the need to develop a comprehensive succession plan and start implementing it. This plan included not only the designation of the child who would run the company but also plans for shifting ownership to both children. The problem was coordinating these two phases of succession planning— leadership and ownership. The father didn't believe that coleadership would work for his business (given the talents and abilities of his two children), but wanted each child to be an equal owner. The way he made this plan work was to hold a family conference at which he ex-

---

Caution

The timing of initiating a gifting program to children who work for the business is critical. While the timing depends in part on the parent's tax picture, it should also consider the psychological impact on the children. There is one school of thought that if the program begins too early, the children may develop a sense of entitlement and cease trying to earn their interest. But other experts suggest that ownership can develop a sense of responsibility. Consider the impact that your gift may have on your child's initiative.

plained what he wanted to do. Equal co-ownership of the business for the children, essentially a legacy from the father, did not prevent eventual leadership by the abler child in this family business. This leadership would then be rewarded with additional compensation.

Providing Children with an Income

Even if your children don't work in the business, you may want to give them an interest in the company as a way of providing them with income. For example, if you own a corporation and give them stock in it, the corporation can pay out a dividend, providing them with an income.

You can't merely assign to them your right to receive dividend income on the stock you own. You need to give them the underlying property—shares in the company—that will entitle them to receive the income. Giving them an income by means of transferring ownership interests is an income-splitting (or income-shifting) device that can produce income tax savings for the family as a whole.

And there's a psychological benefit to this arrangement. You don't have to write out a check to your children in order to give them the income. It comes to them through the business by virtue of their ownership interest.

Keeping the Business in the Family

By transferring ownership interests to family members, you ensure that your company remains a family business. Your children, whether

Example

Let's say you're in the top income tax bracket of 39.6 percent. Your two children are each in the 28 percent tax bracket. If the corporation pays you a dividend of $20,000, you'll have after tax $12,080 ($20,000 less $7,920 tax). This leaves you with the means to give each child $6,040. But now suppose you give your children stock that pays them each a dividend of $10,000. After tax, they'd keep $7,200 ($10,000 less $2,800 tax). In other words, by giving them the stock and letting them pay tax on the dividend, they realize nearly $1,200 of additional money. The only relative that loses in this situation is Uncle Sam.

or not they are active in it, keep control over the business. Of course, this doesn't prevent them from selling out when you die (unless there are restrictions on such transfers). But if you want the company to remain within the family, your gifting to children and allowing them to be owners helps create a tradition of family ownership.

Saving Estate Taxes

As a business owner, you probably have sufficient assets to make you subject to the federal estate tax as it now stands. It doesn't take much to be in this elite group—just over $675,000 in 2001 (rising to $1 million by 2006). When you add in the value of your home, your retirement accounts, portfolio, and other property on top of your business, it's easy to fall into the taxable category.

If you're married, you can postpone the estate tax cost by leaving your property to your spouse. But eventually there's a tax bill to reckon with. If you don't have a spouse, then you must deal with the potential estate tax cost now.

Federal tax rules are designed to ensure that whether you give your property away while you're alive or when you die, you'll pay just about the same in transfer taxes. These transfer taxes—gift tax and estate tax—are unified, sharing the same graduated tax brackets and exemption amounts that can be passed tax free. In figuring the tax on your estate, all taxable gifts that have been made are added in to push up the tax rate on the estate (the taxable gifts aren't taxed twice; they're only added back to increase the tax bracket).

Figure 13.1 shows the graduated estate and gift tax rates. These rates are used to figure the tentative tax—the amount before applying a unified credit. The unified credit effectively translates into an exemption amount that can be passed tax free. The unified credit and exemption amounts are shown in Figure 13.2.

If you give your children gifts throughout your lifetime, you can cut your estate tax bill, while paying little or no gift tax while you're

Example

Your business and other property are worth $5 million. Your spouse dies before you. You die in 2001 and leave your property to your children. Ignoring deductions to which your estate may be entitled, your tentative estate tax would be $2,390,800. Applying your unified credit, your estate tax bill is $2,170,250, or about 43 percent of your property. Only $675,000 of your $5 million passed tax free to your children.

FIGURE 13.1   Estate and Gift Tax Rates

If the Estate or Gift (after Deductions) Is . . .	Tentative Tax Is . . .
Not over $10,000	18% of such amount
Over $10,000, but not over $20,000	$1,800, plus 20% of the amount over $10,000
Over $20,000, but not over $40,000	$3,800, plus 22% of the amount over $20,000
Over $40,000, but not over $60,000	$8,200, plus 24% of the amount over $40,000
Over $60,000, but not over $80,000	$13,000 plus 26% of the amount over $60,000
Over $80,000, but not over $100,000	$18,200 plus 28% of the amount over $80,000
Over $100,000, but not over $150,000	$23,800 plus 30% of the amount over $100,000
Over $150,000, but not over $250,000	$38,800 plus 32% of the amount over $150,000
Over $250,000, but not over $500,000	$70,800 plus 34% of the amount over $250,000
Over $500,000. but not over $750,000	$155,800 plus 37% of the amount over $500,000
Over $750,000, but not over $1,000,000	$248,300, plus 39% of the amount over $750,000
Over $1,000,000, but not over $1,250,000	$345,800, plus 41% of the amount over $1,000,000
Over $1,250,000, but not over $1,500,000	$448,300, plus 43% of the amount over $1,250,000
Over $1,500,000, but not over $2,000,000	$555,800, plus 45% of the amount over $1,500,000
Over $2,000,000, but not over $2,500,000	$780,800, plus 49% of the amount over $2,000,000
Over $2,500,000 but not over $3,000,000	$1,025,800, plus 53% of the amount over $2,500,000
Over $3,000,000	$1,290,800, plus 55% of the amount over $3,000,000*

*For amounts over $10 million, the benefit of the graduated tax rates is phased out.

FIGURE 13.2   Unified Credit and Exemption Amounts

Year	Unified Credit	Exemption Amount
2000 and 2001	$220,550	$675,000
2002 and 2003	$229,800	$700,000
2004	$287,300	$850,000
2005	$326,300	$950,000
2006 and later	$345,800	$1,000,000

alive. This is because the gift tax rules make it less costly to give property during your lifetime than at your death.

Where estate planning is your aim, then gifting to children is not dependent on their participation in the business. One family-owned cosmetic company had two sons who grew up in the business. One loved the daily household conversation about mascara and market share; the other did not. However, the parents still gave stock to the son who went on to a career in technology. Even though he had no active role in the business, the parents felt that an ownership interest was his legacy.

TIP

Giving away an interest in your business not only removes the value of that interest from your estate; it also removes any future appreciation on that business interest from your estate.

Gift Tax Basics

While the tax rates for estate and gift transfers are unified, there are important tax savings to be realized from lifetime transfers in comparison to transfers at death. Each person can transfer annually gift tax free up to $10,000 per person (called the annual gift tax exclusion). This person can be your child, your child's spouse, your grand-

Example

You have two married children. One child has two children; the other has three children. Each year you can give away tax free $90,000 ($40,000 to your children and their spouses and $50,000 to your grandchildren). Over five years, you can transfer to these family members $450,000 *tax free* ($90,000 annual tax-free gifts times five years).

NOTE

The $10,000 annual gift tax exclusion is adjusted annually for inflation after 1998. The adjustment is made in multiples of $1,000. However, to date, with inflation as moderate as it has been in the past several years, there has not been any adjustment to the exclusion. If inflation continues at the rate of 3 percent to 4 percent annually, the exclusion should adjust by 2001 or so.

child, or anyone else you choose. There's no limit on the number of people you can give to each year.

If you're married and your spouse consents to the gift, you can double your annual tax-free gifting to $20,000 per person. In the example, you and your spouse could transfer nearly $1 million tax free in just five years.

The annual exclusion isn't cumulative. If you don't use it this year, you can't carry it over to the next year. But you can make one gift on December 31, 2000, and a second gift on January 1, 2001 (gifts don't have to be spaced a year apart). Also, the exclusion only applies to gifts of "present" interests, such as outright gifts. Gifts in trust, which are considered "future" interests, must be carefully drafted to qualify for the annual gift tax exclusion.

You can transfer larger amounts annually and still owe no gift tax. You do this by using up your lifetime exemption amount. So if you want to give your children $100,000 this year, you'd tap into your $675,000 exemption amount. Once the exemption amount is exhausted, you'd owe gift tax. And your estate would not have any exemption amount to reduce its tentative tax.

The federal estate and gift tax rates are unified. But due to the way in which estate and gift tax laws are structured, it's cheaper to make taxable lifetime gifts than it is to make taxable transfers at death.

How can you be sure that the shares of stock in your company or the interests in your partnership or limited liability company that

Caution

At the time this book went to press there was considerable sentiment in Congress to eliminate or substantially reduce the federal estate and gift tax. (The House voted for full repeal, but President Clinton vetoed the bill.) It's anticipated that there will be some estate and gift tax relief in the future, especially if there is a change in the administration in the presidential election. Relief may be targeted toward family business owners. In designing a gifting program, it's probably not advisable to make any taxable gifts at this time. Adopt a wait-and-see attitude for large gifts, but continue gifting under the annual gift tax exclusion.

Example

Assume you want to give away $500,000 worth of business interests in your business (and you've already used up your exemption amount). The entire $500,000 is subject to tax. Let's assume you're in the 49 percent transfer tax bracket, which we'll round off to 50 percent. If you give the interests while you're alive, you'll need cash of $250,000 to pay the gift tax on the transfer, for a total outgo of $750,000 ($500,000 gift, plus $250,000 gift tax). But if you leave that same interest at death, your estate must have $1 million. Because of the 50 percent tax rate, half goes in taxes, while the other half passes to your heirs. So, by giving interests while you're alive, you save 50 percent of the taxes due on the transfer.

---

you give away are worth no more than the annual gift tax exclusion? Where the company isn't public and stock isn't traded on an exchange, the only way to be sure of value is to rely on an accurate appraisal of the business.

Obtaining an appraisal from an expert can be costly, as discussed in Chapter 12. And since you may be gifting interests each year, it's advisable to work out some fee for making annual updates to the appraisal.

To find an appraiser, contact an appraiser's trade association (see Figure 12.1 in Chapter 12). You may also find appraisers for a business through certified public accountants who perform such appraisals themselves or know of others that do. Attorneys involved in corporate and estate work may also be able to make a referral to an appraiser. But it's not a good idea to use the company's CPA for an appraisal because of the relationship with the business.

Appraisers generally base their determinations on a number of factors. The IRS has provided guidelines for valuing shares in a private corporation. Essentially the same factors apply to valuing interests in unincorporated businesses. Some of these factors include:

- The nature and outlook of the industry in which the business operates
- Book value
- History of the company
- Earnings capacity of the company
- Price of any recent sales of shares/interests in the business

Certain factors can tend to increase or decrease the value otherwise fixed for the business. Valuation discounts for a family business, which allow you to treat the value of an interest at less than its appraised value, are discussed later in this chapter.

While transfer tax savings encourage gifting of business interests, there are drawbacks to consider. You're involving other parties in your business affairs. Even if you retain control of the business (more than 50 percent ownership interest), you may be creating complexities. As owners of the business, your children become entitled to see the financial records of the company. While they can't dictate that the company distribute earnings to them or force the payment of other compensation to them, they can make things uncomfortable for you. If you do give away more than 50 percent of the business to your children, you face the possibility that they could vote together against you on major issues and could even remove you from your leadership position.

And you may be limiting your options for the future. Once you make a gift, you can't take it back. Quarrels with a child, or a child's spouse for that matter, don't give you the right to recoup the interest you've given away.

Basis for Your Children

When you make a gift of your business interests to your children, they step into your shoes and take over your tax basis (which is used for determining gain or loss on a subsequent sale). This may be little or nothing. If they then sell their interest in the future, they face a potentially large capital gain. In contrast, if you retain your interest until you die and they inherit it from you, they get a stepped-up basis equal to the value of this interest at the time of your death. So where your children plan to hold onto the business indefinitely, perhaps passing it on to their children, this basis differential should not be a problem. But if your children plan to sell the company after your death, it may be preferable to hold onto your interests and not make lifetime gifts of them to your children.

Filing Gift Tax Returns

You must file a gift tax return, IRS Form 709, if the value of a gift to any individual is more than the annual gift tax exclusion. This is so even though you don't owe any gift tax. You must also file a gift tax return if your spouse consents to the gift (thereby doubling

> ### Example
>
> You figure the interest you're giving your child is worth $12,000 before any valuation discounts and, with valuation discounts, it's worth less than $10,000. You aren't required to file a return. But if you don't file a return and the IRS decides to review your gift five years from now, this could create big problems. The IRS might disallow the valuation discount, thereby imposing penalties for failure to file a gift tax return. With interest on the penalties, the cost can be high.

your annual gift tax exclusion) or if you are tapping into your exemption amount.

However, you may *want* to file a gift tax return even though you aren't required to do so. As long as there is full disclosure on a gift tax return, the IRS only has a three-year statute of limitations to review the gift and question its value. Full disclosure only means you attach a copy of an appraisal to the return; you don't have to point out what discount you've taken or how that discount was figured. If the IRS fails to act within three years of the time the return was filed, then your claimed valuation can stand.

What's more, valuation on a gift tax return can't be challenged on a later estate tax return. This means that the IRS can't try to bump up the estate tax rate by including gifts in the computation if the statute of limitations on the gift tax return has already run out.

Of course, filing the return to report a valuation below $10,000 might invite IRS review of your transaction. But if you've obtained the necessary appraisals to back up your claimed valuation, this should not present a problem. And the IRS may not bother with an examination unless there are substantial tax dollars at stake.

The gift tax return is due by April 15 of the year after the year of the gift. So if you make a taxable gift (or want to report a nontaxable gift) made in 2000, you must file the return by April 16, 2001 (April 15 is a Sunday). If you obtain an automatic four-month filing extension for your income tax return, you also have this additional time to file your gift tax return.

Gifts to Grandchildren

If you make gifts of business interests to your grandchildren, the same considerations you've seen for gifts to your children apply with equal force to your grandchildren. But there's an additional wrinkle to consider. Gifts to your grandchildren need to be made in light of the generation-skipping transfer (GST) tax. This is a special transfer tax designed to prevent estate tax from being avoided by transferring property across multigenerational lines.

The GST is a flat tax of 55 percent, and it's imposed in addition to any gift or estate tax that might otherwise be due. However, each person can transfer free of GST up to $1 million ($2 million per couple). This $1 million is adjusted annually for inflation (in 2001 it's $1,060,000).

The GST does not apply if you make transfers to your grandchildren and their parents are dead. In this instance, the transfers aren't skipping a generation.

Valuation Discounts

When you give away 1 percent or 10 percent in your business, is the value of that interest the same percentage of the value of your business? If your business is worth $10 million, is a 1 percent interest really worth $100,000? No.

The tax law recognizes that the interests in family business may be discounted from its full value for certain reasons. The main valuation discounts recognized by the IRS and courts include:

- *Minority interest discount.* Since the person receiving the gift owns less than a majority interest, he or she can't dictate company policy and is subject to the decisions of the majority owner. Minority interest discounts can be claimed even where the family together owns a majority of ownership as long as each person receives only a minority interest. Each gift is viewed individually. For example, if a parent owns 100 percent of a company and gives 25 percent to each of three children, a minority interest discount can be claimed for each gift. Even though a total of 75 percent has been transferred, each person still has a minority interest.

- *Lack of marketability.* Where the business isn't a public company, there's no ready market for the interests. An interest can't be easily converted to cash. The person receiving the gift can't simply dispose of that interest, because outsiders may not want to become involved with a family business. Also, interests may be nontransferable to outsiders by means of buy-sell agreements, nontransferability-of-shares restrictions, or other limitations.

- *Potential capital gains.* Where the business owns property that has appreciated substantially and would be subject to capital gains tax if sold, the value of a gift can be reduced to reflect the potential tax cost. This valuation discount is permitted even though the business has no current plans to dispose of the property.

Example

Your business is worth $1 million. Without a discount, you'd be able to give each child only 1 percent ($10,000 per child) gift tax-free. But if you factor in a valuation discount of 25 percent, you can give each child 1.33 percent of the business tax free ($9,975), or one-third more per child.

How much are these discounts worth? Generally, minority interest discounts range between 20 percent and 40 percent, while discounts for lack of marketability range from 10 percent to 35 percent. Smaller discounts have been allowed for potential capital gains. Taken together, it's not uncommon to apply discounts of 25 percent to as much as 40 percent to an intrafamily gift of an interest in a business. This means that an owner can give away a larger percentage of the business without triggering gift tax.

The discounts you apply to gifts of your business interests depend on your situation and how aggressive you want to be about valuation discounts. In planning gifts, as a rule of thumb if you use a 30 percent discount you can transfer a $14,000 property interest for $10,000, keeping the transfer under the annual exclusion.

Gifting to Minors

If you want to make gifts to children or grandchildren under the legal age of majority (18 in most states), you need to use special arrangements. While ownership can be in their name and income distributed from the business will be taxed to them, the interest in the business can be held by someone else.

Custodianships

You can give the interests to a custodian who holds the property in a fiduciary capacity for the minor. Once the minor attains the age of majority, the custodianship ends and the child owns the interest outright.

Custodianships depend on the law in your state. Today most follow the Uniform Transfers to Minors Act (UTMA), which allow the custodianship to continue to age 21 (past the age of majority in most states) and to hold a wider range of property. Some states still use the old Uniform Gifts to

CAUTION

It's generally not a good idea for the donor to act as custodian. While legally allowed to do so, if the donor dies before the custodianship ends, the property is includible in the donor's estate.

Minors Act (UGMA), which limited custodians to holding only cash and securities. These custodianships are set up through banks, brokerage firms, and mutual funds. They may not be able to hold interests in private companies.

Guardianships

Like a custodianship, a guardianship lets an adult act as fiduciary to manage the child's property until the age of majority. This type of arrangement requires court supervision and entails various costs (legal fees, guardian fees if the guardian isn't willing to serve for free, bonding costs, and accounting fees when the guardianship terminates). But it may be necessary to use this arrangement if you are giving a substantial interest in your business to your grandchild and you don't want the child's parent (your own child or his/her spouse) to control the property.

Trusts

Where you transfer or intend to transfer over time a substantial interest in your business to a minor child or grandchild, it's generally a good idea to use a trust for this purpose. The trustee manages the property held in trust for the benefit of your child or grandchild. The trust can provide greater protections for the beneficiary to protect property from the claims of the beneficiary's creditors (including a spouse or former spouse).

There are many different types of trusts. Generally, in order to make gifts to the trust qualify for the annual gift tax exclusion, the trust must be one of two types:

- A trust that ends when the minor reaches 21. Under this type of trust, income and principal do not have to be distributed before age 21. Income and principal can, of course, be used for the minor's benefit during this time. But when the minor turns 21 the trust generally ends and all of the property remaining in the trust, including any accumulated income, must be distributed at that time. However, if within a window provided by the trust, such as 30 days or 60 days, the beneficiary does not elect to take the money from the trust after age 21, then the trust is governed according to its own terms. It may end when the beneficiary is 25, 30, or older, or it may go on indefinitely and ultimately pass to the minor's own children.

- A trust that mandates annual income distributions. Income must be distributed annually to the minor. Principal does not necessarily have to be distributed until age 21. The trust may give the beneficiary the right at 21 to take the funds or leave them in trust.

There is yet another type of trust that can be used to nail down the annual gift tax exclusion. This is a trust that contains a Crummey power. This is a clause in the trust giving a beneficiary (or the beneficiary's parent or guardian if the beneficiary is a minor) the right to withdraw additions to the trust within a limited time. For example, the trust may provide that the beneficiary have a right of withdrawal for 60 days following any addition to the trust.

In structuring gifts to minors, be sure to take in account not only the gift tax cost, but any generation-skipping transfer (GST) tax cost as well (discussed earlier in this chapter).

Grantor Retained Annuity Trusts

Instead of making outright gifts to your children or other family members, you can obtain transfer tax benefits while retaining an income interest from the business. You do this through a trust called a grantor retained annuity trust (GRAT) or a grantor retained unitrust (GRUT). The distinction between the two types of trusts is the way in which the income distribution is figured. For purposes of giving away an interest in your business while retaining an income, the GRAT is usually used to provide an annuity for a term of years.

You set up the GRAT, naming yourself as the income beneficiary with your children as the ultimate beneficiaries of the trust. As the income beneficiary you retain an annuity interest for a set period, say 10 or 15 years. The amount of the annuity is figured under IRS tables.

Example

You put $500,000 worth of shares in your business into a GRAT, retaining a 15-year income interest and naming your children as the beneficiaries of the shares after the 15-year term. Assuming you receive an income interest of about $35,000 annually (the required payment depends on prevailing interest rates), your gift is only about $200,000. In other words, you're taxable on only $200,000 even though you're transferring $500,000 worth of assets.

Caution

If you don't outlive the term of the income interest, then the value of the trust assets—the business—is included in your estate and becomes taxable at that time. But you don't lose anything (other than the cost of professional fees to have set up the GRAT) if you die before the end of the income interest. Your estate can subtract any gift tax it has already paid on the initial creation of the trust.

At the end of that time, the assets in the trust—the business—pass to your children. You are treated as making a gift of the remainder interest in the trust when you set it up. But since this interest can be enjoyed only after your income term ends, the value of the remainder interest is substantially less than the value of the business.

CAUTION

While GRATs can provide substantial transfer tax benefits, don't rush out to create one now. If estate and gift taxes are repealed or reduced, the advantages of a GRAT disappear. Wait to see what Congress does with the transfer taxes before taking any action.

If the GRAT performs better than expected, all that additional income and appreciation of capital inures to the benefit of your child. So, for instance, in the example, instead of transferring $500,000 at a gift tax value of $200,000, if the $500,000 appreciates by 10 percent a year (after making required income distributions), your child would receive almost $1.75 million at the end of the 15-year trust term.

Today short-term GRATs are being used to transfer sizable assets at substantially reduced gift tax costs. Another example, based on an IRS ruling, demonstrates the leveraging impact of GRATs.

Example

A father transferred stock in a public corporation, of which the family controlled 47.5 percent, to a GRAT with a term of just two years. He reserved an annuity of 54.8 percent of the trust's initial value of $22 million, with the balance passing to his children at the end of two years. His annual annuity was $12.2 million, which was made by returning some of the stock to him. The gift tax cost of setting up this arrangement was just $121,000. At the end of two years, despite the two annuity payments, the stock in the trust was worth more than $20 million. In effect, the children received property worth more than $20 million for the same gift tax cost that the father would have incurred for an outright gift of just a fraction of the same stock.

Instead of creating a single GRAT, you can create multiple GRATs with different income terms, such as 5 years, 10 years, 15 years, and 20 years. In this instance, you have a chance that you'll outlive some of the terms, thereby passing on interests to your children on a tax-advantaged basis.

Planning a Gifting Program and Its Impact on Your Business

If you decide that you want to make gifts to your family, you may have to rethink your business organization. For example, if you are now a sole proprietor with children working for the company, you'll have to change your form of business organization to accommodate other owners. You have several choices in this instance: Incorporate (and if desired elect S corporation status), form a partnership (or a limited partnership), or form a limited liability company. This change in organization will allow you to have multiple interests to give away.

If you already have a type of business organization for your business that permits multiple owners, you may not have to make any changes. However, you still might want to change under certain circumstances. For example, if you and your siblings run a partnership, you might want to become a limited partnership when bringing in children or grandchildren as co-owners.

From the company's perspective, changing from one type of business organization to another may entail income tax costs. It is essential to discuss any proposed changes in the business organization with a tax professional.

Gifting Shares in an S Corporation

If your business is an S corporation and you want to keep it this way, there are certain factors to consider with respect to a gifting program. There are two key limitations you need to keep in mind:

1. An S corporation can have only one class of stock.
2. Only certain taxpayers can be shareholders in an S corporation.

If you run afoul of these limitations, you may automatically terminate the S election. So any gifting program entailing S corporation stock must address these two limitations.

One Class of Stock Limitation

If you want to give shares away but retain control, often different classes of stock are used for this purpose. One class, for example, may be preferred stock entitled to receive dividends (i.e., shift income to children), while the other is common stock that enjoys future appreciation. But in an S corporation, you can't use this two classes of stock approach.

You can, however, retain control by giving away shares that aren't entitled to vote. Under tax law, differences in voting rights aren't treated as a second class of stock as long as ownership confers identical rights to distributions and liquidation proceeds. So you can retain all of the voting common shares, while giving away nonvoting common shares.

Permissible Shareholders

If you give shares outright to your children and grandchildren, there's no problem with limitations on S corporation shareholders (assuming none of them are nonresident aliens). However, if you want to make gifts in trust to your descendants, you must use a trust that meets S corporation requirements. You may want to use a trust for several reasons: Your children or grandchildren are minors, you're concerned about them handling money, or you want to make sure the business interests remain in the family in case they divorce or have financial difficulties.

You have two trusts to choose from:

1. Qualified subchapter S trust (QSST)
2. Electing small business trust (ESBT)

Both of these trusts can be structured in such a way that your gifts to the trust qualify for the annual gift tax exclusion. And you may use one type of trust for some descendants and the other type for other relatives.

Qualified Subchapter S Trust

A qualified subchapter S trust (QSST) is a trust that meets certain requirements and the beneficiary (or the beneficiary's parent or legal representative if the beneficiary is a minor) elects to be treated as a QSST. The election must be made no later than two and a half months after becoming a beneficiary or the date on which S corporation stock is put into the trust. The election is simply a signed statement containing certain information, which is then filed with the IRS. If you own more than one S corporation and gift shares of each to the trust, the beneficiary must make a separate election with respect to each S corporation's shares.

> **Note**
>
> In the past, trusts were generally limited in duration because of the "rule against perpetuities." Under this rule, a trust could not be created to run longer than the life of any living person, plus 21 years. But 11 states—Alaska, Delaware, Idaho, Illinois, Maine, Maryland, New Jersey, Ohio, Rhode Island, South Dakota, and Wisconsin—have already repealed the rule against perpetuities (and several others are considering repeal).

A QSST can have only one income beneficiary at a time. For example, you can create a trust for the benefit of your child, with principal passing to your grandchild when your child dies. This trust has only one income beneficiary—your child.

The trust can have successive income beneficiaries—first your child, then your grandchild. Successive beneficiaries don't have to make a new QSST election; the old election continues indefinitely until terminated. In fact, in many states the trust can now go on from generation to generation indefinitely.

You can use one trust to benefit more than one individual at a time in certain instances. If the beneficiaries are husband and wife and file a joint return, it's no problem. So if you name your child and her spouse as income beneficiaries of a QSST, it's treated as having only one income beneficiary. And if it's set up to provide separate shares for multiple beneficiaries, it's viewed as multiple trusts each having only one income beneficiary. So if you have two children, you can use one trust with separate shares for each child. Using separate shares in a single trust cuts down on administrative costs.

The QSST must distribute all income annually to the income beneficiary. The income distributed to the beneficiary is taxed to this beneficiary at the beneficiary's tax rate. So, for example, if the beneficiary is in the 28 percent tax bracket and the S corporation pays a $10,000 dividend on the stock in the QSST, the beneficiary will net after tax $7,200 ($10,000 dividend less $2,800 tax). The trust cannot distribute any principal to someone other than the income beneficiary during the income beneficiary's lifetime.

> **TIP**
>
> You can put nonvoting common stock into a QSST, while retaining the voting stock for yourself. This will limit the trust's control over the business.

Electing Small Business Trust

The other eligible trust to consider when gifting to your children or grandchildren is an electing small business trust (ESBT). This type of trust has different requirements than a QSST. But the ESBT must also make an election that is similar to the QSST election. It too must be made within $2\frac{1}{2}$ months of the creation of the trust. It too must be a signed statement containing certain information, which is then filed with the IRS. But only the trustee, not the beneficiary, must sign the election. The key differences between these trusts:

- The ESBT can have more than one income beneficiary at a time.
- The income can be distributed or accumulated according to the discretion of the trustee or the terms of the trust.
- The ESBT is subject to special tax rules.

SPECIAL TAX RULES

An ESBT is effectively taxed as two trusts. The portion of the trust consisting of S corporation stock is subject to special tax rules; the other portion is subject to regular tax rules. For the S corporation portion, income received with respect to this stock is taxed at the highest noncorporate tax rates. So, for example, ordinary income paid with respect to the S corporation, such as the trust's allocable share of S corporation income for the year, is taxed at 39.6 percent. And capital gains distributed by the corporation to the trust are taxed at 20 percent. These rates apply even though the beneficiary of the trust may be in a lower income tax bracket.

In contrasting ESBTs to QSSTs, there are advantages and disadvantages to each alternative. The former generally are preferred in family-owned S corporations because they offer greater flexibility in estate planning. They have less restrictions than QSSTs. And since one trust can easily be used for more than one income beneficiary at a time, there is an administrative cost savings. But these positives aren't free: ESBTs are taxed at the highest noncorporate income tax rates on their S corporation income. So the tax cost must be weighed against the other advantages.

Tip

In view of the way in which ESBTs are taxed, it makes sense to use them where beneficiaries are already in the highest income tax bracket or the S corporation usually has little or no income. But even where the tax cost is high because beneficiaries are not in the highest income tax brackets and the S corporation regularly reports income, they may still be useful where income accumulations for minors are anticipated.

Example

Your business is valued at $1.5 million and you use a 33$\frac{1}{3}$ percent discount. Assuming you have 10 people you want to bring into the business, you can give away tax free each year 10 percent of the business. After just five years, your family will own half the business and you didn't have to pay a penny of gift tax. Even if you own less than 50 percent of the total value of the business, retention of the general partnership interest means you continue to control the company.

Family Limited Partnerships

Who says you can't have your cake and eat it, too? With a family limited partnership (FLP), you can keep control over your business, while giving away interests to your children for tax-saving purposes. Here's how it works: In a typical family limited partnership, a parent who owns a company sets up the limited partnership. He or she then retains the general partnership interest, typically 1 percent to 2 percent of the partnership, and makes gifts of limited partnership interests to children or others— outright or over time. As the general partner, you run the day-to-day operations of the business and make all important decisions. As limited partners, your family can't compel the company to make distributions or require that any specific actions be taken.

> **CAUTION**
>
> Limited partnerships, even in a family context, must be set up and registered according to state law. You cannot take a casual approach and simply designate gifts to children or others as limited partnership interests. Consult a lawyer to set up your FLP.

There are, of course, both advantages and disadvantages to using a family limited partnership. The advantages include the following:

- *Retention of control.* As a general partner, you keep control over the business operations, even if more than 50 percent of the value of the business is transferred to family members.

- *Transfer tax savings.* Using valuation discounts and the annual gift tax exclusion, you can remove sizable portions of the business from your estate completely tax free.

- *Asset protection.* Business assets are protected from the claims of the partner's creditors since the partnership structure impedes the ability of personal creditors to reach business assets. A creditor of a limited partner who obtains a judgment can only receive a "charging order" entitling the creditor to the limited partner's share of partnership distributions. The creditor can't force any distributions to be made to the limited partner, and the creditor can't obtain the underlying assets of the partnership—the business.

These advantages are certainly impressive. But keep in mind that there are drawbacks to consider:

- *Costs.* To step up the limited partnership and make the transfers you'll incur legal, accounting, and appraisal costs. These can run into the tens of thousands of dollars and only make sense if you plan to make substantial gifts.

- *IRS hostility.* In recent years, FLPs have been used in some situations for other than legitimate reasons. As a result, the IRS now looks very closely at FLPs and attempts to disallow valuation discounts where appropriate. Generally, when a business is involved, there are generally good reasons for the FLP and valuation discounts are allowed to stand as long as they are reasonable. However, in one instance where the general partner ignored the formation of the partnership and deposited partnership checks in her personal account, the IRS chose to ignore the FLP (ultimately including the full value of the FLP property in the general partner's estate).

- *Loss of stepped-up basis for your children.* If you leave your business to your children when you die, they inherit it with a stepped-up basis to the value on your death. If you give them interests while you're alive, they take over your basis, which may be little or nothing. If they ever sell their interests, they'll have to report a capital gain based on your original basis.

Recapitalizations

If you have a corporation, you may want to recapitalize the corporation to facilitate a gifting program. Where the purpose of the gifting program is to reduce the assets includible in the parent's estate, it was common in the past to recapitalize so that the parent retained preferred stock. The parent used common stock as the subject of gifts to children. As a preferred stock owner, the parent received an income—regular dividend payments—while all future appreciation in the business inured to the benefit of the common stock owners, the children (i.e., the future appreciation was kept out of the parent's estate). This is because preferred stock was valued more like bonds than like common stock. But the tax law changed. This so-called freeze arrangement, where the parent's interest in the business was frozen on the date of the recapitalization, is now subject to severe limitations.

Preferred stock is a class of stock entitled to certain preferential treatment. It's entitled to a dividend before any payments to common stockholders. It's also entitled to receive distributions upon liquidation before common stockholders are paid off.

Today, intrafamily transfers are governed by anti-freeze rules that effectively subject otherwise tax-free gifts to current tax under certain circumstances. You don't have to be concerned with these rules when a parent gives away his or her *entire* interest in a business. These rules come into play only when a parent retains an interest in the business (directly or indirectly).

For example, if the parent recapitalizes, retaining preferred stock, then there's a retained interest in the business. Generally, as long as the owner of preferred stock is entitled to receive a cumulative dividend (at market rate) and the common stock is valued at least 10 percent of the total value of the business, the recapitalization won't trigger the anti-freeze rules.

The anti-freeze rules are very complex. You'll need the help of experienced tax professionals to ensure that they are avoided or minimized where possible.

If the anti-freeze rules apply, then they trigger special gift tax rules. These rules require that the value of the gift be determined by subtracting the value of the parent's retained interest from the value of the entire business (with an adjustment to reflect the fragmentation of ownership). You may see this referred to as the "subtraction method." Special rules then determine the value of the parent's re-

---

Example

You own a corporation and recapitalize it, receiving both preferred and common stock. You then give the common stock to your children and retain the preferred stock. Since you've retained an equity interest while at the same time gifting an equity interest, the valuation of the gifts must be figured using the subtraction method. As a result, you're treated as having gifted the entire value of the corporation (your value of your retained interest is effectively discounted in this instance).

---

tained interest, effectively treating the retained interest as having little or no value. The result: The gift to the child is valued according to the total value of the business; the value of the interest retained by the parent is practically ignored.

Transfers Subject to the Anti-Freeze Rules

Transfers of business interests to or for the benefit of family members subject to these rules include a redemption, recapitalization, contribution to capital, or any other change in the capital structure of a corporation or partnership if the donor or donee:

- Receives a retained right (which is a right to certain distributions or payments).
- Surrenders a junior equity interest and receives property other than a retained interest.
- Surrenders a senior equity interest, and the value of the retained interest already held by such person increases.

A *donor* is the person making a gift. A *donee* is the person receiving a gift.

Who are family members for purposes of the anti-freeze rules? Generally they include the donor, the donor's spouse, lineal descendants of the donor or spouse, *and* the spouse of any lineal descendant. Thus, the anti-freeze rules don't apply to transfers to brothers or sisters, nieces and nephews, or cousins. They apply only to children, grandchildren, and their spouses.

CHAPTER 14

Selling Your Business

If you decide to walk away from your business, you can give it away (as explained in Chapter 13) or you can sell it. You may choose to sell some of your interest and keep your hand in the game. Or you may decide to sell all of your interest in the business. The buyer may be your children, grandchildren, and other relatives or it may be outsiders, or a combination of both family and outsiders. You may even decide to sell your business to your employees by means of an employee stock ownership plan (ESOP).

This chapter explains the tax and financial consequences to you of selling your business. It discusses ways to consider selling the business to your children. And it tells you various considerations on selling your business to outsiders, including ESOPs.

Overview of Selling Your Business

You've built up your business over a lifetime. Now you want to turn that equity, which may include considerable sweat equity, into gold. You may have continually plowed everything back into the business and don't have sufficient personal savings needed to provide you with a comfortable retirement income. Or you may want the cash to start another venture.

There are generally two ways you can receive your money:

1. In a lump sum
2. In installments over any period of time agreed upon

Which payout method is preferable for you? The answer depends. If you have any concerns about the ability of your children (or other purchasers) to successfully continue the business, you may want to take your money all at once and run.

If you're comfortable in the knowledge that the business will go on after you leave, then you may want to opt for installments over time. As you'll see later in this chapter, taking installments can produce financial and tax benefits to you.

As in the case of a gift, it's important to properly value the business interest you're selling. This will avoid any claim that you're really making a gift of the business, especially when the buyer is your child.

In valuing the business for a sale you can take into account valuation discounts discussed in Chapter 13. So, for example, if you sell your children a limited partnership interest in an FLP, you'd value that interest in the same way as if you'd given it to them. In other words, the value of that limited partnership interest can be made in light of a minority interest discount, a discount for lack of marketability, or any other applicable discount.

CAUTION

In structuring any sale, if the company is called upon to make payments in any way, then be sure the terms will not have an adverse impact on the business. There's no point in selling a family business to children if the sale itself will jeopardize the very existence of the company.

Straight Sale to Children

You can arrange to sell your interest in the business to your children in a straight sale. Depending of course on the value of your interest, your children may need to borrow in order to raise the cash to pay your price. They can borrow from commercial lenders, using their interest in the business as collateral for the loan. Or they may be able to borrow from the business itself.

In structuring a straight sale, there are three perspectives to consider:

1. The business itself
2. The children who buy the business
3. The parents who sell the business

Business's Perspective

If children borrow from the business to enable them to make an out-right purchase, there are certain things to consider. Make sure the business can afford to make the loan. If the business is put into a cash crush, that can jeopardize its very survival.

In one family-owned construction company, when the dad sold his interest to his three sons who had been virtually running the business for some time, cash wasn't a big problem. First of all, the company had the cash that it didn't have to use for the dad's fat salary (which stopped when he sold out). Secondly, the company was able to bor-row at very favorable terms because it had solid building contracts al-ready in the pipeline. And third, the sons had been putting their own money aside for years in anticipation of the purchase, so they didn't need the business to lend them the full purchase price. The father had discussed his plans about selling out, and the sons had the foresight to make it happen without causing financial problems for the company.

But in another business, using the company to bankroll an out-right purchase by the children almost ruined it. Dad owned all of the shares of stock in regional retail chain stores. He, too, had three sons who were ready and able to take over the company. But they didn't have any cash of their own. And the company's credit line was already stretched almost to the max. They stretched it even further so they could acquire pop's stock. They were fortunate to have made it work because business picked up and interest rates dropped, eas-ing the company's credit position. But had things gone the other way, they could have lost everything.

Children's Perspective

If children borrow from the business to pay the sales price, make sure that the business observes the below-market loan rules. These rules mandate that loans that don't bear a reasonable rate of interest can give rise to "imputed" (or phantom) income to the lender. In ef-fect, the lender—the business—may have to report income even though it hasn't received any.

To avoid the consequences of the below-market loan rules, the loan should bear a rate of interest of at least the applicable federal rate (AFR) for the term of the loan effective at the start of the loan. There are three rates published monthly by the IRS:

1. **Short-term rate** for loans of three years or less. The same rate applies to loans payable on demand. In this case, use the short-term AFR in effect for the start of each semiannual period—January and July.

2. Mid-term rate for loans of more than three but less than nine years.

3. Long-term rate for loans of nine years or more.

In some cases, the children may arrange with the business to borrow the money for free or at low interest rates. If the loan by the business to the children is less than the AFR, then the company is deemed to have received the forgone interest (also referred to as imputed income or phantom income) and must report it as income. The children are deemed to have received compensation equal to this forgone interest as long as they are employees of the business. Such amount is taxable to them as additional compensation. But the business can then deduct this amount (and offset its deemed interest income) as long as total compensation to the children is reasonable. If any of the children don't work for the corporation, then forgone interest is treated as a taxable dividend to them, but is not deductible by the corporation.

It's important to formalize the loan arrangement between the children and the company. Include the loan authorization in the corporate minutes. The children should sign a note agreeing to the loan terms. And the outstanding loan balance should be carried on the company books.

Since the children-borrowers are deemed to have paid interest, they may be entitled to an interest deduction for this amount. Generally, interest on a loan—from the corporation, a bank, or anywhere else—to acquire stock in a C corporation is treated as investment interest. This is so even if the corporation never pays investment income (a dividend) or the loan is taken in order to protect their employment with the corporation. As such, the interest is subject to investment interest limitations. This means that investment interest is deductible only to the extent of net investment income. Unused deductions can be carried forward and used in subsequent years when there is net investment income to offset it.

Interest on a loan to acquire an interest in a pass-through entity—partnership, limited liability company, or S corporation—is treated as a "debt-financed acquisition." As such, an allocation of the loan, and interest on that portion of the loan, can be made according to the assets of the business. To the extent the loan relates to the assets, the interest is treated as business interest. The balance is treated as investment interest subject to the investment interest lim-

Example

Your child borrows $40,000 to buy her interest in your S corporation. The corporation owns equipment of $90,000 and securities of $10,000, based on fair market value. As such, interest on three-quarters of the loan is treated as business interest ($90,000/$100,000); one-quarter is treated as investment interest ($10,000/$100,000).

itations. The allocation of the loan can be based on book value, fair market value, or the adjusted basis of the business assets.

Your Perspective

From your perspective as a seller, a sale of the business is a taxable event. Generally, your gain from the sale of your interest in the business will be treated as long-term capital gain taxed at the 20 percent rate. This treatment applies whether you're selling a sole proprietorship, a partnership interest, or shares in a corporation and regardless of whom you're selling to.

CAUTION

There's no income tax withholding on sales proceeds, so you must account for your gain in quarterly estimated tax payments. In the year of sale, make sure you pay estimated taxes on your gain to avoid estimated tax penalties.

However, if any portion of your gain relates to depreciation on real estate, then any straight-line depreciation is taxed at the 25 percent rate. So, for example, if you sell the assets in your business, one of which is a building that you've been depreciating on the straight-line method, then this depreciation is taxed at the 25 percent rate.

In selling the business to children, it's essential to obtain an expert appraisal. This will ensure that they pay for the full fair market value of the business. If they don't, then you're treated as having made a

Example

In 2000, you sell your public relations business, which you ran as a sole proprietorship. The assets of the business include an office building you bought in 1990 and on which you took straight-line depreciation of $100,000. Let's assume that your gain on the sale of your business is $500,000. In this instance, $400,000 is taxed at 20 percent and $100,000 (the straight-line depreciation) is taxed at 25 percent.

gift of the difference between the business's fair market value and what they actually paid you.

Installment Sale Rules

If you're willing to take your money over time, you can realize tax and financial benefits:

- Gain is deferred, so taxes are deferred as well. You pay tax only on the current gain, not on the deferred gain.

- You receive an income stream. Instead of receiving a lump sum, you're assured of an income for the term of the installment agreement. This income includes interest payable on what is still owed to you.

- There's estate tax savings to be realized. The sale effectively freezes the value of the business so all of the business's future appreciation is enjoyed by your children. As long as the sale price reflects the business's value, there are no gift tax consequences. And if you spend the installments you receive as retirement income, you reduce the size of your estate.

If you sell your interest in the business and will receive payment in more than one year, you've made an installment sale. As such, gain is automatically reported over time as payments are received unless you make an election out of installment reporting.

Perhaps you have basis in your business interest because you invested cash or contributed property to the business. In this case, a portion of each payment you receive represents a return of your investment and is tax free.

Installment payments must carry a sufficient rate of interest. If they do not, then a portion of what you'd consider capital gain is recharacterized as ordinary income. Interest on installment pay-

Example

You sell 1,000 shares of stock in your company to Leslie for $500,000. Payment terms call for $100,000 down, and annual payments of $100,000 (plus interest) over the following four years. If your basis in the stock is zero, then your gain is $500,000 ($500,000 sale price less zero basis). You report $100,000 each year as you receive it.

Example

The situation is the same as in the prior example, except you have a $200,000 basis in your business. In this case, your gain would be only $300,000 ($500,000 less $200,000 basis). As such, two-fifths of each payment is a return of your investment and tax free; three-fifths of each payment is capital gain.

ments is ordinary income to you, in addition to your capital gain from installment payments.

Under current tax law, the installment method to report gain can't be used by accrual-method taxpayers. This ban, which went into effect for sales on or after December 17, 1999, prevents inventory-based businesses from reporting asset sales on the installment method. So if your company is on the accrual basis because it maintains inventory and its assets are acquired by another company, the gain must be reported in full in the year of sale. This rule applies equally to a C and an S corporation. It also applies to a partnership and presumably to any other business entity.

NOTE

There are proposals to repeal the installment sale ban on accrual-method taxpayers. Small business groups all favor repeal and are lobbying for legislation. Watch for possible action by Congress on these measures in the near future.

But in response to the ban on the use of the installment method for accrual-basis businesses, the IRS liberalized the use of the cash method for small inventory-based businesses. It's now possible for the company to use the installment method by changing its accounting method from the accrual to the cash method. Using the cash method will not only simplify accounting and tax reporting for the business now; it will also let the company report gain from asset sales on the installment basis.

The business qualifies to use the cash method if its average annual gross receipts for a three-year period are no more than $1 million and it uses the cash method for its financial reporting (keeping the company books, reports, etc.). Gross receipts for this purpose means total sales, amounts received for services, interest, dividends, and rents. The term does not include sales taxes if the consumer pays the tax. If the company is eligible to make a switch to the cash method and has not already done so, consider filing for a change of accounting. Discuss the switch with the company's accountant or other financial adviser.

But just because the business is on the accrual method does not prevent you from using the installment method to report your gain if

---

Caution

If you're a sole proprietor and your business has depreciable assets, you don't want to use an installment sale for selling the business to certain family members or other related parties. The tax law says that such gain is treated as ordinary income instead of capital gain. The buyer is considered a "related party" to you if it's any corporation or partnership in which you have more than a 50 percent interest or a trust if you or your spouse have an interest in the trust. In figuring 50 percent control, you're treated as owning stock held by your spouse, children, grandchildren, siblings, parents, and grandparents.

---

you sell your interest. If you're on the cash method of accounting, you can use the installment method to report gain on the proceeds you receive over time.

If the installment sale includes assets on which accelerated depreciation was taken, then depreciation recapture must be reported in the year of sale. This recapture must be reported without regard to the amount of proceeds received this year.

If you sell your interest in the business to a relative using an installment sale, you lose the benefit of installment reporting (tax deferral) if the relative resells the interest within two years of your sale. This means you'll have to report your remaining gain even though under the legal terms of the sale you won't receive payment until the future.

This two-year rule isn't triggered if the interest is disposed of following the death of you or your relative or if you can prove to the satisfaction of the IRS that neither your sale to your relative nor your relative's sale to a third party was made for tax avoidance purposes.

Example

You sell your share in the business to your brother for $250,000, of which $100,000 is your profit. Your brother agrees to pay you in five equal annual installments ($50,000 this year and $50,000 in each succeeding year). But later this same year your brother sells the interest in the business that he acquired from you to a third party. You'll have to report your entire gain of $100,000 this year even though you received only one-fifth of the sale proceeds.

Election out of Installment Reporting

You can choose to report all of your gain in the year of sale if it makes tax sense for you to do so. You may want to make the election if you have substantial capital losses from securities sales or other transactions. But remember that the election is irrevocable, so you can't change your mind.

An explanation of the installment sale rules can be found in IRS Publication 537, "Installment Sales," at www.irs.gov.

Special Methods for Selling Your Business to Your Children

You may not want to give away your business to your family. You may prefer to sell it for a number of reasons. Maybe you can't afford to make the gifts and need the money from the sale to fund your retirement. Or maybe you think that your children will value the business more if they have to pay for it.

If you sell your business to your children (and/or grandchildren), it's highly doubtful they'll have the cash to pay you all at once. It may be possible for them to finance their purchase through a bank loan. If they can arrange this loan, then you would receive full payment up front.

It's more common, however, for children to buy a business on the installment plan—so much down and payments over time. You can contract for a straight installment sale as described earlier. You'll realize the income tax advantage from an installment sale: deferral of income. But an installment sale won't result in any estate tax savings for you. You've merely exchanged one asset—your business—for another asset—cash and installment notes. If you die before you've collected all of the payments, the outstanding obligations are included in your estate.

Or you can use one of the following variations on the installment sale theme, which provides *both* income tax *and* estate tax savings to you:

- Installment sales combined with self-canceling installment notes (SCINs).
- Private annuities

The choice depends on your primary objectives in the transaction. Figure 14.1 contrasts the two alternatives, the details of which are explained next.

Installment Sales and SCINs

You can realize income from the installment sale while you are alive but achieve estate tax savings by using an installment sale coupled with

FIGURE 14.1 Self-Canceling Installment Notes (SCINs) versus Private Annuities

Your Objective	Alternative to Use
Deferring income tax on your gain	Either alternative
Avoiding estate tax	Either alternative
Obtaining the most retirement income	Private annuity (the older you are at the time of sale, the larger the annuity payments)
Obtaining security for the transaction	SCIN

> **CAUTION**
>
> While the arrangement saves you estate taxes, it can wind up costing your child income taxes. This is because the cancellation of debt may result in income to your child.

self-canceling installment notes (SCINs). You make a regular installment obligation. But you agree that if you die before receiving all of the payments, the balance is automatically canceled. This avoids inclusion of the notes in your estate and saves estate tax accordingly. To make this arrangement work as planned, the installments cannot be set to run longer than your life expectancy. And the purchase price for the business interest usually is higher than the price for an ordinary installment sale to account for the value of the self-canceling feature.

If your children don't have income from the cancellation of the notes, your estate could wind up having to report such income. Proper wording, however, can save the estate from this income tax result.

Instead of having the initial sales agreement provide for cancellation of debt on your death, you may choose to cancel the obligations in your will. If you use this method, your estate must still include the value of the outstanding obligations. In other words, you won't save estate tax in this case. But if you're not sure you want to cancel the obligations—for example, you may want your children to pay the funds into the estate to provide income for your spouse—then using your will to make a bequest of the debt forgiveness provides you with flexibility. You have some time to decide whether to forgive any outstanding amounts.

Private Annuities

Private annuities are like commercial annuities in that you're buying an income interest for life. You're exchanging your interest in the business for an income interest for the rest of your life (or the joint lives of you and your spouse). In a family business context, private annuities offer a number of important tax advantages to consider:

Caution

The factors from the IRS tables cannot be used if there's a more than 50 percent chance that you'll die within one year of creating the annuity. So, for example, if you're diagnosed with a terminal illness from which death can be anticipated within the year, you must use the actual life expectancy, which means the annuity runs for only a year. In effect, you really can't use the private annuity if you have serious health problems. But if you choose to do so and outlive the creation of the annuity by at least 18 months, then you can presume retroactively that you weren't terminally ill and can rely on the IRS tables to figure the required annuity.

- Property is moved out of your estate. You no longer own the business. And when you die, the annuity ends so there's nothing to include in your estate.

- Gain from the appreciation in your business interest is reported over your lifetime instead of in full in the year of a sale. A part of each annuity payment represents capital gain from the sale of your business interest. This capital gain is the difference between the present value of the annuity and your basis in the business interest, divided by your life expectancy. The present value and your life expectancy are determined from IRS tables. As in the case of installment reporting, if there is any depreciation recapture, it must be reported in full in the year you purchase the annuity in exchange for your business interest.

- There's no gift tax involved. Since you're selling, not giving, your interest, you don't have to be concerned with gift taxes. To make sure that you aren't making a gift, you must receive an an-

Example

Let's assume that you're age 70 and exchange your business interest worth $1 million for a lifetime annuity that your child agrees to pay. If the applicable AFR is 6.4 percent, then the annuity factor taken from the IRS tables is 8.0062. Divide the value of the property exchanged, your business interest of $1 million, by this annuity factor, to find the annuity payment that must be made in order to avoid any gift tax. In this case, the required annuity payment is $124,903 ($1 million divided by 8.0062). If you die after two years, your child has acquired a $1 million business for a cost of just $249,806.

nuity that has a present value equal to the business interest you're giving up. This requires both an accurate appraisal of the business interest and reliance on the IRS tables to determine the value of the annuity.

Present value is figured under IRS tables that use an interest rate of 120 percent of the applicable federal mid-term rate (AFR) in effect for the month of the valuation (when the annuity starts). The applicable federal rate fluctuates and is published monthly by the IRS.

As interest rates rise, the required annuity increases as well. For instance, in the example, if the applicable AFR was 8.4 percent, the required payment would increase to $141,980.

If you outlive your life expectancy, then all remaining payments to you are treated as ordinary income (you've already covered your basis and have no further capital gain to report). If you die before fully recovering your cost basis, the unrecovered amount is deducted on your final income tax return.

From your child's perspective, he or she gets a stepped-up basis for the interest in the business. When that interest is sold, gain or loss is determined according to this basis. In contrast, if the child receives the interest by gift, the basis in the business interest is your basis, which may be little or nothing.

Before you rush out to create a private annuity, consider some of the drawbacks you'll need to take care of:

- *Valuation can be problematic.* The avoidance of any gift tax is dependent on an accurate appraisal. So you probably have to incur appraisal fees for a qualified appraiser to obtain a reliable value. And, since the private annuity being is created between a parent and child, the IRS generally looks closely at whether the arrangement is legitimate. It must make as much economic sense here as it would in an arm's-length transaction between strangers.

- *Security of payments.* With a commercial annuity, you are assured of payment by a large company regulated by a state insurance department. With a private annuity, payments are unsecured. They cannot be secured by assets, such as your child's stock in the company. If the payments are secured, then you're immediately taxable on your gain. So you need absolute trust in your child that payments will be made on schedule. If your child dies before you, there's no guarantee that your child's estate will continue to make payments.

TIP

If you opt for a private annuity, consider buying life insurance on your child's life. Since it's your child, you have an insurable interest. And the cost of the coverage may be modest given your child's age.

- *Professional fees.* To value the business and create the annuity, you'll probably have to pay sizable fees to appraisers (to value the business), attorneys (to draft the annuity agreement), and accountants (to figure the annuity). Generally, your accountant will have special software to compute the annuity.

All of these drawbacks affect you. But there's an important drawback to your child, one that may prevent the private annuity from getting off the ground. Your child may have difficulty coming up with the necessary funds to pay the annuity payments. The older you are and the more valuable the business, the larger the annuity payments. While a recent change in IRS tables has reduced the required annuity payment (because life expectancies have increased), the burden on your child may still be too much to handle.

Depending on how the business is doing, your child may be able to increase his or her compensation to cover the annuity payments (assuming total compensation remains reasonable). But your child will owe income tax on the added compensation. And your child can't deduct the payments made to you. Also, you and your child will need the services of an accountant to figure the basis in the business interest acquired. The computations, made under IRS guidance, are quite complex.

Part-Gift, Part-Sale Techniques

If you can afford to give away some of your interest in your business, you can combine the advantages of gifts with the advantages of sales. You'll remove more assets from your estate and make it easier for your children or other relatives to acquire their interests. Here are some alternatives to consider:

- *Gift plus a private annuity.* You give your children an interest in the business. Then you sell the balance of your interest in ex-

Tip

If you're married, set up the private annuity as a joint and survivor annuity with your spouse. This will reduce the size of required annuity payments. It will also provide an income to your spouse after you die. To make this work, your spouse needs to be an owner in the business and exchange his/her interest when you do. But you can give your spouse an interest tax free in order to arrange an ownership interest before creating the annuity.

change for a private annuity. This minimizes your children's annuity payment obligations to you.

- *Gift plus a redemption of the balance of your shares.* You give your children an interest in your corporation. Then you have the corporation redeem the balance of your shares. If the redemption is properly structured, you can extract funds from your corporation at a 20 percent tax rate. (Redemptions are explained in Chapter 12.)

Sale of Part of Your Interest

If you want to shift ownership to your children while retaining an interest in the business, you can sell them some of your ownership interest. Instead of simply giving them an interest, you sell it to them for fair market value. The sale avoids any gift tax issues that arise on gratuitous transfers. However, from an estate planning perspective, a sale merely substitutes cash for property (the interest in the business), although future appreciation on the business interest is removed from your estate.

You might consider using a family limited partnership (explained in Chapter 13) to retain control over the daily business operations. Instead of gifting limited partnership interests to your children, you sell them their interests. As long as the interests are properly valued, gift tax issues are avoided.

Selling rather than giving the children an interest may have nontax and nonfinancial benefits. The children may feel a greater connection to the business because they paid for it.

Selling Your Business to Outsiders

You might not have children or other family members who want to buy your business. In this case, you may be forced to sell to outsiders when you want out.

Since the buyer isn't sitting at your dinner table, you may have to look around to find a candidate willing and able to make the purchase. You have many options for finding a buyer. You can use the services of a business broker to bring you together with interested buyers. You can even find buyers through the Internet.

Or you may be able to sell your business to key employees or to all company employees through an employee stock ownership plan (ESOP), discussed later in this chapter.

From your perspective you probably want to construct the sale as a lump-sum cash payment. In this way you receive your funds up

front and don't have to rely on contractual obligations for payment. To obtain a lump-sum buyout,
you may have to agree to a lower selling price
than you could command on an installment sale.

If you want the full price for your company, you
probably have to agree to payments over time.

Using ESOPs

If your business is incorporated, you may effectively use the business itself to buy you out. You do this by setting up an employee
stock ownership plan (ESOP). An ESOP is a qualified plan that holds
company stock for the benefit of employees who
participate in the plan. The corporation makes annual contributions to the ESOP that are used to
buy shares. The corporation claims an income tax
deduction for its contributions.

When participants leave the company, vested
benefits in the plan can be paid in stock. But the
plan is permitted to pay the equivalent amount in
cash, retaining the stock and keeping the business
within the family.

As an owner, generally you're taxed on gain
from the sale of your shares to the ESOP. However, under a special tax rule, you can defer recog-
nition of your gain by reinvesting the proceeds in

TIP

Depending on the nature
of your business, you
may be able to take your
company public and ease
out from ownership
over time.

CAUTION

While S corporation
owners can sell their
stock to an ESOP without
causing termination of
the S election, they can't
use the deferral rule to
postpone gain on their
sale by reinvesting in
other securities. That
deferral break applies
only to C corporation
shareholders.

Note

Employee stock ownership plans (ESOPs) can be used by S corporations
without running afoul of the 75-shareholder limit. An ESOP is treated as one
shareholder for purposes of the shareholder limit, so it doesn't matter how
many participants are in the ESOP. And to protect the future integrity of the S
election, the ESOP may provide that participants can't demand their
distributions in the form of employer securities. Instead, the plan can pay them
out in cash.

Also, items of income or loss of the S corporation are not treated as
unrelated business taxable income to the ESOP, so there's no double tax on the
ESOP and again when benefits are distributed to ESOP participants. Only the
participants ultimately pay the tax on items of income or loss of the S
corporation.

TIP

If you invest in qualified replacement property that isn't yielding the return you'd like, you can borrow against the value and invest the loan proceeds for additional income. This may be wise where you can earn a higher rate of return than you'll pay on the loan interest. Generally you can deduct the interest on the loan as investment interest (provided you have sufficient investment income).

other securities (called "qualified replacement property"). These securities are limited to stocks and bonds issued by U.S. corporations.

You qualify for this tax break as long as you've held your shares for at least three years before the sale to the ESOP and, immediately after the sale, the ESOP owns at least 30 percent of each class of the corporation's outstanding stock or at least 30 percent of the total value of all of the corporation's stock.

The deferral lasts as long as you continue to hold the qualified replacement property. Once such property is sold, then the deferred gain, plus any additional appreciation on the property, is recognized. You're not permitted to make a rollover of the proceeds to other such property in order to continue the deferral. But if you hold onto the qualified replacement property until your death, your heirs receive a stepped-up basis for the value at the time of death. The result: All of the deferred gain escapes income tax forever.

Selling to Strangers

Mom and Dad may have had a dream—a family business that would go on generation after generation. Not all dreams can come true. Even though you may own a family business, you may not want or be able to keep it in the family forever. There may be sound reasons for selling to strangers. If you don't, you may watch your business go down the tubes.

You may want to sell to outsiders if any of the following conditions exist in your company:

- *There's no management talent in the next generation.* As much as you love your children, you must make a realistic appraisal of their ability to run the company. If you've concluded that unfortunately the acorns fell far from the tree, you may need to sell in order to preserve wealth for the family.

- *Your children don't want the business.* While you love your company, your children may have other feelings toward it. They don't like the line you're in. They don't see growth potential. Or they're already into something else. You can't force them to buy you out.

- *You fear that family feuds will undermine the business.* If your children can't get along at family functions, they won't be able to work together in the business. This friction will probably kill the business, and you're better off selling it to outsiders.

- *You receive an offer you can't refuse.* You may have built up a business that's highly attractive to another company. That company may want yours as another division to expand its product line or territory or for any number of other reasons. Usually, economics doesn't dictate decisions in a family-business context. But in some cases the dollars can't be ignored. Such was the case with a Midwestern auto parts maker that was sold by its fourth-generation owners in response to a fabulous offer. The money was great, and the owners were having trouble finding a suitable successor within the family.

The methods for selling to outsiders are the same as for intrafamily sales: outright or in installments. However, in negotiating the price to outsiders, the method of sale may have an impact on the net dollars you'll realize. Generally, you can command a higher price if you're willing to take payments over time. Of course, you trade off not only the security of having the money in hand, but also the time value of the money. While you'll be paid interest on the outstanding balance, the reasonable rate of interest may be less than you could realize by investing the funds on your own. For example, you might receive 9 percent interest on installments, but could realize 15 percent by investing the money in the stock market.

ASSET SALE VERSUS STOCK SALE

There's another wrinkle in selling a corporation. There's a choice in how to structure the sale: as a sale of the company's assets or by selling your shares. Again, the structure can dictate the sale price as well as the net amount to you.

From your perspective, an asset sale generally results in a double tax, leaving less cash after tax for you. This is because the corporation pays a tax on the sale of its assets. Then it distributes the after-tax amount to you, and you pay tax on the amount you receive. The combined tax on the asset sale can be as high as 53 percent. So if the selling price is $1 million, you'd net out only $470,000. In contrast, if you sell your stock directly to the buyer, you have only one level of tax: You pay tax on the gain on your stock. But a stock sale typically commands a lower price tag than an asset sale. Obviously, the method of sale is something to be negotiated.

GOING PUBLIC

In lieu of selling the entire company, it may be possible for you to cash out part or all of your equity by taking the company public.

Whether this is feasible depends on your company—its financial position, industry, size, and many, many other factors.

Going public means opening up your family business to outsiders. But it's also a way to keep control of the business within the family. Other families have done it. Wal-Mart, for example, is still a family business even though its stock is traded on the New York Stock Exchange. Sam Walton's children are still substantial owners of the company.

CHAPTER 15

Estate Planning for Your Family Business

You've probably spent most of your life building up your business. It's probably your largest single asset. You want to make sure it passes to the family member or members you intend—those you believe to be the most capable of ensuring the continued life of the business and those you want to benefit financially. And you want to avoid erosion of this asset by federal and state death taxes.

In order to accomplish your intentions, you need to make plans. If you don't, state law says who will inherit your property. And you'll lose out on opportunities to minimize or avoid estate taxes.

This chapter discusses general estate planning considerations. It explains basic estate tax rules to consider in making estate plans. And it tells you about special estate tax breaks for family business.

Estate Planning for Your Business

If you want, like many family business owners you can take a Louis XV attitude and let the chips fall where they may after you die. But this approach seems ridiculous in view of the fact that you've spent your life building up a business. If you don't take steps now to plan for the business after you die, there's no telling what will result.

NOTE

It's been estimated that more than 40 percent of business owners don't have succession plans in place. This failure may explain why 70 percent of family-owned businesses don't survive to the next generation.

Without any succession planning:

- The business may pass into the hands of family members you'd prefer not to inherit an interest. They may not be competent to run the business. They may not get along with each other. The result: Those who inherit your business may run it into the ground.

- Estate taxes may seriously cut into the amount you can pass on and may even put your heirs into debt. For example, if you leave to your children an estate worth $5 million consisting primarily of the value of your business, they'll have to come up with $2.2 million within nine months of the day you die to pay Uncle Sam his estate tax due.

To leave a lasting legacy and prevent these catastrophic results, you need to take steps now. These steps should be designed to accomplish two main goals: passing your business to your children or other family members as you prefer, and avoiding or minimizing estate taxes in the process. In effect, you need a comprehensive succession plan.

Outline of a Comprehensive Succession Plan

A succession plan is comprised of two main parts: designating who will *run* your business and who will *own* your business. In some cases, this is the same person or persons. But in other cases, you may want one child to be the head of the company while you want both children to co-own it.

In order to ensure that your succession plan will be actualized, you need to put things in motion. Naming a successor is the first step

Caution

You should recognize that your leadership designation may not come to pass. Unless a transition takes place while you're alive, your heirs may wrangle over power after you die. Based on their ownership interests, they may fight for control. The two sons of Harry Winston fought over control, and burned up millions of dollars in legal fees, for more than 20 years after Winston's death.

that needs to be taken in your succession plan. This process is discussed in Chapter 11.

Then you need to address the transfer of ownership from you to your family. This transfer can take place entirely while you're alive, after your death, or a combination of the two.

Lifetime Steps

How much of your business do you want your children or other family members to own? You must decide the portions that each will receive from you. Estate planning can't be viewed only as measures taken at death. It must be viewed as a total approach to passing property that includes lifetime measures as well. You may want to give away interests in your business while you're alive (explained in Chapter 13) or sell business interests before your death (explained in Chapter 14). If you have a buy-sell agreement in place, you'll want to coordinate your estate plan with the terms of the agreement (explained in Chapter 12).

Death-Planning Steps

If you hold onto some or all of your interest in the business until your death, you need to put your wishes into effect through your will. Your will allows you to pass property in your name—an interest in a partnership; shares in a corporation—to whomever you choose. You can leave the business entirely to your spouse or to your child or in combination to both.

> **NOTE**
>
> You're not required to leave *anything* to your children. State law only dictates what children inherit in the absence of a will. You can, by will, make any bequests you want. For example, you can leave everything to one child and disinherit another. You aren't even required to explain why (although you may want to do so if this is your intention).

The beauty of using your will for succession planning is that it allows you complete flexibility to make changes. This lets you retain complete control over the business for as long as you want. In contrast, if you give away your interests while you're alive, you can't change your mind and recover those gifts. They're out of your hands. But if you sign a will leaving your business to one relative and later want to provide for another, you can write a new will. As long as you are legally competent to write a will (you're not suffering from any condition that diminishes your mental capacity), you can make changes up to the day you die.

Instead of using a will, you can use a trust to accomplish the same dispositions of business interests to family members after your death. Generally, a living trust is used for this purpose. A living trust is a trust you set up while you're alive. It's usually a revocable trust because you retain the right to revoke the trust and recoup trust assets until your death (or incapacity). After setting up the trust, title to your assets, including your business interests, is transferred to the trust. Taxwise, the living trust doesn't change a thing. You remain taxable on income earned by the trust throughout your lifetime. At your death, the assets of the trust are included in your estate as if you had kept title to them in your own name. However, a living trust can include all of the same estate tax saving strategies that can be used in a will, such as the unlimited marital deduction.

Where you have more than one child, you may need to make special arrangements. You can, of course, leave each child an equal interest in the business. This may be advisable where the children all work in the business. Equal ownership doesn't prevent one child from assuming the leadership of the company—something that may already be in place before your death.

To paraphrase George Orwell's *Animal Farm*, all children are created equal but some children are more equal than others. After all, equal may not necessarily be fair. But say you have two children, one who works in the business and one who does not. If you leave them equal interests, the working child may become answerable to your other child. There may be an ongoing tension about whether to reinvest profits to grow the business or distribute them for current income. And your working child may have a feeling of unfairness about your bequests.

If you want to provide the nonworking child with some ownership interest, you won't have any standard allocation formulas to guide you. What you leave is entirely up to you. Your only guidance is to make sure that control is held by the child who works in the business.

Instead of leaving equal shares, you can make bequests of property of equal value. The child who works for the business would receive your ownership interest; the other child would inherit other property of equal value.

What if you don't have property of equal value to leave the child who's outside the business? Creativity comes into play. You may be

Example

You own a retail store worth $1 million. You have two children: a daughter who's been working in the business for years and a son who's an artist. You leave your daughter your ownership interest in the company. You leave your son your IRA worth $600,000 and home worth $400,000. Each child inherits property of approximately equal value.

able to buy life insurance on your life to make up the difference. Depending on your age and your health, you may be willing to pay the premiums on this policy to ensure that your children receive equal treatment upon your demise.

Or you can leave your children different interests in your business. For example, you can leave your child who works for the company all of the voting stock and your other child only nonvoting stock. This will eliminate issues of control over company business after you die.

Or you can provide that the child you leave the business to must pay out a dollar amount to your other child over a number of years. What you don't want to do is make dispositions that will generate hostility between family members.

Bequests to Grandchildren

Where you want to pass on interests in your business to minors, you may want to use trusts for this purpose. The business interest is held by the trust for the benefit of the minor. Upon turning 18, 21, or whatever age you specify, the interest is then distributed to the beneficiary.

If your business is an S corporation, a trust can be a shareholder if it is a specific type of trust. In a testamentary context, consider using the following trusts to pass on interests to grandchildren:

- *Electing small business trust.* This is a special type of trust in which the trustee elects to be treated as an electing small business trust (ESBT). This trust can have multiple income beneficiaries—for example, several grandchildren. The trustee can be given discretion to distribute or accumulate trust income. However, this trust pays tax on income related to S corporation stock at the highest individual income tax rates. ESBTs are explained in Chapter 13.

- *Testamentary trust.* Where S corporation stock passes into a trust created under the terms of a will, the trust can remain as an eligible shareholder for two years after the owner's death. Thereafter, if the trust continued to hold the stock, the S corporation would have an ineligible shareholder and its election would terminate automatically. So if a trustee didn't elect ESBT treatment, the trust would remain a testamentary trust subject to the two-year limit.

TIP

To keep the insurance proceeds out of your estate, use a life insurance trust to own the policy for the benefit of your child. You can give the trust cash each year to pay the premiums. As long as the trust contains a Crummey power allowing the beneficiary the right to withdraw additions to the trust, then your contributions qualify for the annual gift tax exclusion.

Bequests to a Spouse

If you have a spouse you want to provide for after your death, you need to consider his/her role with respect to your business interests. If your spouse is already a co-owner, you may wish to increase your spouse's ownership share by leaving your interest to your spouse. But if estate taxes are a concern, you may not want to unduly burden your spouse's estate with additional business interests, and may instead opt to pass them on to your children.

If your spouse has no involvement in the operations of the business and your interest in the business is your primary asset, you need to devise a way to provide your spouse with income while ensuring that your spouse isn't thrust into the company's daily operations. If you have sufficient assets outside of your business—IRAs, real estate, a securities portfolio—you can provide adequately for your spouse with these other assets, leaving your business interests to your children. But if your only (or primary) asset is your business interest, you have no choice but to leave this interest to your spouse. As in the case of bequests to children where only one works for the business, you can limit the types of interest that pass to your spouse (e.g., nonvoting stock).

If you have concerns about your spouse's ability to manage an inheritance or want to retain control over who ultimately receives your property, you may want to use a trust (the type of trust you use depends on estate tax considerations). The trustee, who may be your adult child or a third party (or your spouse in conjunction with someone else), manages the assets of the trust for the benefit of your spouse. Income is paid to the spouse for life. Trust assets can be used if necessary to maintain the spouse's standard of living. Upon your spouse's death, the assets of the trust pass to your children or other beneficiaries (again depending on the type of trust you use). For example, if you want to say who ultimately receives the property from the trust—your business interest—then you would probably use a QTIP trust.

A *QTIP* trust is a type of trust designed to qualify for the marital deduction even though the surviving spouse does not receive a required interest in the property. With a QTIP you give a spouse a lifetime right to income from the trust. When the spouse dies, the assets remaining in the trust pass to the beneficiary or beneficiaries you've designated (your children or others).

In devising your estate plan, you should work with a knowledgeable attorney. The attorney can coordinate all of your documents, such as buy-sell agreements and lifetime trusts you may have already created, to ensure that things are clear. You want to avoid conflicting documents and ambiguities concerning your business interests that would have to be resolved after your death—at great expense.

Overview of Estate Taxes

According to one survey, family business owners are more concerned about estate taxes than income taxes (including capital gains). There's good reason for this concern. Federal estate taxes are designed to limit wealth transfer from generation to generation. People of very modest means aren't subject to the tax. There's an exemption amount of $675,000 in 2001 (rising to $1 million by 2006). Very wealthy individuals can use a wide range of devices to avoid estate tax. It's primarily those in the middle—business owners who are rich enough to have property but too poor to be able to afford to give it all away—who often fall into the estate tax trap.

> **NOTE**
>
> States may impose their own estate or inheritance taxes on transfers at death. Some states use only a "pickup" tax equal to the federal credit for estate taxes. But some impose additional taxes.

If you're married, you can postpone the estate tax cost by leaving your property to your spouse. There's an unlimited marital deduction that lets bequests to a spouse pass tax free. These bequests can be made outright or in certain trusts. But after the spouse dies, there'll be an estate tax bill to pay. If you don't have a spouse and can't postpone estate tax, then you must face the potential estate tax cost now.

Whether you give your property away while you're alive or when you die, you'll pay just about the same in transfer taxes because the estate and gift taxes are unified. These transfer taxes—gift tax and estate tax—share the same graduated tax brackets and exemption amounts that can be passed tax free. In figuring the tax on your estate, all taxable gifts that have been made are added in to push up the tax rate on the estate (the taxable gifts aren't taxed twice; they're only added back to increase the tax bracket). Gifts are explained in Chapter 13. The graduated unified estate and gift tax rates and an illustration of how they apply are also found in Chapter 13.

The tentative tax from the unified estate and gift tax rate table applies to the value of the property included in your estate minus certain deductions to which it may be entitled. These deductions include the unlimited marital deduction, charitable contributions, the deduction for administrative expenses (such as attorney's fees and probate costs), and the family-owned business deduction discussed in the next section. In valuing realty used in a closely held business, special valuation rules, discussed next, may apply.

Special Adjustment Due to Gift Valued under Anti-Freeze Rules

If you gave away interests in your business while retaining rights, there's a possibility that your retained rights (that were given a zero value for gift tax purposes) will be subject to a double tax when you die and those rights are included in your estate. (The anti-freeze rules are discussed in Chapter 13.) To prevent this double taxation, your executor can make a special adjustment in figuring the estate tax.

Generation-Skipping Transfer Tax

If bequests are made to grandchildren whose parents are still alive, there is a potential generation-skipping transfer tax cost. The GST is a flat tax of 55 percent and it's imposed in addition to any estate tax that might otherwise be due. However, each person can transfer free of GST up to $1 million ($2 million per couple). This $1 million is adjusted annually for inflation (in 2001 it's $1,060,000).

Paying the Estate Tax

The big concern for owners of family businesses and others who may be subject to estate tax is payment. The tax is due nine months after the owner's death. And payment must be made in cash; you can't hand over property in lieu of cash.

To ensure that there's sufficient cash on hand to pay the tax, many owners carry life insurance for this purpose. Life insurance on the life of the business owner is included in his or her estate if the business owner was the owner of the policy or retained "incidents of ownership" in it. Incidents of ownership are powers over the policy, such as the power to cancel the policy and recover the cash surrender value, the power to borrow against it, or the power to name new beneficiaries. Generally, both ownership and incidents of ownership concerns are avoided by having an irrevocable trust own the policy. If the trust takes out the policy and the insured doesn't have any powers over the trust (for example, there's an independent trustee), the proceeds aren't included in the insured's estate. If the business owner already owns insurance, the policy can be transferred to a trust. As long as the insured outlives the transfer by at least three years, the proceeds aren't includible in his or her estate.

The trust can provide that the trustee may lend money to the estate or any heirs on commercially reasonable terms. Thus, the trust can act as a bank to provide the necessary cash to pay estate taxes.

> **CAUTION**
>
> The trust should not be *required* to pay estate taxes. Doing so can subject the proceeds to inclusion in the insured's estate and result in additional estate taxes.

Other methods for paying estate tax include:

- Redemption of stock
- Sale to an ESOP
- Payment in installments

These methods are discussed later in this chapter.

Deduction for Family-Owned Businesses

Whether your business is a sole proprietorship, partnership, limited liability company, or corporation, your estate may qualify for a special deduction that, when added to the exemption amount, allows you to pay tax free up to $1.3 million of closely held business property. The deduction is the difference between the $1.3 and the exclusion amount for the year of your death. If your estate uses the maximum deduction, then your exclusion amount is limited to $625,000. In effect, if you live to 2006 and your estate qualifies for this special deduction, you can pass $300,000 more tax free than those who don't own family businesses.

Eligibility Requirements

These requirements are numerous; some may be confusing and some may be difficult to meet. But if you think your estate may qualify for this special break, it affects your lifetime succession planning. To qualify for the special deduction, all of the following conditions must be met:

- You are a U.S. citizen or resident at the time of death.
- Your "qualified business interest" is more than 50 percent of the adjusted gross estate (referred to as the "50 percent liquidity test"). This liquidity test is figured using a ratio that's rather complicated.
- You must meet material participation requirements prior to death. This means that you actively work in your company.
- You must leave your interest to certain qualified heirs. These include your family members—spouse, your or your spouse's children, grandchildren, parents—as well as any individual who has been actively employed by the business for at least 10 years prior to your death. So, for example, while your cousin isn't a family member, he may still be a qualified heir if he has worked for the business long enough.
- Your qualified heirs must continue to materially participate in the business for at least five years of any eight-year period within the

10 years following your death. If the heirs fail to meet this requirement, there's a recapture that applies, the percentage of which depends on how long they actually participated. (See Figure 15.1.)

• You must own a qualified business interest whose principal place of business is in the United States. Such interest means owning at least 50 percent of the business by one family, 70 percent of the business by two families, or 90 percent of the business by three families (as long as your family owns at least 30 percent of this percentage). Your family for this purpose includes your spouse, parents, their lineal descendants, and spouses of any lineal descendants. Ownership in public companies doesn't qualify even if they're closely held.

And the business must be an active one and not merely a personal holding company for investments.

Special Use Valuation for Real Estate Used in Business

Realty used in a closely held business may be specially valued for estate tax purposes. This means that instead of valuing the property at its highest and best use, the general standard for valuation, it can be valued according to its actual use. This may bring down the value of the property for estate tax purposes, thereby saving estate taxes. However, there's a limit on how much special valuation can bring down the size of the gross estate. Special use valuation cannot reduce the gross estate in 2000 by more than $770,000 (this figure is indexed annually for inflation).

Eligibility requirements for special use valuation are similar to but not always identical to those for the family-owned business deduc-

FIGURE 15.1   Recapture of Family-Owned Business Deduction

Nonmaterial Participation Starts in the Year Following the Year of Material Participation . . .	Applicable Recapture Percentage Is . . .
1 through 6	100%
7	80%
8	60%
9	40%
10	20%

tion. To be eligible for special use valuation, all of the following conditions must be satisfied:

- You must be a U.S. citizen or resident at the time of your death.
- The value of the property (reduced by any mortgages) must be at least 50 percent of the adjusted gross estate (the gross estate less any debts and expenses). This 50 percent requirement is figured before applying special use valuation.
- At least 25 percent of the adjusted gross estate must be used in a closely held business. Again, this 25 percent requirement is figured before applying special use valuation.
- The property must pass (directly or in trust) to a qualified heir. This includes a spouse, parents, siblings, children, stepchildren, and lineal descendants of these relatives. If the heir disposes of his or her interest within 10 years of your death, there's a sliding scale for a recapture tax.
- The property must have been owned by you or a member of your family and used in the business for five of the eight years before your death.
- You or your family must have materially participated in the business for five of the eight years before your death, disability, or retirement.
- Your executor must elect special use valuation on the estate tax return.

> **NOTE**
>
> An estate may be eligible to claim *both* special use valuation for business use realty as well as the deduction for family-owned business interests. Eligibility requirements are similar but not identical and need to be checked carefully.

Using Charitable Arrangements to Minimize Estate Taxes

As a family business owner you usually think about passing your ownership interests directly to your children or other relatives. But doing so may result in sizable estate taxes and impose an undue burden on your heirs. Instead of leaving your interests directly to your family, you might want to use a charitable arrangement. These charitable arrangements:

- Reduce estate taxes.
- Provide a benefit for charity.
- Keep ownership of the business within the family. The arrangement prevents the need to sell off interests to pay estate taxes.

Charitable Lead Trusts

You can use the same technique used by Jacqueline Kennedy Onassis to reduce substantially the amount of her estate tax while ensuring that her property ultimately passed to her children and grandchildren. It's called a charitable lead trust. It provides that for a term of years—typically 10 to 20 years—the income from the trust is payable to a charity. At the end of this term, the trust ends and the property remaining in the trust passes to your children or other designated beneficiaries. The estate can claim a charitable contribution deduction for the discounted present value of the charity's income interest. The numbers really explain it better (see example).

The charitable lead trust may pay an income to the charity for the term of the trust. Technical tax rules dictate the parameters of what that income must be. But the trust need not actually pay out cash to the charity. The "income" distribution can be made in company stock held by the trust.

The corporation may buy back the stock from the charity each year. As long as the buyback isn't prearranged or required by contract or otherwise, this arrangement lets the charity realize cash while retiring the stock and keeping control within the family.

Charitable Remainder Trusts

This trust is the complement to the charitable lead trust. It provides an income to beneficiaries for life or a term of years not exceeding 20 years. At the end of that time, the assets of the trust pass to a named charity. As long as the trust conforms to tax law requirements, the owner's estate can claim a charitable contribution deduction for the present value of the charity's remainder interest.

Where such trust is funded by interests in a family-owned business, the charity may wish to sell its interest back to the business. Again, as long as the sale isn't prearranged and the charity isn't required to sell back its interests, then the goals of the owner are pro-

Example

Assume a business owner of a family corporation owns $10 million worth of stock at his death. In round numbers, his estate would owe a tax of $5.5 million. But if the owner's will creates a charitable lead trust for 20 years to benefit a charity (even a family's own private foundation), the tax bill can be cut to $2.2 million, or 60 percent less than it had been.

tected. The owner's estate claims a charitable contribution deduction, and the ownership interests remain within the family.

Private Foundations

You can set up your own charity to provide for your own philanthropic concerns. Like other charitable arrangements, property left by will to a private foundation enables the estate to claim a charitable contribution deduction. Family members—children or others—can be named to the board of the foundation and oversee its management. Thus, control is kept within the family.

Paying Estate Taxes

The federal estate tax is due nine months after the date of death. States may require payment even sooner than that. Payment must be made in cash; property can't be paid over to the U.S. Treasury in satisfaction of estate tax liability.

Coming up with the cash needed to pay a large estate tax bill may be a serious problem. Unless a person has sizable liquid assets, such as marketable stocks and bonds, or had the foresight to carry a large life insurance policy, paying the tax bill isn't easy. It could even require the estate to sell off assets at fire-sale prices to raise the cash.

But the tax law provides some mechanisms designed to help estates of private businesses meet the burden of paying estate taxes. There are three main alternatives:

1. Redemptions of stock in a closely held business
2. Using ESOPs
3. Installment payments of estate tax

Redemptions to Pay Estate Taxes

If you die owning shares in your corporation (C or S), these shares can be redeemed to pay federal and state estate taxes, funeral costs, and other administrative expenses. The redemption produces capital gain treatment.

To qualify for this special redemption rule, the value of the stock must be more than 35 percent of the adjusted gross estate (your gross estate less deductions for expenses and losses). If you own stock in two or more corporations, then each must be 20 percent or more of your gross estate in order to be lumped together for purposes of the 35 percent threshold. If the redemption is more than the limit for capital gain treatment (the amount redeemed exceeds death taxes and expense), it's still possible that capital gain treatment may apply.

Example

You own stock in a family business worth $1.5 million and other assets worth $1.5 million (for a total estate of $3 million). If you were to give each of your four children and six grandchildren $10,000 worth of stock each year (total gifts of $100,000), in just five years you'd be under the 35 percent threshold and your estate would be ineligible to use this special redemption rule.

Generally, the redemption must take place within three years and nine months following the shareholder's death. Where the redemption is more than four years after death but within the statute of limitations for assessing estate tax, then capital gain treatment is limited to the lesser of the total of death taxes, funeral expenses, and administrative expenses unpaid immediately before the redemption, or the total amount of death taxes and expenses paid within one year of the redemption.

If you plan to hold onto the bulk of your shares until death and pass them to your family under the terms of your will, then be sure to limit any gifting program so you don't slip under the 35 percent threshold for special redemption treatment.

If you do plan to make gifts, be sure to balance gifts of business interests with gifts of other property to retain the proportion of the business interest to your total estate. So if you give away say $100,000 worth of stock in your corporation, you can keep above the 35 percent threshold by also giving away $100,000 of art, bonds, or other property.

Alternatively, if you now see that your estate would fall below the 35 percent threshold, you can take steps to make sure it will satisfy this requirement by selling or gifting nonbusiness assets. This will boost the percentage of your estate in stock in your corporation.

If you plan to have your estate use this special redemption provision, you need to take steps to ensure that your corporation will have sufficient cash on hand to go through with the redemption. Generally a C corporation cannot accumulate more than $250,000 ($150,000 for personal service corporations) of earnings without being subject to penalty. However, the corporation is permitted to accumulate earnings for the reasonable needs of the business. This includes accumulations for the purpose of redeeming a deceased owner's shares.

Alternatively, the corporation can maintain life insurance on your life to finance its redemption of your shares. Where the corporation is the beneficiary of the policy, this ownership arrangement can result in a big income tax bite on the corporation when it collects the proceeds, thereby diminishing the cash available to make the redemption.

However, if you're the sole or controlling shareholder owning more than 50 percent of the voting stock at the time of death and the proceeds aren't payable to the corporation or a third party for a valid business reason, then the life insurance proceeds are treated as includible in your estate. This serves to boost your estate taxes accordingly.

Using ESOPs

An employee stock ownership plan (ESOP) can be used by an owner of a corporation for lifetime and death planning. For example, an owner may sell shares during life for tax advantage (explained in Chapter 14).

These are qualified plans that must meet stringent IRS and Department of Labor rules to maintain qualification. Corporate contributions to the plan are deductible, even if made with company stock.

An ESOP can also buy shares from an owner's estate. The ESOP in effect becomes a ready buyer for the shares that might otherwise have no market. The purchase by the ESOP provides cash for the estate. This cash can be used to pay estate taxes or administrative expenses, or to fund bequests.

Installment Payments

If after all your planning, your estate still faces a sizable tax bill, it may be possible to pay it off in installments at very favorable interest rates. This avoids the need to sell the business or interests in it at distressed prices or to borrow at burdensome interest rates.

The federal estate tax ordinarily is due nine months after a person's death. Nine months can roll around in no time. But under a special break for estates of business owners, the estate may be able to use a 14-year installment payment plan for the part of the estate tax attributable to interests in the business. To qualify, the same 35 percent threshold for special redemptions applies to installment payments. In other words, the value of the business must be more than 35 percent of your adjusted gross estate (your gross estate less deductions for expenses and losses).

But unlike the redemption break that applies only to corporations, the special installment rule can be used by owners of sole proprietorships, part-

TIP

Qualification for installment payments doesn't depend on the estate's need. Even if the estate has the cash to pay the tax, it can choose to make installment payments if eligible to do so. This means that if the estate can earn more money than the favorable interest rates charged on installments of tax, it would be better advised to make the election and put its money to better use.

Example

In 2001, an owner of an S corporation valued at $3 million dies and her executor elects to pay the estate tax attributable to this interest in installments. The portion of the estate tax attributable to the value of the business between $675,000 and $1,675,000 is subject to a 2 percent interest rate. This works out to $414,000 ($634,550 tentative estate tax on $1,675,000, less $220,550, the unified credit amount for 2001). The portion of the estate tax on the value of the business exceeding $634,550 has an interest rate of 45 percent of the IRS underpayment rate (which currently amounts to 4.05 percent).

CAUTION

The estate tax payments are accelerated if more than 50 percent of the business interest is disposed of or liquidated before the full payment of estate tax.

ners in a partnership having 15 or fewer partners or in which the partner owns 20 percent or more of its capital, or shareholders of a corporation having 15 or fewer shareholders or in which the shareholder owns 20 percent or more of the voting stock.

If your estate qualifies for special installment payments and your executor elects to pay estate tax in installments, then no taxes are due for the first four years. Only interest payments are required. But starting in year five, interest plus one-tenth of the estate tax must be paid. The interest rate is 2 percent on the tax attributable to the first $1 million in taxable value (which means the amount in excess of the exemption amount). For 2001, the 2 percent portion is equal to the tentative tax figured on the value of a family business between $675,000 (the exemption amount for this year) and $1,675,000 ($1 million plus $675,000). Excess amounts are taxed at just 45 percent of the IRS rate otherwise applicable to underpayments. For the third quarter of 2000, the general underpayment interest rate for noncorporate taxpayers is 9 percent so the rate on excess amounts would be 4.05 percent (45 percent of 9 percent).

OTHER INSTALLMENTS

If your estate doesn't qualify for this special installment payment break because it falls short of the 35 percent threshold, it may still be able to pay tax in installments. The IRS has discretion to grant extensions of time to pay estate tax where there is reasonable cause. Reasonable cause generally means that immediate and full payment would impose undue hardship (for example, the estate would be forced to sell off the business at fire-sale prices).

Family Business Programs

A number of universities now offer programs designed to train specialists in helping family businesses. Others offer programs in conjunction with the Small Business Administration to provide services to family-owned businesses. Through these programs and services you may find counseling, forums, and publications of assistance to family business owners within your area. If you do not see a listing for a program near you, contact the closest university to inquire about family business forums, centers, or institutes.

Institute	Contact	Web Site
Alfred University Center for Family Business	Saxon Drive Alfred, NY 14802 (800) 541-9229	www.alfred.edu/cfb.html
American University	4400 Massachusetts Avenue N Washington, DC 22016 (202) 885-1000	
Baylor University Institute for Family Business		http://hsb.Baylor/edu.htm/ cel/ifb/ifb/home.htm
Bryant College Institute for Family Enterprise	1150 Douglas Pike Smithfield, RI 02917-1284 (401) 232-6477	www.bryant.edu

California State University Fresno Family Business Institute	5150 North Maple Avenue Fresno, CA 93740-8026 (559) 278-4240	www.csufresno.edu
Canisius College Family Business Institute	2001 Main Street Buffalo, NY 14208 (716)-883-7000	www.canisius.edu/canhp. departments/cfe/fbi/fbi.html
Case Western Reserve University Weatherhead School of Management	10900 Euclid Avenue Cleveland, OH 44106-7166 (216) 368-2041	www.cwru.edu
Cornell University Family Business Research Institute	Ithaca, NY 14853-4401 (607) 255-2591	www.cornell.edu
Creighton University Center for Family Business	2500 California Plaza Omaha, NE 68178 (401) 280-5521	www.creighton/edu
DePaul University Family Business Program	1 E. Jackson Chicago, IL 60604 (312)-362-8000	www.depaul.edu
Duke University's North Carolina Family Business Forum	Fuqua School of Business Box 90118 Durham, NC 27708-0118 (919) 660-7716	www.duke.edu
Fairleigh Dickinson University—The George Rothman Institute's Family Business Forum	285 Madison Avenue Madison, NJ 07940 (201) 443-8842	www.fdu.edu/academic/ rothman/htm
Florida International University Family Business Institute		www.fiu.edu
George Washington University's The Center for Family Enterprise	School of Business and Public Management 710 21st Street, NW Suite 206 Washington, DC 20052 (202) 994-6380	www.sbpm.gwu.edu/ research/centers/cfe/
Harvard Business School Executive Education: Families in Business		www.exed.hbs.edu
Indiana University Family Business Forum	Office of Communications and Marketing (812) 855-4248	www.iuinfo.indiana.edu/ ocm/releases/fambus.htm
Kennesaw State University—Family Enterprise Center	(770) 423-6045	www.kennesaw.edu/ fec/index.html
Loyola Center for Closely-Held Firms	Loyola College in Maryland 4501 N. Charles Street Baltimore, MD 21210 (410) 617-2395	http://chf.loyola.edu/

McMurry University Family Business Center	Fourteenth and Sayles Blvd. Abilene, TX 79697 (915) 691-6430	www.mcm.edu/academic/ sevlead/fambus/member.htm
Montana State University Family Business Program	(406) 994-6187	
Northeastern University's Center for Family Business	(781) 320-8015	
Nova Southeastern University Institute for Family Business	3301 College Avenue Ft. Lauderdale, FL 33314 (800) 541-6682	
Oakland University Center for Family Business		www.sba.oakland.educ
Oregon State University Austin Family Business Program	College of Business Bexell 201 Corvallis, OR 9733	www.familybusiness.orst.edu
Saint Louis University's EWEB	(314) 977-3850	www.slu.edu/eweb
State University of New York at Buffalo Family Business Center	School of Management Buffalo, NY 14210 (716) 645-3959	www.mgt.buffalo.edu/cei/fbc
Temple University Family Business Alliance	1510 Cecil B. Moore Avenue Philadelphia, PA 19121 (215) 205-4555	www.sbm.temple.edu/~fba
Tulane University Family Business Center	(504) 862-8482	
University of Alabama Family Business Forum	Culverhouse College of Commerce and Business Box 870221 Tuscaloosa, AL 35487-0221 (205) 348-7270	
University of Cincinnati Goering Center for Family and Private Business	ML 177 Cincinnati, OH 95221 (915) 556-7126	
University of Connecticut—Family Business Program	U-41FB 368 Fairfield Road Storrs, CT 06269-5740 (860) 486-5740	www.sba.uconn.edu/Fam Bus/FBhome.htm
University of Louisville Family Business Center	(502) 852-1518	
University of Massachusetts Family Business Center	Division of Continuing Education Box 31650 Amherst, MA 31650 (413) 545-1537	

University of Memphis—Family Business Forum	Fogelman College of Business Room 431 Memphis, TN 38152 (910) 678-4799	http://fbf/memphis.edu/ index.html
University of Pennsylvania Wharton School of Business—FCCP	Family-Controlled Corporation Program 3733 Spruce Street Philadelphia, PA 19104 (215) 898-4470	www.fccp.com
University of San Diego Family Business Institute	School of Business Administration San Diego, CA 92110 (619) 260-2376	www.acusd.edu/fbf/index.html
University of Southern California Family Business Program	School of Business Administration Bridge Hall 5B Los Angeles, CA 90089-1421 (231) 740-0416	www.usc.edu/entrepreneur~ /familybusiness.toc.htm
University of Texas at El Paso Family and Closely Held Business Forum	College of Business Administration (915) 747-7724	www.utep.edu/coba/fbf/ welcome.html
University of Toledo Center for Family Business	College of Business 2801 West Bancroft Street Toledo, OH 43606-3390 (419) 530-4058	
Virginia Commonwealth University Family Business Forum	School of Business 1015 Floyd Avenue Box 844000 Richmond, VA 23284-4000 (808) 828-7288	www.vcu.edu/businweb/ ufbf/index.htm

Family Business Resources

In addition to family business institutes at various universities and the publications they offer, there are a number of other resources geared specifically for the family business.

Resource	Web Site (or Phone Number)
Arthur Andersen Center for Family Business (seminars, books, comprehensive survey on American family business today)	www.arthurandersen.com/cfb
Business Owner Resources (publisher of monthly newsletter called *Family Business Advisor*)	members.aol.com/busowners/bor.htm
Center for Family Business (seminars and books)	216-442-0800
Family Business (a quarterly magazine for owners and managers of family businesses)	www.fambuspub.com/subscrib.htm
Family Business Publishing Company (publisher of handbooks for the family business)	www.fambuspub.com
The Family Business Report (compiled by law firm Hale and Dorr, LLP)	www.haledorr.com/publications/family/FamilyDirectory.html
Family Business Resource Network Inc. (information and links for family business)	www.familybusinessresource.com

Family Business Roundtable (information)	www.fbrinc.com
Family Firm Institute (consulting services)	www.ffi.org
Massachusetts Mutual Life Insurance Co.'s Family Business Network (statistical data, educational programs)	www.massmutual.com/fbn
NetMarquee, Inc. (family business search engine)	www.fambiz.com

Index